Vietnam

SECOND EDITION

VIETNAM
The Struggle for National Identity

D. R. SarDesai
University of California, Los Angeles

WESTVIEW PRESS
Boulder • San Francisco • Oxford

To the children of Vietnam
who will ultimately determine
that country's national identity

Copyright © 1992 by Westview Press, Inc.

Published in 1992 in the United States of America by Westview Press, Inc., 5500 Central Avenue, Boulder, Colorado 80301-2847, and in the United Kingdom by Westview Press, 36 Lonsdale Road, Summertown, Oxford OX2 7EW

First edition published in 1988 by Promilla & Co., Publishers

Library of Congress Cataloging-in-Publication Data
SarDesai, D. R.
    Vietnam : the struggle for national identity / D. R. SarDesai. —
2nd ed.
        p. cm.
    Includes bibliographical references (p.   ) and index.
    ISBN 0-8133-8196-7 — ISBN 0-8133-8197-5 (pbk.)
    1. Vietnam—History—20th century. 2. Nationalism—Vietnam—
History. I. Title.
DS556.8.S26 1992
959.704′4—dc20   91-45349
                                                                            CIP

Printed and bound in the United States of America

The paper used in this publication meets the requirements
of the American National Standard for Permanence of Paper
for Printed Library Materials Z39.48-1984.

10   9   8   7   6   5   4   3   2   1

Contents

Preface

Vietnam has evoked more interest internationally among scholars and diplomats, militarists and peace activists, journalists and the public than most other countries in recent times. The spectacle of a small nation, with far less sophisticated weaponry than its opponents and hardly any air power, immobilizing the most advanced, militarily best-equipped nation moved people across the globe. What motivated the Vietnamese men, women, and children to make such supreme sacrifices? Was it communism or nationalism? Or a combination of both?

My interest in Vietnam was further aroused by numerous Vietnamese students at UCLA who had immigrated to Southern California as "boat people" in the wake of the 1975 "fall" of Saigon. Their plaint about a persistent bias in most of the Western accounts about Vietnam and their plea that I write an objective history of the modern period in the perspective of its long historical past have been primarily responsible for this book. I have profited most from discussions with them, in particular Nguyen Dao Phan, who completed a thesis on the National Liberation Front under my supervision. My thanks are also due to Pham Cao Duong, whose scholarly insights into the agrarian policies and successes and failures of governments in Vietnam have benefited my understanding of rural Vietnam. For the recent period, I have drawn extensively from the most well informed and fairly objective and analytical reports of Nayan Chanda, special correspondent and expert on Vietnam for the *Far Eastern Economic Review*.

I should acknowledge my debt of gratitude to Charlotte Spence, the recently retired Indo-Pacific bibliographer of the University of California, Los Angeles, for her unfailing assistance in locating materials, and to Dr. Ingelise Lanman, my former doctoral student research assistant, for her help in the writing of this book. I am very grateful to Jane Bitar, manager of the word processing department for social sciences and humanities at UCLA, and Nancy Rhan, also in the word processing department, for their professional expertise in the preparation of the manuscript. Finally, as always, I am beholden to my wife for providing consistent encouragement and inspiration in all my scholarly and writing endeavors.

D. R. SarDesai

VIETNAM

Source: Bill Gausman, *Red Stains on Vietnam Doves* (Kiowa, Colo.: Veracity Publications, 1991). Reprinted with changes with permission.

CHAPTER 1

Ethnicity, Geography, and Early History

The Southeast Asian littoral, the promontory at the extremity of mainland Southeast Asia, constitutes Vietnam. It extends from about 8° to 23°N and 102° to 109°E. The long coastline of Vietnam uncoils in the shape of an S from China's southern border to the tip of the Indochina Peninsula. It is bordered on the north by China, to the west by Laos and Cambodia, and to the east and south by the South China Sea. Nearly 1,240 miles long, the country extends unevenly at widths ranging from 31 to 310 miles and covers an area of 127,300 square miles. Vietnam is as large as the British Isles, smaller than Thailand, with a population estimated at 66 to 68 million in 1989.

Vietnam's two fertile alluvial deltas—Red River, or Hong-ha, in the north and Mekong in the south—have inspired the image of the typical Vietnamese peasant carrying two rice baskets suspended at the ends of a pole. Connected by a chain of narrow coastal plains, the deltas produced enough rice before the war not only to feed the population but even to export. Although these delta regions constitute only about a quarter of the country's area, they support almost 80 percent of its population. The rural population density in some of the provinces of the Red River Delta is as high as 1,000 per square mile. The Mekong Delta is the richer of the two and extends well into Cambodia. Both the deltas are known for their intensive agriculture; the Red River Delta has long reached the point of optimum agricultural expansion. The country's historical, political, and economic development has taken place in these two separate areas partly because of a mountain range dividing the country. The Truong Son, or Annamite Cordillera, runs approximately north and south along the border of Laos and Vietnam, cutting the latter almost in two and also extending along the Vietnamese-Cambodian border. At certain points, the mountains have elevations of up to 10,000 feet.

1

Communications between Vietnam and Laos or Cambodia are possible through certain strategic passes. Of these, the more difficult ones are located in the north at an altitude of more than 3,000 feet at the head of the valleys of the Song Da (Black River), the Song Ma (Red River), and the Song Ca. Further south, the communications are, by comparison, not as difficult. Thus the Tran Ninh area can be reached through the town of Cua Rao whereas the Cam-mon Plateau can be reached from the Nghe An area through the Ha-trai and Keo Nua passes at an altitude of more than 2,000 feet or further south through the Mu Gia Pass at a somewhat lower altitude. From Quang Tri one can traverse just north of the Kemmarat rapids through the Ai Lao Pass (at an altitude of about 1,300 feet), regarded as the gateway to Laos. Between the Red River Delta and central Vietnam, communications go through several passes and corniches at Hoanh Son, the gateway to Annam, at elevations of between 1,300 and 1,500 feet. The geographical configuration and the varied accesses are extremely significant for understanding the movement of people and armies in the military encounters in ancient as well as recent times.

VIETNAM—THE NOMENCLATURE

For most of their history, the Vietnamese people lived only in the Red River Delta. During the first millennium of the Christian era, from 111 B.C. to A.D. 939, Vietnam was a directly ruled province of the Chinese Empire. The separate kingdom of Champa, south of the empire's border in central Vietnam, existed until 1471, when most of it was overrun by independent Vietnam. The remnant of Champa was absorbed by the Vietnamese in 1720. Thereafter, taking advantage of an extremely weakened Khmer Empire, the Vietnamese gradually expanded into the Mekong Delta, completing the conquest by the middle of the eighteenth century and reaching the modern borders of Vietnam.

Vietnam has had a succession of names, reflecting its rule by various people at various times. The Chinese called the country Nan Yueh and the Red River Delta the Giao. In the seventh century, after putting down a series of revolts by the Vietnamese, the Chinese renamed the territory Annam, meaning "pacified south." After the Vietnamese overthrew the direct Chinese rule in A.D. 939, the kingdom was called Dai Co Viet (country of the great Viet people). As the kingdom extended its borders, the three natural divisions of Vietnam—north, central, and south—came to be known to the Vietnamese as Bac Viet, Trung Viet, and Nam Viet, respectively. The territory was divided into two political parts in the sixteenth and seventeenth centuries and ruled by two families: the Trinh in the north and the Nguyen in the south, both of whom recognized the Le as kings (see Chapter 2). The country was unified for the first time by

Emperor Gia Long in 1802 and was named Vietnam. Because France conquered Vietnam in three different stages and later tried through official policies to submerge the nationalist identity and spirit of the Vietnamese people, the French referred to the three regions only by the names of their administrative units, insisting also that these corresponded to three separate cultural entities. Cochin China in the south was a French colony; Annam, or central Vietnam, with its imperial capital of Hué, was a protectorate; and Tongking, with Hanoi as capital, was regarded as a separate protectorate. The French vivisection of Vietnam was regarded as an insult by Vietnamese nationalists, who vowed to liberate their country from the French (and later from the Americans) and to bring about its reunification as the single nation-state of Vietnam. This they accomplished in 1976, after a relentless struggle of several decades.

THE HUMAN FABRIC AND LANGUAGES

The Vietnamese

The Vietnamese, who form 85 percent of the population, are a mixture of non-Chinese Mongolian and Austro-Indonesian stock who inhabited the provinces of Kweichow, Kwangsi, and Kwantung before the area was brought under Chinese rule in 214 B.C. Further racial intermixture probably came about through marriages between the Vietnamese and a Tai tribe long after the Vietnamese had moved into the Tongking Delta.

The mixed racial descent of the Vietnamese is reflected in their language, which is both monotonic like the Malayo-Indonesian and variotonic like the Mongolian group of languages. It is also influenced by the Mon-Khmer languages in its grammar (no declension or inflection) and even more so in its vocabulary (up to 90 percent of words in everyday usage). Vietnamese owes its multitonic system as well as a large number of words to the Thai language. By the time the Vietnamese came under Chinese rule in 111 B.C., they already had a well-developed language of their own. Thereafter, the monosyllabic Vietnamese language drew heavily on the Chinese for administrative, technical, and literary terms. For most of their history, the Vietnamese used Chinese ideographs for writing. Since the seventeenth century the Vietnamese have employed a system of writing developed by a Jesuit missionary. *Quoc-ngu*, as it is called, shows the differing levels of pitch as well as vocal consonant elements by diacritical marks.

The Tribals

Several tribal groups live in the extensive mountainous country to the north and west of the Red River Delta. The Meo, the Muong, and the Thai, all of Mongolian origin, are the most important and numerous. Together, all the tribals account for about 2 million people. The Tai speak languages closely allied to those of Thailand and Laos. Except for the 20,000 Muong, who use a language akin to Vietnamese, the other tribes speak dialects of Tibeto-Mongolian origin. The vast plateau and hilly areas of central Vietnam are inhabited by several ethnic minorities numbering nearly 1 million people and collectively called the Montagnards by the French. Six of the larger groups account for nearly half of the tribal population. These are the Rhade, Sedang, Jarai, Stieng, Bahnar, and Roglai, certainly a heterogeneous people, whose skin color ranges from brownish white to black and whose languages are drawn both from the Malay-Polynesian and the Mon-Khmer groups. They were pushed into the mountains by the Vietnamese moving south.

Traditionally, there is not much love lost between the tribal people and the plains people. Renowned as warriors and as masters of the strategic passes, the tribals have been able to move swiftly across the borders of Vietnam into Laos and Cambodia. They may be fewer in number than the Vietnamese and their weapons far less sophisticated, yet they were never completely subdued by the Vietnamese. Because of their bravery, skills, and knowledge of the terrain, the tribals were wooed by the Chinese as they considered an invasion of Vietnam, later by the French, and by both sides in the recent drawn-out war. The tribals have held all outsiders, including the ethnic Vietnamese, in contempt and have viewed them with strong suspicion. They do not have the Vietnamese enthusiasm for wet rice cultivation, preferring instead to burn the brush on the mountain slopes and resort to dry rice cultivation. Their ways of life, languages, dress, social organization, and house structures have all been distinct from those of the Vietnamese. Generally speaking, the Montagnards have never displayed a high regard for the law and government of the plains people.

Despite governmental efforts to improve their lot, the tribal population of Vietnam still follows primitive ways of life, eking out a miserable existence exploiting the infertile and inhospitable terrain constituting four-fifths of the country's area. After 1954, the North Vietnamese government introduced several programs to improve their economic condition. This was perhaps because of the valuable assistance the tribals gave to the Viet Minh, who had operated from their hideouts in the mountainous territory of the northwest during the struggle against the French. The present government of Vietnam has a twofold policy toward the tribal population. On the one hand, it allows them autonomy, thus helping them to maintain their ethnic identity through retention of age-old social institutions and practices. On the other hand, it encourages assimilation through education and common participation in the life of the lowlands.

The Chams

Also in central Vietnam are the Chams, numbering about 40,000. The descendants of a former dominant and highly civilized people who controlled central Vietnam for nearly fifteen centuries, they are of Indonesian stock and have reverted to a tribal life-style. Their former kingdom, called Champa (or Linyi in Chinese records), was founded in A.D. 192 by a local official who overthrew the Chinese authority. Taking advantage of the weak Chinese control over Tongking in the declining days of the Han dynasty, the Chams extended northward. Although they controlled portions of Annam at various times, Champa proper extended from a little south of Hué to the Cam Ranh Bay and westward beyond the Annamese Mountains into the Mekong valley of Cambodia and southern Laos. The history of the relationship between China and Champa was one of alternating hostility and subservience on Champa's part. With the reconsolidation of China under the Chin dynasty, Champa sent the first embassy to the Chinese emperor's court in A.D. 284. But whenever the Chinese authority in Tongking slackened, the Chams seized the opportunity to raid the northern province. During this early period, the center of the Champa kingdom was in the region of Hué.

Champa came under Indian influence around the middle of the fourth century A.D., when it absorbed the Funanese province of Panduranga (modern Phan Rang). Funan was an early kingdom based in Cambodia, extending its authority over the Mekong Delta, southern Laos, Cambodia, and Thailand from about the first century A.D. The political center of Champa had by then moved from near Hué to the Quang Nam area, where famous Cham archaeological sites of Tra Kieu and Dong Duong indicate profound Pallava impact of the Amaravati school of art. In the same area, the most notable archaeological site is that of My-son, a holy city whose art demonstrates Gupta influence as well as that of the indigenous pre-Khmer concepts of Cambodia. After the sixth century, the center of Cham activity moved south to Panduranga, or Phan Rang, where the south Indian influence increased, as is seen, for instance, in the towers of Hoa-lai. In the opinion of the eminent French scholar Georges Coedès, it was the Indianization of Champa that lent it strength against its Sino-Vietnamese enemies.[1]

Although the kingdom was divided into several units separated from each other by mountains, the Chams rallied dozens of times in the defense of freedom against attacks by the Chinese, the Vietnamese, the Khmers, and, later, the Mongols. In such conflicts Champa's mountainous terrain and easy access to the sea provided considerable scope for military maneuver. At last, after a millennium and a half of survival as an independent state, the Chams suffered a severe defeat at the hands of the Vietnamese in 1471. More than 60,000 Chams were killed and about half that number were carried into captivity. Thereafter, Champa was limited to the small area south of Cape Varella around Nha Trang. The remnant state lingered until 1720, when it was finally absorbed by the Vietnamese, the last Cham king and most of his subjects fleeing into Cambodia.

The Cham society was and is matriarchal, daughters having the right of inheritance. Following the Hindu tradition, the Chams cremated their dead, collected the ashes in an urn, and cast them into the waters. Their way of life resembled that of the Funanese. Men and women wrapped a length of cloth round their waists and mostly went barefoot. Their weapons included bows, arrows, sabers, lances, and crossbows of bamboo. Their musical instruments included flutes, drums, conches, and stringed instruments. Today about 40,000 southern Vietnamese and about 85,000 Cambodians claim Cham ancestry. Their social organization, marriage, and inheritance rules did not change despite their later conversion to Islam.

The Khmers

Not far west of Saigon and south of the Mekong live about 500,000 Khmers in what were once provinces of the Khmer Empire (founded in the ninth century A.D.) and its precursors, the kingdoms of Chenla (seventh to eighth century A.D.) and Funan (first to sixth century A.D.). Like the Chams, the Funanese were of Indonesian race, whereas the Chenlas and the Khmers were kindred to the Mons of Burma. At its height the Khmer Empire extended over the southern areas of mainland Southeast Asia, including the Mekong Delta. The Funanese and the Khmers were extremely active as a maritime commercial power, serving as intermediaries in the trade between India and China. Both were Indianized kingdoms that adopted the Sanskrit language and Indian literature and religions and grafted Indian concepts of art and architecture to indigenous forms, producing (among others) the world-renowned monuments of Angkor. After the sack of Angkor by the Thais in A.D. 1431, the Khmers became subservient to the Thais but still retained control of the Mekong Delta. With the Vietnamese conquest of Champa and the final absorption of the Champa kingdom, the Mekong Delta region of the Khmer kingdom was exposed to the aggressive Vietnamese policies. The present-day Khmers of Vietnam are descendants of the population that chose to stay on in the Mekong Delta after its conquest by the Vietnamese in the eighteenth century. An indeterminately large number of them were used by the Vietnamese as an advance column in their march into Cambodia in December 1978.

The Chinese

Until the recent exodus, there were over a million Chinese in Vietnam, mostly in the south and especially in Cholon, the twin city of Saigon (now called Ho Chi Minh City). Some of them are descendants of very old families, whereas ancestors of most others migrated in the wake of the French colonial rule in the nineteenth century, principally from the Canton area. As in most other countries of Southeast Asia, the Chinese dominated the economic life of their adopted country, acting as traders, bankers, moneylenders, officials, and professionals. They maintained close ties with relatives in their homeland. Because of their economic power, they invited the hatred and distrust of the Vietnamese people and governments, including the present Communist government. More recently, they became the target of official persecution in 1978–1979, resulting in their large-scale migration to China and as boat people to other destinations. A large number perished on the high seas.

One of the most persistent themes throughout Vietnamese history is a love-hate relationship between China and Vietnam. If the Vietnamese appreciated, admired, and adopted Chinese culture, they despised, dreaded, and rejected Chinese political domination. Such a mixture of envy and hostility is seen in the contemporary Vietnamese attitudes toward the ethnic Chinese in Vietnam, who have been by far superior to the Vietnamese in trade, commerce, and finance. Historically, Vietnam was the only country in all of Southeast Asia with close political and cultural ties to China, all the other Southeast Asian countries being heavily influenced by Indian culture, at least in the first millennium of the Christian era. As David Marr observes, there is "the subtle interplay of resistance and dependence which appeared often to stand at the root of historical Vietnamese attitudes toward the Chinese."[2]

The long history of Sino-Vietnamese relations was marked by significant Vietnamese absorption of Chinese culture both through imposition and willful adoption. Vietnamese intellectuals through the centuries have regarded their country as the "smaller dragon" and a cultural offshoot of China. Nonetheless, their history was punctuated by numerous valiant efforts to resist the deadly domination of their land by their northern neighbors. Vietnamese nationalism took a virulent form whenever fear of Chinese takeover loomed large. Some of the greatest Vietnamese legends have been woven around the exploits of heroes who led the struggle against the Chinese. It is, therefore, no surprise that a significant section of the historical museum in Hanoi is dedicated to exhibits on the numerous instances of Vietnamese resistance to Chinese domination. The Vietnamese never allowed their culture to be totally overwhelmed by the Chinese, taking care periodically to review, rearticulate, and maintain their identity as a people distinct from the Chinese. The hostility born of Chinese domination for long centuries sharpened a militant nationalism against any alien rule.

EARLY VIETNAMESE HISTORY

The Vietnamese have attempted to give their country a history as hoary as China's. According to one of the numerous legends concerning the origin of their state, a Vietnamese prince named Lac Long Quan came to northern Vietnam from his home in the sea. He married a princess from the mountain, Au Co, who is also described as the wife of a northern (Chinese?) intruder, on the top of Mount Tan Vien some time around 2800 B.C. Instead of the commonplace result of such a union, the princess laid 100 eggs, a son eventually hatching from each. For some unknown reason, the parents separated, the mother leading half the progeny across the northern mountains, where they became the ancestors of the Muong, and the father leading the remaining fifty sons to the sea, where they became ancestors of the Vietnamese. The most valiant of the sons was chosen to be the first of the eighteen Hung kings. Lac Long Quan, a prince of the sea, and Au Co, a princess of the mountains, are regarded by the Vietnamese as their primal ancestors. Does this imply that the Vietnamese were originally of the Malay-Polynesian, sea-oriented race who came to terms with the Mongolians of the southern Chinese plains?

The Dong-son Culture

The earliest name for Vietnam was Van Lang, founded by King Hung. Seventeen kings or generations, all styled Hung, succeeded him. They ruled throughout the Bronze Age from Phung Nguyen, in the Hong River valley (site of the Early Bronze Age, third millennium B.C.) to Dong Dau (site of the Middle Bronze Age at the midpoint of the second millennium B.C.) and Go Mun (peak of the Bronze Age, 1200–800 B.C.) to Dong-son (the most famous site of the Late Bronze Age, 800–300 B.C.). Although the archaeologist's spade has uncovered substantial quantities of bronze arrowheads in Dong Dau and Go Mun, a fairly centralized state probably did not emerge until the Dong-son period. The Hung era is rightly termed "legendary" by most historians inasmuch as no eighteen kings or generations could have spanned the nearly two millennia of prehistoric development in the Tongking Delta. It is possible that the rule of the eighteen Hung monarchs relates to the Dong-son period, which marked the displacement of the economic and social leadership of primitive agricultural practices by a monarchical apparatus responsible for the building and maintenance of an irrigation system of dikes and canals, providing against nature's vagaries of droughts and floods.

The new state, based on the irrigation system in the region of the three rivers in Upper Tongking, must have produced excess wealth, requiring protection against predator enemies from the exposed borders to the north and the south. Hence the need for extensive use of bronze technology for varied weaponry. By the Dong-son period, the kingdom of Van Lang extended to Hunan in southern China. The capital was moved to Vinh Phu, where the three rivers—Song Da, Song Ma, and Song Ca meet.

The evidence of the bronze-using Dong-son culture is spread not only along the northern and central Vietnamese coastline but also as far away as Yunnan and Szechuan in China and in Malaya and Flores in the Moluccas. A large number of ornate bronze drums as well as hoes, axes, knives, spears, and plates of armor, among other archaeological artifacts, speak of a flourishing culture noted for agriculture, handicrafts, pottery, silk, music, and maritime activity on a substantial scale.

The Dong-son people were undoubtedly seafarers who built their own canoes for domestic communications but also modest-sized ships for distant trips, guiding their navigational movements with some understanding of astronomy. Their trading contacts with the outside world must have brought them the knowledge of metallurgy. The discovery of the Dong-son culture demolished the earlier theory that bronze was introduced by China (where iron was not used until the third century B.C.) and iron by India. As for religion, the art of Dong-son demonstrates the practice of ancestor worship and animism. Gods were related to agriculture; temples were built on hills or elevated platforms. The ashes of the dead were buried in jars or in megalithic dolmens, although the people seemed to believe that the dead passed away to some place in the direction of the sinking sun. In their elaborate cosmology, the dualistic elements of mountain and sea, winged beings and water beings, mountain dwellers and plains people provided the core themes. A substantial part of the Dong-son culture eroded among the Vietnamese during the subsequent long period of Chinese rule. Essentials of the proto-Vietnamese language of the Dong-son people have survived among the Muong tribal people, including the Dong-son title for princes—*quan lang*—used by Muong hereditary chiefs.

The reasons for the fall of the Hung rulers of Van Lang, known to us partly through the Dong-son cultural remains, cannot be established by historical evidence. By 300 B.C., it seems the people in the region of Kwantung and Tongking were divided into Tay Au, namely, Vietnamese of the highlands, and Lac Viet, Vietnamese of the plains. They were politically united into the kingdom of Au Lac by An Duong Vuong, about whom similarly little is known. It is not clear whether the Au Lac people were partly descendants of Van Lang or Dong-son or whether they were the Viets, "real" ancestors of the Vietnamese people who, under pressure from the Han Chinese, migrated from their habitat in Lower Yangtse round 300 B.C. southward into the Red River Delta.[3] Most scholars now accept that the Vietnamese are not descended from one single racial group but are instead a racial mixture of Austroasiatic-Indonesian and Mongolian races.

The capital of the new kingdom of Au Lac was built further along toward the delta, at Co Loa, about 20 miles north of Hanoi. It was a fortified city, a model for later capitals, with three walls, the outer one nearly 9,000 yards long. Au Lac followed both land-based and water-based techniques of warfare in which the Tay Au and Lac Viet, respectively, specialized. Co Loa must have been involved with some very heavy fighting in its early days, judging from the thousands of bronze arrowheads found in the Iron Age layers under its ramparts. By the time Au Lac was overthrown by the Chinese general Zhao Tuo, it was already well into the Iron Age.

Vietnam Under Chinese Rule

With the first consolidation of the Chinese Empire by Shih Huang Ti, the builder of the Great Wall, in the third century B.C., the Vietnamese living in the Kwangsi, Kwantung, and the Red River Delta areas came under increasing pressure. In 207 B.C., Zhao Tuo, who commanded the Kwantung and Kwangsi provinces, also brought the Red River Delta under his jurisdiction, carving out a wholly independent kingdom called Nan Yueh or Nam Viet (*Nam* meaning "south"). The capital of the new state was near modern Canton. Nam Viet was thus ethnically a composite Sino-Vietnamese state. Zhao Tuo encouraged local customs of the Vietnamese and promoted intermarriage between the Chinese and the Vietnamese people. The kingdom retained its independence for roughly a century.

In 111 B.C. the expansionist Han emperor Wu Ti (140–87 B.C.) sent his forces against Nam Viet, liquidating its independence and turning it into a province of the Chinese Empire. It took a long time, however, for the outlying provinces of the Chinese Empire to be absorbed into the Chinese central administration. In fact, it was after the Trung sisters' rebellion in A.D. 39–43 that the Chinese seriously undertook to impose their culture on the Vietnamese. North Vietnam remained a province of the Chinese Empire for the next millennium, until the ouster of the Chinese rulers in A.D. 939. For administrative purposes, the Han emperors divided Nan Yueh into three commanderies: Giao Chi (or Tongking), Cuu Chan (or Thanh Hoa), and Jenan (or Nhat Nam).

The two essential elements that contributed to the molding of the early Vietnamese social organization have been the struggle against nature and the struggle against a mighty neighbor to the north. In the process, the Vietnamese developed into one of the most determined, persistent, and tenacious people anywhere. Frequent flooding of the Red River as well as disastrous droughts compounded the misery of the people of the Red

River Delta. In a dry year, water may drop by five-sixths; in a year of heavy monsoons, the floods may raise the water level to forty times the normal height of the river. Early in Vietnamese history, possibly before the Christian era, the Vietnamese developed an elaborate system of dikes and canals and the rudiments of governmental authority to control and channel the supplies of water. The dikes cover an area of more than 1,500 square miles in the Tongking Delta today, assuring the peasants their sustenance but exposing them to the risks of an avalanche if the hydraulic installations are damaged. According to some scholars, the collective work on the building of dams and the regularly compartmentalized field system to provide protection against flooding were techniques introduced by Chinese rulers. They may have also brought the water buffalo and the plow to Vietnam and taught the Vietnamese how to use human excrement as field manure. The Chinese may also have introduced methods of intensive pig rearing and market gardening, which have contributed substantially to the alleviation of the peasants' financial woes in China and Vietnam to this date.

The millennium of direct Chinese rule accounts for numerous Chinese traits in the Vietnamese culture. Even before the Chinese rule began, as inhabitants of the composite state of Nan Yueh or Nam Viet, the Vietnamese had come into contact with the Chinese culture; once Chinese governors and county chiefs gained control, a certain amount of deliberate sinicization of Vietnamese culture took place. Further intensive and extensive introduction of Chinese culture came about in the first century A.D., when floods of Chinese refugees poured into the Red River Delta. These were not needy peasants but well-accomplished scholars and officials who had fallen out with the Chinese government under the usurper Wang Mang (A.D. 9–23). They became agents of intensive propagation of Chinese culture through the introduction of Chinese classics, Confucian ethics, and Chinese ideographs. Until the adoption of the romanized *quoc-ngu* in the seventeenth century A.D., Vietnamese was the only language in Southeast Asia that used the Chinese characters and was therefore not alphabetical. Beginning in the fifth century A.D., the Mahayana form of Buddhism was introduced to Vietnam by Chinese scholars and preachers, some of whom passed through Vietnam on their way to India for higher studies in Buddhism or for pilgrimage to Buddhist holy places. The Chinese traveler I-Ching attests that Hanoi had become a great intellectual center of Buddhism by the seventh century.

EARLY NATIONALISM

Chinese rule was punctuated by several violent expressions of hostility on the part of the Vietnamese subjects. A number of factors led to intense

Vietnamese resentment of Chinese rule. The large numbers of mandarins who flowed into Nam Viet in the wake of Wang Mang's ascendancy occupied lands previously owned by high Vietnamese officials. The Chinese also made heavy demands for various tributes, maintained a monopoly on salt and iron, and embarked upon a program of Vietnamese conversion to Chinese culture.

Vietnamese revolts occurred during periods when the central government in China was weak and its authority consequently less effective in the outlying province of Tongking. The first of these uprisings took place in A.D. 39 and is notable for giving Vietnam two heroines remembered for their bravery and patriotism. A powerful local chieftain, Thi Sach, violently resisted the Chinese policy of acculturation and was executed at the orders of the Chinese governor, Su Ting, who wanted the event to serve as a warning to other recalcitrant chiefs. The Vietnamese reaction was exactly the opposite of what the Chinese intended. The chieftain's widow, Trung Trac, is said to have set aside her personal grief, not even wearing the traditional mourning headdress. Instead, she raised troops, boosting their morale with her oath:

> I swear, first, to avenge the nation;
> Second, to restore the Hungs' former position;
> Third, to have revenge for my husband;
> Fourth, to carry through to the end our common task.[4]

She and her sister, Trung Nhi, pushed the Chinese out and proclaimed themselves joint queens of almost all of Nam Viet for two years. It proved a short-lived liberation but was remarkable for its support not only by the nobility but also by the peasantry. When the Chinese retaliated and crushed the revolt, the two sisters committed suicide.

The Vietnamese later deified the two martyred sisters; for centuries legends came to be woven in their memory as they continued to inspire Vietnamese resistance to alien domination. Many pagodas were built to honor the sisters, the most notable being the Hai Ba pagoda in Hanoi and the Hat Mon pagoda in the Sontay province. The government of Vietnam has proclaimed them national heroes. To this day, Vietnamese girls honor their memory on Hai Ba Trung Day in March, and troops marching to battle have been known to take along pictures of the two sisters to encourage them.

The Trung sisters' revolt was followed by a campaign of severe physical, psychological, and cultural suppression of the Vietnamese. Ma Yuan, the Chinese general in charge of the operation, pillaged and broke up Vietnamese feudal estates, executed hundreds of members of the nobility who were even remotely linked with the revolt, humiliated others, and exiled still others to South China. Chinese garrisons were set up at numerous strategic points to eschew the possibility of future revolts. Nam Viet was divided into three prefectures (*quan*) and fifty-six districts (*huyen*), all under the control of Chinese mandarins. A vigorous campaign was launched to further assimilate the Vietnamese into the Chinese culture through more intensive adoption of the Chinese script and educational system, subordination of Vietnamese laws to Chinese jurisprudence, and, above all, enforcement of Confucian ethics of submission of subjects to emperor, son to father, and wife to husband.

The Vietnamese proved diligent pupils, mastering the Chinese classics and quickly demanding posts in the civil service. Their industry and intelligence were not readily nor adequately rewarded. The Chinese never intended to treat them on equal footing; moreover, they resented that the Vietnamese scholars, despite adopting all the external trappings of Chinese culture, in fact managed to retain Vietnamese cultural traditions. Among the old customs that persisted even among the sinicized Vietnamese elite during the period of Chinese domination were tattooing, coating the teeth with black lacquer, chewing betel nut, and giving women a high place in society. Although the Vietnamese looked upon such customs as proud symbols of their cultural nationalism, the Chinese regarded them as barbarous practices that justified keeping the Vietnamese out of the Chinese civil service. The numbers of Vietnamese who managed to enter the civil service remained small until the Tang dynasty (A.D. 618–906).

Such "collaborators" were far fewer than those who consistently hated the Chinese rule and spared no opportunity to demonstrate the sentiment. Rebellions against Chinese domination were staged by nobility and peasantry alike and even by those Vietnamese who were conscripted into the Chinese army of occupation. The Vietnamese have recorded in extensive verse the exploits of their heroes in the struggle against Chinese rule. The Socialist Republic of Vietnam has enshrined the memory of such deeds in a special museum in Hanoi.

Among such revolts or wars of independence, the Trung sisters' rebellion was indeed the most notable. But there were others, too, that held down Chinese troops for long periods. Some of the more important uprisings were those led by Chu Dat in A.D. 160, by Luong Long in 178, and by Si Nhiep in 187. Si Nhiep had been a governor of Giao Chi under the Han and was successful in maintaining peace during times of trouble. After the overthrow of the Chinese, Si Nhiep made Nam Viet virtually independent from 187 to 226. In the middle of the third century A.D., a major rebellion was again led by a woman. In 248 Ba Trieu, the nineteen-year-old sister of a headman in Thanh Hoa, helped her brother raise an army of more than a thousand to be given guerrilla training in the neighboring mountains. The guerrillas killed the Chinese governor of Chiao Chih (a port in central Vietnam) and resisted Chinese reinforcements for several months. In the end, superior Chinese forces crushed the resistance, Ba Trieu committing suicide on Tung Mountain, where a tomb and a temple perpetuate the inspiring memory of her sacrifice.

In the sixth century, Ly Bi, a Vietnamized Chinese of the seventh generation, led a revolt in Thai Binh province. With considerable help from Vietnamese aristocracy and peasantry, he brought the country from Thai Binh (at the southern end of the Tongking Delta) to Langson (in the northeast, near the present-day border with China) under his newly proclaimed independent kingdom of Van Xuan. The independence lasted a brief four years before it was ruthlessly ended by the Liang emperor's army in 548. The resistance was continued by Bi's brother, Ly Thien Bao, in Cuu Chan. He was forced to withdraw into Laos, where he proclaimed himself the independent king of Dao Lang. Another of Ly Bi's associates, Trieu Quang Phuc, meanwhile, called himself king of the Viets in the swampy area of Da Trach. A decade later, both he and Ly Thien Bao's cousin shared authority in most of Nam Viet. The confusing history of that turbulent period brings out the valiant exploits of Trieu Quang Phuc (also called Trieu Viet Vuong, king of Viet), who seems to have successfully eluded the Chinese for three to four decades.

The Tang dynasty, more powerful and centralizing, was noted for several revolts in Nam Viet and Laos, some of them involving non-Viet minorities. Notable of these was the rebellion of Ly Tu Tien, who in 687 succeeded in occupying Tong Binh and killing the Chinese governor. In 722, led by Mai Thuc Loan, the Muong people of Ha Tinh revolted against the excessive economic exactions requiring delivery of lychee fruit to the Tang imperial court. The rebellion spread to Thanh Hoa, Nghe An, and Ha Tinh. Although Mai Thuc Loan also secured help from the king of Champa to the south to overthrow the Chinese governor and occupy the capital of Tong Binh, he was eventually defeated by superior Chinese forces and retreated to his mountain base, Ve Son. A citadel named Van An Thanh (Citadel of Peace) and a temple in Nghe An remind people to this date of Mai Thuc Loan's valiant fight against the Chinese.

Later in the century, two brothers, Phung Hung and Phung Hai, led a guerrilla movement in Ha Tay and succeeded in capturing Tong Binh. They proclaimed their independence from Chinese control, an independence that lasted under Phung Hung and his son Phung An until 791.

In the last decades of the once powerful Tang dynasty, Nam Viet was attacked and held by the Thais (863–866) from Nan Chao in Yunnan. Although the Chinese rulers of Nam Viet were also able to throw out the Nan Chao forces, the weakness of the Tang dynasty and its inability to control its distant southern province were bared. When the Tang dynasty actually fell in 906, the Vietnamese would no longer recognize the suzerainty of the southern Han dynasty based in Kwantung. At this point, China was undergoing the rule by Five Dynasties (A.D. 906–960). First in 906 a Vietnamese notable, Khuc Thua Du, and later his son, Khuc Hao, and Khuc Hao's son, Khuc Thua My, proclaimed themselves governor of what they called Annam. The Khuc family did not want openly to confront the Chinese rulers with independence for Nam Viet. They had hoped that the disintegration of central Chinese rule alone would in time confirm Vietnamese independence. In 923, however, the last-named Khuc governor was replaced by a Chinese governor left behind by the invading forces of the southern Han dynasty. Less than a decade later, Ngo Quyen (son-in-law of Duong Dinh Nghe, a general of the Khuc family) truly ended the thousand-year Chinese rule. A brilliant strategist, he is believed to have used underwater iron spikes to wreck the invading Chinese ships. It gave a crucial victory to Ngo Quyen, who proceeded boldly to restore the country's name to Nam Viet, with its capital in the ancient city of Co Loa. The independence he established was conclusive despite the chaos caused by disputes over succession after Ngo Quyen's untimely death in 944. But for a short reinstatement of Chinese rule (1407–1428), the Vietnamese enjoyed virtual independence until the nineteenth-century conquest by the French.

Summarizing the complex Sino-Vietnamese relationship, King Chen notes: "Sino-Vietnamese relations in the past were an enterprise of mutual interest. Politically and militarily, China was for Vietnam an administrative tutor as well as an aggressor; economically, China was a promoter and an exploiter; and culturally, China was both teacher and indoctrinator."[5] It has been pointed out that, thanks to the Chinese rule, the Vietnamese made substantial advances in technology and material life: use of the iron plow, the art of printing, minting of coins, silkworm breeding, porcelain manufacture, and a great involvement in international trade.[6] If we keep in mind the Vietnamese drive and dynamism of the Dong-son period before the Chinese rule, though, we might well believe that the Vietnamese would have progressed in a number of these or other directions, to import technology and knowledge in a variety of fields of human endeavor on their own. The different Chinese roles were imposed on the Vietnamese, who preferred to be left alone to develop themselves as an independent state.

It is difficult, however, to estimate the depth of assimilation of Chinese culture by the Vietnamese. As in the other Southeast Asian countries, in Vietnam probably only the court and the elite were able to appreciate and absorb these alien cultural importations, whether Indian or Chinese. The Chinese mandarin system, with its Confucian values, helped the elite to erect a wall of authority that further buttressed their social and economic position vis-à-vis the peasantry.[7] Most of the hierarchical, bureaucratic

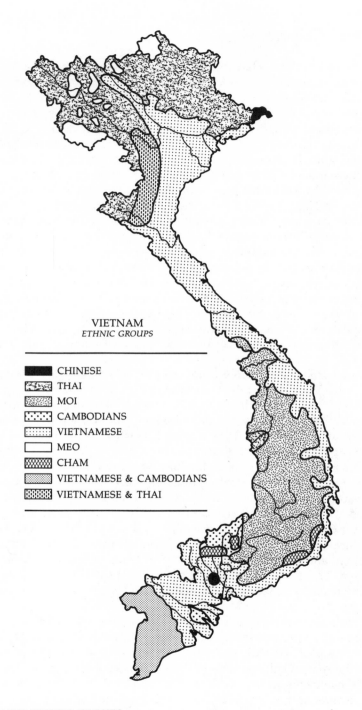

VIETNAM
ETHNIC GROUPS

■	CHINESE
	THAI
	MOI
	CAMBODIANS
	VIETNAMESE
□	MEO
	CHAM
	VIETNAMESE & CAMBODIANS
	VIETNAMESE & THAI

VIETNAM'S ETHNIC GROUPS

positions were filled by the elite through a civil service examination, held as in China on the district, provincial, and imperial levels. The examinations were rigorous, requiring a long period of study of Confucian classics, which were highly regarded not only as scholarly works but also as a conceptual aid to finding solutions to contemporary problems. Because only the elite could afford the luxury of a long-term education in the Confucian classics, the bulk of the people remained outside the pale of sinicization. The Chinese language written in Chinese characters remained the administrative and literary language of the elite. The masses retained the Vietnamese language, customs, and religious beliefs rooted in animism and ancestor worship. Vietnamese villages, with their closely knit families, helped preserve the distinct culture and remained firmly resistant to outside influences.

Paradoxically enough, the sinicization of the Vietnamese elite resulted in the latter's desire and ability to acquire and retain their independence from China. As Joseph Buttinger puts it: "The more they [the Vietnamese] absorbed of the skills, customs, ideas of the Chinese, the smaller grew the likelihood of their ever becoming part of the Chinese people. In fact, it was during the centuries of intensive efforts to turn them into Chinese that the Vietnamese came into their own as a separate people, with political and cultural aspects of their own."[8]

The phenomenon was not unlike what took place in the nineteenth and twentieth centuries, when Asian nationalism grew in the face of Western powers' efforts to Westernize the colonial peoples. Chinese rule and intensive efforts to sinicize promoted Vietnamese nationalism. Throughout its history, Vietnamese culture remained distinct enough for the Vietnamese people to resent and revolt against China's political domination.

CHAPTER 2

A Millennium
of Freedom

In the tenth century, taking advantage of the fall of the once powerful Tang dynasty, the Vietnamese declared the establishment of an independent kingdom. Between A.D. 939 and the imposition of French colonial rule in the nineteenth century, Vietnam enjoyed a thousand years of freedom from alien rule. The only exception was a short period of twenty-one years from 1407 to 1428, when the Ming rulers of China overran Vietnam and again brought it under direct Chinese rule. Because the millennium of freedom from foreign domination followed a millennium of intensely hated Chinese rule, one would naturally have expected a revulsion for Chinese political and cultural institutions in the new era of freedom. The reaction was, however, mixed, not unlike what Westerners witnessed in the postcolonial, independent states of Asia and Africa, where a strong revival of indigenous values, traditions, and development of political culture took place within the general constitutional, administrative, economic, educational, and military frameworks inherited from the erstwhile colonial rulers.

As a mark of political expediency, Vietnam maintained formal though nominal links with the Chinese Empire during the period by sending triennial tribute to the Chinese court through 1885. The expediency can be explained on several grounds. First, the long Chinese rule, particularly the liberal phase toward its end, had produced a Chinese-Vietnamese aristocracy with intellectual and institutional loyalties to a Confucian court. Such an elite perceived its vested interests to be more secure within the Chinese political system to which they were by then accustomed than in a completely independent monarchy without any links whatever with the Chinese Empire. Second, the new Vietnamese state had reason to be concerned about potential attacks from the Thai state of Nan Chao (in Yunnan), which had overrun Tongking in the eighth and ninth centuries

A.D. while the latter was still under Chinese rule. Tongking had also suffered from a maritime invasion from the south, from the Sailendra kingdom of Java in the eighth century. And, indeed, there was Champa, the perpetual thorn in the Vietnamese side. The Vietnamese rulers therefore felt that a Chinese connection established through the tributary overlord-vassal relationship would serve as a deterrent against any potential aggressive designs of its enemies, particularly the Thais.

The overlord-vassal relationship did not, as in Europe, necessarily obligate the vassal to send troops or funds to help the military adventures of the overlord. It did not really diminish independence except in a legal, formalistic sense. Yet the benefits of deterrence were real because a vassal could appeal to his overlord for assistance in times of need. Thus as late as 1884, when Annam was threatened by the French, the Annamese emperor appealed to the Chinese emperor, who sent his forces across the southern border to fight the French at Langson.

After the Vietnamese won their independence in 939, the leader of the independence movement, Ngo Quyen, moved the capital of his new kingdom to Co Loa (upstream from Hanoi), the base of the ancient kingdom of Au Lac. The decision to relocate the capital reflected the intense nationalist shift of the new leadership of Vietnam. The new kingdom was, however, plagued by internal conficts from the very beginning because of rival claims to the throne made by ambitious chieftains. The first seventy years of independence saw the rise and fall of three dynasties, each of them founded by a man of great vigor and dynamism, who was, however, not followed by equally competent successors. Ngo Quyen, who was responsible for pushing out the Chinese rulers, lived for only five years thereafter. He had not had much opportunity to consolidate his kingdom and establish an institutional structure that would balance and contain the ambitions of numerous feudal lords. Twelve warlords divided the country among themselves not long after his death. It was reunited only in 968 by Dinh Bo Linh.

Dinh Bo Linh came from a peasant background and was by contemporary accounts a forceful person who put down the various ambitious and greedy feudal nobles, consolidated his kingdom, and called it Dai Co Viet, country of the great Viet people. He tried everything possible to bring about unity among his people. To end the challenge to the country's integrity, it is said, he threw some of the recalcitrant nobles into cauldrons of boiling oil or to be devoured by his tigers. Unfortunately, Bo Linh, too, died early. His family having been murdered by certain nobles, the only surviving member was a six-year-old boy-king, who in 980 was overthrown by the army chief Le Hoan, founder of the early Le dynasty.

One significant legacy of Dinh Bo Linh was the sending of a triennial tribute to the Sung emperor of China in return for assurance that China would not interfere in Vietnam's internal affairs. Though this made him a vassal, Dinh Bo Linh still wanted to be designated emperor (*de* in Vietnamese, *ti* in Chinese). The Chinese preferred that the Vietnamese monarch be called governor. Realizing that it would be difficult if not impossible to reestablish control over their southern province, the Chinese finally agreed to a compromise: The Vietnamese ruler would be designated a vassal king of China; he could style himself emperor in relation to his own subjects and in dealing with his vassals.

Both the Ly and the Tran dynasties had excellent rulers, at least for the first hundred years of each dynasty. Several of the rulers had long periods of reign, the first four Ly kings ruling for a total of 117 years. The Ly rulers moved the capital to Thang Long (present-day Hanoi), renamed their kingdom Dai Viet, and gave it a strong centralized government. In order to facilitate closer administrative ties, a network of roads linking the provincial capitals to the royal capital was built by 1044. A postal courier service was also established by the middle of the century.

Although Vietnam had become an independent monarchy in the tenth century, it was only in the first half of the following century that major institutional changes came about. The power of the court and the civilization that the Ly dynasty created lasted for 400 years. The Ly rulers set up an elaborate apparatus to promote the Confucian cult at the court. During the last quarter of the eleventh century, they established a Confucian Temple of Literature and the Han-Lin Academy for Study in Confucianism at the highest level. In 1076 the National College was founded to train civil service officials. Only scholars well versed in Confucian classics would be able to pass the examinations. The principles guiding the government, then, were Confucian, and the mandarins who were regarded as social and intellectual leaders would, through their personal example, propagate Confucian values among the Vietnamese elite. The Ly rulers adopted the Chinese model of hierarchical bureaucracy in 1089, creating nine levels of civil and military officials. Thus despite strong political hostility toward the Chinese, the Vietnamese rulers deliberately set their nation on a course of sinicization.

The Tran dynasty produced a number of great rulers, the most notable being Tran Thai Tong (1225–1258). The many innovative administrative, agrarian, and economic measures he introduced were extended more or less along the same continuum by his successors. Tran Thai Tong reinforced the Confucian-based civil service examination after the Chinese model, consolidated the hierarchy, and glorified it further by creating new, more impressive bureaucratic titles. The kingdom was divided into twelve provinces ably administered by scholar-officials. Tran Thai Tong revamped the taxation system by categorizing the rice fields according to quality and imposed a land tax. Additionally, he introduced a poll tax payable by landowners. During his reign and throughout most of the Tran dynasty, public works were energetically pursued, embankments being constructed all along the Red River, down to where it emptied into the sea. Many other irrigation and water-control projects were undertaken to assure good crops and general prosperity for most of the long period of the Tran dynasty.

A mighty achievement toward the end of Tran Thai Tong's reign was the repulsion of the Mongol invasion in 1257. In a bid to conquer all of China, the Mongols had taken over the southern province of Yunnan in 1253. In order to consolidate their southern flank against the Sung dynasty's armies, the Mongols sent ambassadors to Burma and Dai Viet demanding tribute. Both refused to recognize the rising Mongol political power. Tran Thai Tong imprisoned the ambassadors. In retribution, the Mongol armies, under the leadership of Uriyangadai, swooped down and reached the Vietnamese capital in 1257. At this point, Tran Thai Tong and his heir apparent, Tran Thanh Tong, pushed the Mongols across the borders into China.

MONGOLS INVADE VIETNAM AND CHAMPA

After the conquest of China in 1279, the Mongol emperors became heirs to Chinese culture as well as political traditions. They followed the age-old policy of keeping a close watch on neighboring countries to see that they would remain weak and fragmented, never strong enough to attack China. They enforced the tributary system and at times insisted on a visit, in person, by the vassal kings at the court in Beijing (which the Mongols established as their capital). Most of the Southeast Asian monarchs lent a grudging cooperation. Champa was the most recalcitrant on mainland Southeast Asia; the Cham king, Indravarman V, sent tribute to Beijing but did not comply with the Chinese emperor's invitation to appear in person. Even the visit of the great Mongol General Sogetu, sent by the Chinese emperor to the Champa court in 1281, failed to persuade the Cham king to visit Beijing. At this rebuff, Kublai Khan sent a punitive expedition under Sogetu by sea because Dai Viet refused to allow Mongol troops to pass through its territory. Fortunately for the Chams, their relations with the Vietnamese were very cordial during the reign of Indravarman V. They perceived the common Mongol threat to their independence and decided to act in unison.

In the face of superior forces, the Cham king withdrew from his capital and for several years engaged two separate Mongol expeditions in guerrilla warfare from his refuge in the mountains, marking a precedent for similar struggles against a militarily superior enemy in recent Vietnamese conflicts against the French and American forces. Indravarman V proffered all kinds of excuses to avoid a personal meeting with Sogetu but showed readiness to send tribute and hold negotiations. In 1285 Kublai Khan sent a third expedition numbering 500,000 men under his own son, Prince Toghani; this time the Mongols traveled by land through the Dai Viet to help Sogetu's naval expedition, which landed directly in Cham ports. The Mongol troops suffered heavy casualties both in the Tongking Delta and in Cham territory. The guerrillas killed General Sogetu; Prince Toghani suffered an ignoble defeat. Cham guerrilla tactics and sudden ambushes paid off. Kublai's troops finally withdrew without getting the Cham king to appear in person at Beijing. Both Dai Viet and Champa, however, sent ambassadors to the Mongol emperor in the same manner that they had done before to previous Chinese emperors.

During the Mongol attack, the Vietnamese monarch vacated his own capital and repaired to the countryside to fight the invaders. The hero of the Vietnamese resistance was Prince Tran Quoc Toan, whose exploits are recounted as among the most celebrated in the valiant annals in the Vietnamese history of resistance against China. The proud Vietnamese king refused to agree to Mongol demands that he send his sons as hostages to the Mongol court and supply troops for the Mongol army. Thereafter, the Mongols decided that discretion was the better part of valor and meekly accepted the Vietnamese and Cham triennial tribute in return for peaceful mutual relations.

FALL OF CHAMPA

Vietnam's relations with Champa did not always remain cordial. Three provinces to the north of the Col Des Nuages (just north of Hué and south of Vinh) long remained a bone of contention. Even a matrimonial alliance between the two kingdoms (the Vietnamese emperor's sister was given in marriage to the Cham king) in 1306 failed to bring an enduring peace. Finally, in 1312, the Vietnamese emperor Tran Anh-tong was able to inflict a major defeat on Champa, retrieving the contested territory and making Champa a vassal state until 1326.

All through the fourteenth century, Vietnam and Champa were continually at war with each other. From 1369, when the Vietnamese emperor Tran Du-tong died heirless, until the end of the century, the Vietnamese monarchy was beset with instability and palace intrigues that resulted in a series of uncertain successions to the throne. The king of Champa, the famous Che Bong Nga (1360–1390), took sides in these palace plots and attacked Vietnam by sea in 1372, 1377, and 1388, sacking Hanoi on the first two occasions. Champa was able to retrieve the disputed northern provinces. It would have brought the Tongking Delta under its rule but for a valiant defense organized by Le Quy Ly, an official of Chinese origin who was related to the Vietnamese imperial family. From 1394 to 1400, he served as a regent while his infant cousin from the Tran family was the nominal king. The Tran dynasty had practically ended in 1394 but lingered in name until 1400.

A notable feature of the Tran dynasty was the rulers' tenuous relationship with China, the Trans never enthusiastically serving as vassals of the Mongol rulers. In the fourteenth century, in the declining days of that dynasty and the beginning decades of the Ming dynasty (1368–1644), the Vietnamese sent no tribute to China. Champa, however, improved its relations with China largely to buttress its position vis-à-vis Vietnam. Recognized by the new Ming dynasty as early as 1369, the Chams kept the Ming rulers well posted on the succession disputes and rivalries in Vietnam in the last decades of the fourteenth century. The Champa kings openly sided with China in the ensuing Chinese invasion of 1407 because five years before the Chams had lost the northern provinces of the kingdom of Quang Nam again to the Vietnamese under Le Quy Ly.

In 1400 Le Quy Ly himself ascended the Vietnamese throne in a brand new capital, Tay Do, which he established in Thanh Hoa province in the southern part of the Red River Delta. He changed his surname and assumed a new name, Ho. The new dynasty, called the Ho dynasty, became the shortest in the Vietnamese annals (1400–1407).

CHINESE OCCUPATION AND
THE BIRTH OF THE LE DYNASTY

In the fifteenth century, Vietnam once again suffered a Chinese invasion and occupation. The early rulers of the powerful Ming dynasty sought to augment Chinese influence in all of Southeast Asia. In 1407, Ming troops of Emperor Yung-lo entered Vietnam on the pretext of restoring the kingdom from the usurper Ho rulers to the rightful rulers, the Tran dynasty. Instead, the Chinese plainly annexed Vietnam to the Chinese Empire. Ho Quy Ly (the former Le Quy Ly) and his son were captured and taken to China, where they languished and died. Vietnam witnessed the most intensive sinicization ever, every effort being made to demoralize the Vietnamese. Chinese civil service officials were imported and imposed on the Vietnamese. A Chinese-style census was undertaken to make it the basis both for conscription to the Chinese army and to levy heavy taxes. The Chinese system of *baojia* (collective responsibility) was rigorously enforced. Vietnamese ways of life and religious practices were banned, and the people, particularly the higher echelons, were compelled to wear Chinese costumes, women to wear Chinese dress, men to wear long hair. The Vietnamese language was not allowed to be taught in schools. Literature extant in Vietnamese was confiscated and carried to China. Those Vietnamese who resisted, about 100,000 intellectuals and artisans, were exiled to Nanjing, where they were drafted to serve the empire. A number of Vietnamese were also sent to various parts of Vietnam to procure precious metals, gems, pearls, and ivory for the Ming emperor. All Vietnamese were treated as suspect and were required to carry identity cards.

Such actions naturally provoked the Vietnamese spirit of nationalism and age-old hostility against China. Vietnamese reaction was swift and conclusive. By 1418 Le Loi, an aristocratic landowner from Thanh Hoa province, had emerged to lead a guerrilla resistance that ended a decade later in the capture of Hanoi and expulsion of Chinese troops and civil officials. The proclamation of independence Le Loi issued reflected the Sino-Vietnamese tensions as well as Vietnamese pride and patriotism:

Our Great Viet is a country where prosperity
abounds. Where civilization reigns supreme.
Its mountains, its rivers, its frontiers are its own;
Its customs are distinct, in North and South.

Trieu, Dinh, Ly and Tran
Created our Nation,
Whilst Han T'ang, Sung and Yuan
Ruled over Theirs.

Over the Centuries,
We have been sometimes strong, and sometimes weak,
But never yet have we been lacking in heroes.
Of that let our history be the proof.[1]

Though Le Loi liberated the country from Chinese rule, he could not liberate the peasantry from want of land and pangs of hunger. Le Thanh Thong (1461–1497) solved that problem by conquests in the south at the expense of Champa in 1471. The conquest of Champa made possible the Vietnamese expansion first into central Vietnam and then eventually into the Mekong Delta in the eighteenth century. Le Thanh Thong also made Laos (then known as Lan Chang) a vassal of Vietnam. Although the Vietnamese thus received tribute from their vassals, they in turn sent tribute to the Chinese emperors, who recognized them as kings of Annam, the "pacified south."

Le Thanh Thong deliberately consolidated the Chinese system of administration, including its recruitment method, through the competitive, Confucian-style civil service examination. Whether this mode of cultural acceptance was simply designed to keep the Chinese out through flattery or whether it was born out of a genuine belief that such Chinese institutions lent social and political stability to a state will never be known. Under Le Thanh Thong, all the traditional Chinese cultural traits, such as language, the art of writing, the spatial arts, as well as Mahayana Buddhism, were adopted. The central administration was patterned on the Chinese model, with six ministries—finance, rites, justice, personnel, army, and public works. The civilian bureaucracy and military establishment were divided into nine grades each. A board of censors carefully watched over the bureaucracy and reported to the emperor any infractions of rules or procedures. The bureaucracy did not reach the village level. Rather, local affairs were managed through a council of notables, whose charge was to maintain order, execute official decrees, collect taxes for the imperial government, and recruit conscripts for the imperial army.

Recruitment to the civil service was dependent upon success in the examinations specially conducted for the purpose. They were based on the Confucian classics and were held annually at the provincial level, triennially at the regional and national levels. As in China, the candidates successful at the national level were granted an audience by the emperor himself and were given high positions in the administration. Because the social and economic status of the elite was dependent upon their administrative rank, Vietnam became thereafter and until the nineteenth century a Confucian state dominated by the mandarins. The cultural impact of the system persisted until modern times. Even after the civil service examination was abolished in 1905 in China, the system continued in Vietnam for several years longer. The Vietnamese intellectual elite was drawn from the Confucian-oriented families.

The intense cultural impact of China on Vietnam was a mixed blessing. The system of civil service examinations produced an educated elite, encouraged a family-oriented hierarchical loyalty, and promoted a well-regulated mandarin bureaucracy, all resulting in a relatively stable, social administrative order. Yet these same factors bred condescension toward people of other walks of life and a tendency to look to the past for precedents and for solutions to problems. The system discounted initiative, originality, and creativeness. The doctrine of the mandate of heaven underlined the ruler's moral responsibility to the people and allowed the people the right to revolt against inadequate or oppressive rule. Unquestioned loyalty to the emperor, father, husband, and older brother were mandatory in "normal times." A way of life and philosophy that regarded non-Confucian outsiders, including Westerners, as barbarians developed chauvinism and parochialism. This head-in-the-sand attitude could only contribute to stagnation of political and social institutions, as it inhibited the borrowing of scientific and technological knowledge from others. Vietnam's (like China's) relations with Western powers in the nineteenth century must be seen against this backdrop of constricting Confucian legacy.

Notwithstanding the administrative framework and the civil service examination that reflected such immense Chinese influence and impact, Le Thanh Thong consciously sought to move away from Vietnam's intellectual bondage to the Chinese in at least one or two major aspects. The Code of Hong-Duc, promulgated in 1483, brought together within a single conceptual and legal framework all the laws, rules, and regulations issued from time to time by previous Vietnamese emperors. Another area of Vietnamese assertion was art. The Le dynasty witnessed a large-scale program of construction of temples, tombs, and ceremonial halls all over the kingdom, notably in Hanoi, Lamson in Thanh Hoa province, and Hué. These edifices, along with steles, balustrades, and ornamental gateways, still survive, attesting partly to the continuing Ming influence but also to significant Vietnamese variations on traditional Chinese themes. The best example of such Vietnamese artistic assertion is seen at Hoa-lu (south of Hanoi), which had been the capital of the Dinh dynasty in the tenth century.

VIETNAM'S PARTITION

The inclusion of the former Champa territories made the expanded Vietnamese kingdom an administratively awkward unit. The southern portions of the kingdom hardly felt the impact of the central administration based in Tongking. At the same time, pressures of population in the Tongking Delta and an opportunity to fulfill political ambitions encouraged some Vietnamese princes and generals to move to the new territories in the south. The central government's authority weakened progressively. The reign of the last real Le ruler, Le Chieu Tong (1516–1526), was marked by rivalries for power among three families—the Mac, the Nguyen, and the Trinh. In 1527 the ruling Le family was deposed by General Mac Dang Dung, who seized power in Tongking. The Le family's cause was upheld by a loyal nobleman, Nguyen Kim, who fled to Laos, raised an army there, and in 1533 put a Le prince on the throne in Thanh Hoa. Nguyen Kim died in 1545 and was succeeded by his son-in-law, Trinh Kiem.

This series of events marked the beginning of a protracted civil war punctuated by intervals of truce that did not really end until the middle of the eighteenth century. The long periods of relative peace were made possible by China's intervention, which was sought by rival parties. The first such mediation by China as Vietnam's overlord brought about the initial "partition" of the country in 1540. The Macs were recognized by China as the rulers of Tongking, whereas the Le-Nguyens were allowed to make Thanh Hoa their capital and seek their fortunes in the present central Vietnam. The settlement was not as significant for its lasting value as it was for setting a precedent for Vietnam's future partition. The Mac rulers were stoutly opposed by Nguyen Kim's son, Nguyen Hoang, as well as by his son-in-law, Trinh Kiem. By 1592 Trinh Kiem's son, Trinh Tung, overthrew the Mac regime in Tongking and restored the throne to the Le dynasty. He brought the nominal Le ruler from Thanh Hoa to Hanoi, thus unifying the divided kingdom of Vietnam. As the suzerain power, China undid the previous "partition," recognizing the Le dynasty as the only legitimate ruler of all of Vietnam.

In point of fact, however, there were two centers of power as before, the Trinhs ruling in Tongking (with Le as nominal rulers) and the Nguyens in the south also ruling in the name of the Le dynasty. The situation long remained fluid and tenuous. Technically, the Nguyens were self-appointed governors of the southern province, slowly carving out a kingdom for themselves at the expense of the Khmers. Yet they regarded themselves as loyal appointees of the Le rulers who were extending the Le empire. The Nguyens were generally well regarded by the Le rulers and, more importantly, by the people under their charge in the south. In contrast, the Trinhs, who had captured all the important posts at the capital, Hanoi (then known as Thang Long), were considered usurpers. In 1620 an open conflict broke out between the Trinh and the Nguyen forces, the latter refusing to pay the Trinh taxes collected in the south in the name of the Le rulers. A military stalemate was eventually reached. In 1673 a durable peace was worked out by China. The territory was partitioned. A wall—some called it the "Small Wall of Vietnam"—was erected from the Annam Mountains to the sea near Dong Hoi, very close to the 17th parallel, which marked the dividing line under the Geneva agreements of 1954. The Nguyens were now officially recognized as independent rulers of the territory from Dong Hoi to Cape Varella, or Song Cau. The event ushered in an era of peace extending for nearly a century.

THE TAYSON REBELLION

Once the Trinh threat was removed, the Nguyen power grew rapidly in the south. In the early eighteenth century, the Nguyens liquidated the remainder of the old Champa kingdom, thereby reaching the borders of the Khmer-controlled Mekong Delta. No major battles took place for the conquest of these rich and fertile lands. Vietnamese control came about like ink spreading on blotting paper. The Nguyen rulers encouraged their retired soldiers to establish colonies beyond the Vietnamese frontiers in Khmer areas. Minor skirmishes with Khmer authorities produced prisoners of war who, along with weaker ethnic communities, were used to help the Vietnamese cultivate the lands. By the middle of the eighteenth century, virtually all the Khmer territories of present-day southern Vietnam had become part of the Nguyen kingdom.

The last quarter of the eighteenth century was a period of great social and political convulsions for Vietnam. The old established regimes were overthrown both in the north and in the south. In 1773, three brothers from the village of Tayson in central Vietnam—Nguyen Van Nhac, Nguyen Van Lu, and Nguyen Van Hue (who had adopted the name of the southern ruling family) raised the standard of revolt. They quickly became dominant in the provinces of Qui Nhon, Quang Ngai, and Quang Nam. The Trinh family ruling in Hanoi (with Le as effete emperor) took advantage of the situation, sent troops southward, and captured Hué in 1777. A decade later, feuds developed within the Trinh family, which gave the Tayson brothers the opportunity to capture Annam and Tongking, eliminate the Trinh, and depose the Le dynasty. By 1788 the Taysons obtained control of all of Vietnam: Nhac was proclaimed emperor of Annam, with Van Hue and Van Lu in charge of the Red River and Mekong basins, respectively. In a sense, Vietnam was unified under the three brothers, though Vietnamese historians prefer to regard the Tayson revolt as a catalyst for the real unification brought about by Emperor Gia Long in 1802.

The Tayson success was helped by the public's disgust with the nepotistic, corrupt Trinh administration in Tongking and its belief that the Trinhs had lost the mandate of heaven. But if in the north the Taysons were hailed as deliverers, in the south they were seen as unscrupulous usurpers. They were accused of taking advantage of the tragedy in the Nguyen family, the king having died without leaving an adult heir. The teenage prince, Nguyen Anh, received sympathy and secret support from large numbers of people in the Ca Mau Peninsula, where he had taken refuge. Nguyen Anh's adversity lasted slightly over a decade. His family's numerous allies eventually enabled him to capture the environs of Saigon from the Taysons. The people believed the mandate of heaven had been passed from the Le-Trinh not to the Taysons but to the Nguyens to rule over all of Vietnam.

UNIFICATION AND CONSOLIDATION

Among the supporters of Nguyen Anh was a French missionary, Pigneau de Béhaine, who regarded Vietnam as his second homeland. In 1787 he went to the court of Louis XVI with Nguyen Anh's son, Canh, to seek military assistance for restoring Nguyen Anh to power. Considering the domestic preoccupation and plight of the French monarch, it was a miracle that a Franco-Vietnamese treaty was signed, providing French military aid in exchange for a grant of monopoly of external trade and the cession of Poulo Condore Island off the coast of south Vietnam and the port of Da Nang to the French. The French government directed its colonial governor of Pondicherry (in south India) to provide the military assistance, an order he failed to carry out. De Béhaine, however, raised 300 volunteers and funds in Pondicherry—enough to purchase several shiploads of arms. He arrived in Vietnam on June 19, 1789, barely a month before the fall of the Bastille.

French help was marginal to Nguyen Anh's success. Even before its arrival, he had captured Saigon in 1788; when he conquered Hué in 1801 and Hanoi a year later, there were only four Frenchmen in his army. Bishop de Béhaine, who himself participated in the military campaigns, died in 1799. The French helped in the construction of numerous forts, casting better and larger cannons and creating a navy. Vietnamese Communist historians have lambasted Nguyen Anh for accepting even this limited foreign assistance, comparing him with Ngo Dinh Diem and likening the French volunteers of the late eighteenth century to the U.S. military advisory group of the 1950s and 1960s.

In 1802 Nguyen Anh proclaimed himself emperor of Annam, giving himself the title of Gia Long to signify the political unification of the Red River and Mekong deltas. (The title itself was a contraction of Gia Dinh, the name of the region around Saigon, and Thang Long, that of the region around Hanoi.) In the following year, he sent tribute to the Chinese court; for the first time, China recognized the Nguyen dynasty.

Emperor Gia Long (1802–1820) is considered the first unifier of Vietnam. As remarkable a leader in peace as he was in war, Gia Long reorganized the entire country into three parts and twenty-six provinces. The traditional center of Nguyen power, Hué, became the capital of the kingdom. Tongking was divided into thirteen provinces, Annam into nine, and Cochin China into four. The provinces were subdivided into districts, subdistricts, and villages. Gia Long allowed the Red River and Mekong basins considerable autonomy, a policy reversed by his son, Minh Mang.

Gia Long revived the imperial government as constituted by Le Thanh Thong in the fifteenth century, which was in turn based on the Chinese model. The emperor and six ministers (in charge of public affairs, finance, rites, armed forces, justice, and public works) constituted the Supreme Council. The civil service examination on Confucian lines was reinstituted and a code of laws based on Chinese principles of jurisprudence was proclaimed.

Emperor Gia Long also devoted himself to reconstructing the country, which had been ravaged by a three-decade-long civil war. The most urgent task was to restore the age-old, intricate irrigation system of the Red River Delta. Among his notable public works was the construction of the Mandarin Road (dubbed Route 1 in the 1950s by U.S. soldiers from California) along the coast, linking Saigon, Hué, and Hanoi, a distance of 1,300 miles, which could be covered on horseback in eighteen days. Fortifications dotted the strategic points along the entire route to maintain firm control over most of the country. Communist criticism apart, such remarkable work has earned for Gia Long the undying gratitude of the Vietnamese people as their country's unifier and greatest monarch ever.

CHAPTER 3

The French Conquest
of Vietnam

Despite the long history of French presence in Vietnam, major French territorial conquests did not take place until the second half of the nineteenth century. Like that of the Portuguese, French activity in Asia began under royal patronage and with similar aims: God, gold, and glory. The first French expedition reached Asia in 1601. Two years later, an East India Company was formed in Paris. At least in the initial decades, however, its trading activities did not flourish because of persistently successful Dutch raids against French shipping in the Indonesian waters. An additional reason for the French company's failure was its official sponsorship by the royal court, which meant that its fortunes were dependent upon the whims of the reigning monarch and subject to court intrigues.

VIETNAM AND THE FRENCH MISSIONARIES

For the first two centuries of their presence in Asia, the French were far more successful in religious activities than in trade or acquisition of territories. In 1615, Jesuits opened a mission at Fai Fo, south of Tourane (Da Nang). Its most illustrious member was Alexandre de Rhodes, who beginning in 1627 spent nearly four decades in missionary effort. A great scholar, his most notable contribution to Vietnam was his invention of *quoc-ngu*, a method of writing the Vietnamese language in Roman script instead of the traditional, cumbersome Chinese characters. De Rhodes's motivation, like that of many a missionary compiling glossaries, grammars, and dictionaries of different languages and dialects in Asia, Africa, and Polynesia, was to use the script to reach the masses more easily and convert them to Christianity.

De Rhodes had a checkered career in Vietnam. Born in Avignon, France, in 1591, he joined the Order of the Jesuits at the age of twenty and traveled to the East in 1619. Under instructions from the Vatican, all Catholic missionaries going to the East had to land first in Goa. After a short stay in Goa, Malacca, and Macao, de Rhodes received orders from the Vatican to proceed to Japan. While on his way, de Rhodes learned that there was an official ban on missionaries entering Japan. He therefore stopped in Vietnam. In 1627 he received the Vietnamese emperor's permission to work in the north, but by 1630 he was suspected of political links with Western powers and was expelled. A decade later, he returned to south Vietnam and was again expelled for similar reasons in 1649. After three years in Rome, he returned to France and established the Society of Foreign Missions (Société des Missions Etrangères) in Paris. The society sent scores of missionaries to Vietnam who were successful in converting thousands of people to the Catholic faith. By the end of the eighteenth century, French missionaries claimed about 600,000 converts in south Vietnam and about 200,000 in the north, mostly in the coastal provinces.

Successive French governments demonstrated a consistent interest in proselytization, and missionaries generally maintained close links with the French court right up to the French Revolution. As a French historian of Vietnam, Charles Maybon, notes:

> The history of the new Society [of Foreign Missions] is closely associated with the history of French influence in Indochina. One of its founders, Palu, tied the first knot of relations between the French and the Annamese royal courts. The most illustrious of all missionaries was the Bishop of Adran (Pigneau de Béhaine) who officially strengthened these ties: the acts of the Society's members provoked the first French armed intervention in Vietnam.[1]

Even though Bishop de Béhaine was posthumously given the honors due a duke of the Vietnamese kingdom, his role in converting the young Prince Canh during his visit to France was neither forgotten nor forgiven. Vietnamese monarchs no longer trusted the French missionaries. During Gia Long's rule Christian converts received harsh treatment, their numbers dwindling by 60 percent.

Large-scale persecution of converts and missionaries began in the 1820s under Emperor Minh Mang (1820–1841) and was continued by Thieu Tri (1841–1847) and by Tu Duc in the early part of his reign (1847–1883). The Chinese experience with foreigners (during the Opium War and its aftermath) and missionaries (the Taiping rebellion) had done little to reassure the Vietnamese court. There was a marked increase in hostility toward the Catholics and toward foreign influences in general. Such an attitude was enhanced by continued missionary involvement in court politics. The close association of the missionaries with the semi-independent, rebellious governor of Cochin China, Le Van Duyet, who attempted to prevent Minh Mang's succession to the throne when Gia Long died in 1820, earned them the extreme wrath of the monarch. The revolt posed a serious threat to Minh Mang because Thailand took the opportunity to send its troops to Cochin China. Recent research indicates that the real reasons for the revolt were not so much religious as political. Contrary to his father's policy of devolution of power, Minh Mang had attempted to control Tongking and Cochin China from Hué, even though the one was 600 miles north and the other 600 miles south of the capital city. The Cochin Chinese rebellion was a protest against Minh Mang's ambitions. The emperor was, however, a forceful personality in religion and war. He pushed the Thai troops out of Cochin China and crushed the rebellion with an iron hand.

Minh Mang was an ardent Confucian who believed in ancestor worship. Missionaries encouraged Roman Catholics to oppose such practices. In 1833 the French missionary Father Marchand was suspected of involvement in an uprising in Cochin China led by Le Van Khoi. It was no surprise, therefore, that Minh Mang issued a series of proclamations to eliminate Catholic converts and their institutions. In 1825 Minh Mang forbade the entry of missionaries to his country because he regarded them as agents of an alien power and friends of his major political foe at home. Eight years later, an extremely severe decree ordered churches to be demolished and made profession of the Catholic faith an offense punishable by death.[2] Though the order was not literally applied, many Catholics, including priests, were killed. In 1836, almost at the same time the Chinese restricted foreign trade, the Vietnamese monarch closed his ports to European shipping.

If the Chinese experience held lessons for Vietnam, the British success in "opening" China emboldened the French, who employed similar tactics to open up Vietnam by using the excuse of religious persecution. French missionaries had made it a practice to ignore or violate the laws inhibiting travel in the interior of some of the Asian states, particularly China and Vietnam, and carried on their work of proselytization. As John Cady observes: "In the absence of any French Far Eastern commerce to protect, the missionaries constituted the only tangible aspect of national interest with which [French] naval officers could concern themselves."[3] In the 1840s, French merchant ships and the navy, whose presence in the South China Sea had increased following the opening of five Chinese ports, intervened to secure the release of some missionaries awaiting death sentences in Vietnamese prisons. In 1846, French ships blockaded Tourane (Da Nang) for two weeks and then bombarded the port, demanding the release of Monseigneur Dominique Lefèbvre, who had been condemned to death by the Vietnamese government. Figures of Catholic casualties as well as those of French bombardment of Da Nang have been grossly exaggerated. Buttinger writes: "In seventy minutes, French guns had taken a hundred times more lives than all the Vietnamese Governments in two centuries of religious persecution."[4] According to the U.S. *Catholic Digest*, "In the persecutions of the last century, tiny Vietnam had 100,000 martyrs, far above any single nation's quota since the early Roman persecution."[5] Such exaggerated accounts ignore the gap between the letter of the imperial edicts prescribing persecution and their actual implementation. It should be noted that during Tu Duc's reign, when the persecutions had been taken to a higher level through a decree ordering the subjects to seize missionaries, tie rocks around their necks, and dump them into the sea, a Vietnamese Catholic, Nguyen Truong To (1827–1871), still served as a high court official. He was able to go with a missionary to Europe, see the pope, bring home Western books, and advise Emperor Tu Duc to institute reforms in Vietnam. He could not have survived if the imperial edicts had been strictly enforced.

CONQUEST OF COCHIN CHINA

By responding to reports of persecution of Catholics, the French government of Napoleon III hoped to compensate for its fiasco in Mexico with success in Cochin China. The new French imperialism of the time was widely based on a coalition of diverse interests of the church and traders and manufacturers in search of new markets, and it was aided by the egotistic emperor's lust for colonies to augment national power and prestige. The business interests were aware of the exclusive geographic advantages their position in Vietnam could give them for seeking access to the lucrative markets of interior China. The opening of five Chinese ports in 1842 and eleven more in 1860 gave equal opportunity to almost all foreigners by virtue of the most-favored-nation clause in the treaties of Nanjing and Tianjin. French businessmen interested in overseas markets supported the government of Cochin China because of the prospect of establishing a base in Saigon rivaling Singapore and Hong Kong for funneling South China trade.[6]

In 1858 a joint Franco-Spanish expedition proceeded to Vietnam to save the missionaries. In that year, two priests—one French and one Spanish—had been killed in Vietnam. The Spanish quit after the Vietnamese government gave assurances of nonpersecution, but the French continued the fighting for three years, until they secured a treaty from Tu Duc in 1862. The provisions of the treaty revealed the French intentions clearly: The Vietnamese emperor ceded three provinces in Cochin China, including Saigon, to France and assured that no part of his kingdom would ever be alienated to any other power except France, a clause the latter interpreted to mean that Annam had agreed to be a potential French protectorate. Tu Duc further agreed to pay an indemnity of 4 million piasters in ten annual installments and open three ports in Annam to French trade. Christianity would be tolerated in the future. Significantly, the treaty gave France the right to navigate the Mekong. Five years later, the French obtained the remaining provinces of Cochin China to enable it to establish full control over the Mekong Delta.

How does one explain French success in Cochin China? Most historians have based their analyses on French accounts, blaming the Vietnamese debacle on the inadequate and inefficient administration in the Mekong Delta. If this were so, it is difficult to comprehend how the Annamese court directed a war lasting three and one-half years against France, an enemy with far more sophisticated equipment and economic power than Vietnam. In fact, what made the Vietnamese emperor capitulate in 1862 was the need to divert his forces and attention to putting down a rebellion that had just broken out in north Vietnam under the leadership of a descendant of the old Le dynasty. More accurate explanations are provided by Bernard Fall and Lê Thanh Khoi. Fall attributes the French success to the alienness of the Vietnamese in Cochin China, which they had "colonized" only recently. In his view, there they were "the least secure in their social structure and institutions." Hence the comparative lack of resistance among the non-Vietnamese population to the colonial penetration in the south; the French found it more and more difficult as they advanced further north.[7] Lê Thanh Khoi, an eminent Vietnamese historian, holds that the mandarins hid from the ruler, who was isolated from his people by the high walls of the Forbidden City, "national realities as well as the gravity of the crisis in foreign relations." In Lê's opinion, it was their "blind pride as well as their narrowness of views which bears a large measure of responsibility for the fall of Vietnam."[8]

There is no doubt that along with Burma and Thailand, Vietnam was the most advanced administrative polity in all of Southeast Asia. The Confucian mandarinate recruited through the civil service examination was still capable of governing the country and conducting a war with the French that lasted over three years. It continued to govern central and north Vietnam for another two decades until the French progressively brought the rest of Vietnam under their control. What was basically wrong was the mandarins' habit of looking to Confucian classics for solutions to the challenges posed by the scientific and technological innovations from the West. Under those circumstances, a national debacle at the hands of an aggressive, Western power was only a matter of time.

DE LAGRÉE-GARNIER EXPEDITION

Undoubtedly the most important provision of the 1862 treaty was France's right to navigate the Mekong, which was believed to originate in southwest China. That, and not the protection of Christianity, was the real reason for the occupation of Cochin China. After all, Vietnamese Christians were not located only in Cochin China. Within four years of the treaty, the privately endowed Paris Geographical Society sponsored the exploration of the Mekong under the leadership of two naval officers, Francis Garnier and Doudart de Lagrée. It is significant to note that the president of the society was Chasseloup Laubat, head of the Ministry of the Navy, who was intent upon securing the interests of the traders. The society itself was a front for business interests. In 1873, in cooperation with the Paris Chamber of Commerce, a Society for Commercial Geography was established that sponsored and financed future explorations overseas. Garnier, then a young naval officer, was a scion of a royalist family who, like Joseph François Dupleix before him in India, held grandiose visions of a French empire in the East rivaling that of Britain. Garnier's consuming personal ambition was born of a sense of manifest destiny that he was the divine instrument for elevating France's declining prestige in the world. He had been administrator of Cholon near Saigon for four years when he volunteered to join de Lagrée on the Mekong expedition.

In its exploration of the Mekong, the de Lagrée-Garnier expedition, which left Saigon in June 1866, soon had to pass through Cambodia. Unfortunately, Cambodia had been in grave political trouble for quite some time, and its kings had appealed to France for intervention. With the conquest of Cochin China in 1862, France claimed to have succeeded Vietnam as overlord of Cambodia. In the following year, the French offered to establish a protectorate over Cambodia, a proposal readily accepted by King Norodom, who had succeeded his father, Ang Duong. A Franco-Khmer treaty was drawn up on August 11, 1863.

There was one major legal hurdle before the treaty could be valid. Norodom had not been formally crowned: The royal insignia was in Bangkok, and the Thai monarch insisted on the coronation of his vassal king at his own hands. If Norodom were to become the vassal of Thailand, the French would not be able to establish a protectorate over Cambodia without Thailand's consent. French gunboats therefore blocked Norodom's way to Bangkok. Thailand then revealed a previous secret treaty between Bangkok and Phnom Penh confirming Thailand's suzerain rights and acknowledging the Cambodian monarch's status as Thai viceroy of Cambodia. The ensuing Franco-Thai negotiations finally produced a treaty in 1867 whereby Thailand gave up all claims to suzerainty over Cambodia in return for French recognition of Thai sovereignty over the two western Cambodian provinces of Battambang and Siem Reap.

GARNIER'S TONGKING ADVENTURE

The de Lagrée–Garnier expedition had reported on the unsuitability of the Mekong as a commercial artery into South China. The frequent water-falls and gorges in northeast Cambodia and Laos impeded navigation on the Mekong. De Lagrée lost his life in the upper reaches of the Mekong. Garnier managed to proceed to Yunnan and return to Saigon via Hankow. In a two-volume report on his journey, Garnier recommended exploration of the Red River route. He had discovered while in Yunnan that the bulk of the south Chinese trade in silk, tea, and textiles passed through the Red River valley rather than Canton. Garnier argued that the exploration of the Red River route would offer France, in addition to commercial benefits, an opportunity to extend its "mission civilisatrice" (civilizing mission) to the Red River Delta and beyond.[9]

The serious domestic crisis in which France was engulfed following its disastrous defeat by Prussia arrested all plans for exploration in Indochina for some time. By 1873, however, a chorus of mercantile agitators in Paris and Saigon demanded that France strengthen its hold on Indochina and precipitate access to the markets of interior China before the other Euro-peans in the region did. Three principal actors of the drama to be enacted that year in the Red River Delta were Admiral Marie-Jules Dupré, governor of Cochin China; Francis Garnier; and a French adventurer-trader, Jean Dupuis.

Dupuis had been in Asia since 1858. An extremely able but unscrupu-lous man, he had established an official arms procurement agency for the Chinese government to enable the latter to suppress the series of revolts in south and southwest China following the Taiping rebellion there. Du-puis's interests soon extended to trafficking in minerals and salt between Yunnan and Tongking, violating the monopoly interest of Vietnamese mandarins in those items. In Hankow in 1868 Dupuis discussed with Garnier the possibility of opening the Red River route to facilitate the flow of trade. Both of them were eager to "take Tonkin for a French granary and obtain an opportunity to exploit the mines of Southern China."[10] Four years later, Dupuis enlisted the support of the French Ministry of the Navy, which agreed to have "a naval vessel to rendezvous with him off the Tonkin coast and provide him with information and at least moral support in his negotiations with the Vietnamese."[11] While in Paris, Dupuis also met the governor of Cochin China, Admiral Dupré, and apprised him of future plans.

In the decade before Dupuis's incursions into the Red River Delta, the Vietnamese emperor's hold over his northern possessions was at best tenuous. It had taken five years to suppress the anti-Nguyen revolt of 1862 in the Red River Delta, but a series of new disturbances had broken out in the almost inaccessible, mountainous terrain on either side of the Sino-Vietnamese border. Hordes of fugitive Chinese bandits and rebels who had participated in the Muslim rebellions of South China for over a decade moved across the border, preying on the produce and property of Vietnam's Montagnard population. Two of the largest, best-organized bandit armies were the notorious Black Flags and Yellow Flags, who soon vied with each other for control of the trade and customs revenue collection of the upper Red River valley. Such a local context of "rebellion, banditry and social disorder"[12] was further muddied by the activities of Dupuis, who was determined to open the Red River route to Yunnan to facilitate his illicit trade in salt, minerals, and guns. In addition to some covert support from French officials, Dupuis had a well-trained and well-armed force of 150 men, loaned to him by the Chinese commander in chief of Yunnan.

Dupuis's force clashed with local Vietnamese elements in Hanoi in May 1873. The mandarins there were apprehensive of Dupuis's trading activities because they cut into their monopolies. They refused to allow the Frenchman to proceed upstream on his second attempt with a cargo of salt and arms to China. Dupuis's response was to occupy a section of Hanoi with the help of his Chinese troops and to appeal to Governor Dupré for mediation with Vietnamese authorities. Ironically enough, unaware of the secret ties between Dupuis and Dupré, the Vietnamese emperor, Tu Duc, also appealed to Dupré to order the French intruder out of Hanoi. This was, indeed, a heaven-sent opportunity for Dupré, who wanted an excuse to fish in Tongking's troubled waters. He decided to send a "mediation force" of two gunboats, two corvettes, and 100 men, including sixty marines, under Garnier, ostensibly to evict Dupuis from Hanoi. Garnier had resigned from the navy and, after receiving adequate funds from merchants in France for exploration of new trade routes, had returned to China.[13] He was in Shanghai when Dupré sent for him and entrusted him with the Tongking mission. Ever since he had become governor of Cochin China in 1871, Dupré had harbored an ambition to open the Red River Delta to French influence in order not only to be able to reach South China before the British did but also to help Cochin China's economy, which had been depressed for some time. He was so keen on achieving these objectives that he even disregarded a dispatch from the new minister of the navy and defense in Paris advising patience toward the Tu Duc government and specifically requesting him to abstain from any military involvement. In the absence of a flat veto from the minister,

Dupré and Garnier decided to go ahead with plans to occupy the Red River Delta and present Paris with a fait accompli.[14]

Once in Hanoi at the head of a group of forty men, Garnier threw to the winds the assurances given to Emperor Tu Duc that he would evict Dupuis from Tongking. Instead, he joined forces with Dupuis, picked a quarrel with the local mandarins over the quarters provided for his men, and initiated other measures that were bound to infuriate the mandarins. On November 16, Garnier unilaterally declared the Red River open to international trade and revised the customs tariffs to make them more advantageous to foreigners. Five days later, in a brash action, Garnier stormed the citadel of Hanoi and proceeded to do likewise in all important towns of the Red River valley. Within three weeks, lower Tongking, including Haiphong and Ninh Binh, was under French military control, and Dupuis seemed well entrenched in Hanoi. But the spectacular success was too easy to last long. The mandarins, whose pride, position, and profit were hurt by Garnier's actions, used another group to get rid of him. Garnier had already declared himself opposed to Black Flags then roaming and raiding the Tongking countryside. The mandarins instigated them to attack Garnier. On December 21 Garnier lost his life during a skirmish with the Black Flags.

It is difficult to know whether Garnier and Dupré were acting on their own or as part of a skillfully disguised scheme of the French government, which could always disclaim the venture if it went awry. Ostensibly, at least, the news of Garnier's undertaking dismayed Paris. France officially denounced his actions, ordered Dupuis out of Tongking, and signed an essentially conciliatory treaty with Tu Duc. Nonetheless, a number of Garnier's objectives had been accomplished: The Red River was declared open to foreign commerce and three ports of the delta were also opened, with a French consul and garrison stationed in each. Both Garnier's death and the episode as a whole, however, were a serious setback to further French expansion for at least a decade.

FRANCE COMPLETES THE CONQUEST OF VIETNAM

In spite of the Garnier affair and domestic strife within France, certain groups still advocated expansion in Southeast Asia. Those enthusiastic about increasing overseas markets and desirous of a predominant role in the international competition for colonies demanded immediate French initiative in Asia and Africa. Members of the emerging geographical societies were often the most ardent supporters of such an initiative, arguing that colonization projects would afford desirable outlets for surplus population and capital and help the reestablishment of French prestige and power. Such geographical organizations, including the influential

Paris Geographical Society, were critical of the lack of support for Garnier and Dupré's intervention in Tongking. They insisted that the area would not only be a commercial asset but one where the French could pass on the benefits of their superior culture to the "barbaric" inhabitants.

By 1881 the exponents of imperialism had enlisted the aid of the new premier, Jules Ferry, who was prepared to take the risks of pursuing an active and aggressive policy in the Far East. A one-time, self-styled economic liberal, Ferry had changed his views on the value of colonies at the behest of colonial traders and investors interested in opening profitable markets. "There needs to be no hesitation," he had come to believe, "in affirming that colonies in the present state of the world is the best affair of business in which the capital of an old and wealthy country can engage."[15] He emphasized the importance of colonies to French commerce, which was then suffering from the prevailing depression. For his own efforts toward the conquest of the Tongking Delta, he gave another reason: "It is not a question of tomorrow but of the future of fifty or hundred years; of that which will be the inheritance of our children, the bread of our workers. It is not a question of conquering China, but it is necessary to be at the portal of this region to undertake the pacific conquest of it."[16]

The treaty of 1873 gave France the rationale for its subsequent action. The French alleged that the Vietnamese court had contravened the protectorate clause implicit in that treaty by continuing to send the traditional, quinquennial tribute to China. Besides, the Vietnamese mandarins had hindered a French expedition led by Henri Rivière to push the piratical Black Flags out of the Red River valley. The Vietnamese emperor was forced to sign further treaties in 1883 and 1884 that made Vietnam a French protectorate, gave France administrative control of Tongking province, and turned Hanoi and Hué into French residencies. The powerless emperor appealed to his Chinese overlord for help in stopping further French encroachments on Vietnamese territory.

As the French approached the Chinese borders, frequent clashes took place between the Chinese and French troops. With the defeat of French forces at the border post of Langson on March 28, 1885, the Ferry ministry collapsed. But France struck back by attacking Keelung in Formosa, capturing the Pescadores Islands, and blockading the port of Fuzhou, crushing the Chinese navy that defended it. Ultimately, the well-armed French troops overcame the ill-equipped Chinese forces. At Tianjin on June 9, 1885, the Middle Kingdom signed a treaty recognizing the French protectorate over Annam and Tongking, permitting French traders in South China, granting preference to France over all other European powers in Yunnan, and allowing France to build a railway paralleling the Red River valley from Hanoi to Kunming. The treaty brought to an end the subordination of Vietnam by China that had lasted nearly 2,000 years—and completed the French conquest of Vietnam.

Although Vietnam had been unified under the Nguyen emperors since 1802, the French divided it into three administrative units: Cochin China, Annam, and Tongking. With the conquest of three provinces of Cochin China in 1862, the French governed the new acquisition as a colony. Its administration was placed under the navy, which had been responsible for its conquest in the first place. Until 1879, its governors were appointed by and accountable to the Ministry of the Navy and Colonies. Meanwhile, in 1867 a protectorate had been established over neighboring Cambodia, where the old court and nobility continued to have nominal authority whereas the French nominee at the Cambodian monarch's court exercised real power.

The annexation of Tongking and Annam to the French empire was also effected through treaties of protectorate concluded with the Vietnamese emperor in 1874 and 1883, respectively. In 1885 they were ratified by China, thereby terminating Vietnam's status as a vassal state of the Chinese empire. In 1887, four French acquisitions—Cochin China, Cambodia, Annam, and Tongking—were brought under a new colonial entity called the Indochinese Union. It created a French governor general, headquartered in Hanoi, with authority over all four French units. Cochin China was treated as a direct colony under a French lieutenant governor; a French official styled the "resident" was placed at the courts of the emperor of Annam at Hué and of his viceroy at Hanoi. A resident was similarly accredited to the Cambodian king's court at Phnom Penh. Although the newly established Indochinese Union appeared to be a combination of direct and indirect rule, in effect, power came to be increasingly concentrated into the hands of the governor general in Hanoi.

Further centralization of authority over Indochina came about under the strong-willed Paul Doumer, governor general from 1897 to 1902. A few years before his arrival, the French had brought the kingdom of Laos under its protection. In 1897 Doumer abolished the post of Vietnamese viceroy in Tongking, instead appointing a French "resident superior" to represent that region in Hanoi. Another French "resident superior" at Hué would exercise all authority in the name of the emperor. Residents were also placed at the courts of the kings of Cambodia and Laos; there was no change in Cochin China's status. By the end of Doumer's administration, all semblance of indirect rule had disappeared, though the emperor of Annam and the kings of Cambodia and Laos were allowed to maintain their courts and advisory councils.

LUANG
PRABANG

HANOI

THANH-HOA

HAI-NAN

QUANG BINH

QUANG TRI
HUÉ
TOURANE

PHNOMPENH

BIEN HOA
MY THO   SAIGON
BARIA

SOCTRANG

UP TO THE 10th CENTURY   17th CENTURY

11th-15th CENTURY   18th CENTURY

16th CENTURY   19th CENTURY

VIETNAMESE SOUTHWARD MOVEMENT

CHAPTER 4

The Nationalist Movement

 The Vietnamese are a freedom-loving people who have often had to fight to obtain and maintain their liberty. As Marr observes: "The continuity in Vietnamese anti-colonialism is a highly-charged, historically self-conscious resistance to oppressive, de-grading foreign rule. Possessors of a proud cultural and political heritage, many Vietnamese simply refused to be cowed."[1]

Vietnamese nationalism began as opposition to the direct Chinese rule from 111 B.C. to A.D. 939 and again from 1407 to 1428. As late as the end of the eighteenth century, the Chinese Emperor Jianlong lamented: "The Vietnamese are, indeed, not a reliable people. An occupation does not last very long before they raise arms against us and expel us from their country. The history of past dynasties has proved this fact."[2]

Despite a policy of sinicization of Vietnam, whether enforced by the Chinese rulers or voluntarily adopted by the Vietnamese emperors, Chinese culture failed to obliterate the Vietnamese social traditions, particularly in the countryside, where the bulk of the people lived. Sinicization affected mainly the upper classes. Left to themselves, the villagers continued to worship village genies, ancestors, mountains, and rivers in rites that predated the advent of Chinese culture. Chinese domination never threatened the traditional modes of Vietnamese social behavior as much as did French rule, especially toward the end of the nineteenth century.

The French administration destroyed the Vietnamese peasant civilization that had survived with nominal foreign interference for two millennia. Before the French conquest, each bamboo-fenced Vietnamese village was an almost autonomous social entity governed by a council of village notables who collected taxes on behalf of the central government, assigned agrarian chores, distributed the rice, and dispensed justice. The imperial government intruded only to take census or to recruit soldiers. The rural folk believed that the laws of the emperor were less significant than the customs of the village. The French disrupted the village system, instituting regular registration of births and deaths to allow more accurate tax polls and more efficient tax collection and generally establishing a tight control over fiscal matters. Later they substituted elections for co-optation of council members. The right to vote was based on education in French and high property qualifications, which limited the benefits of the new system only to Western-educated individuals, who had neither a traditional following nor influence among the peasants. The changes made the traditional notables join the ranks of the opposition.

EARLY RESISTANCE TO FRENCH RULE

Under diverse leaders, including peasants, resistance to French rule began almost as soon as it was introduced in Cochin China in 1862 and expanded to revolutionary scale after the French conquest of Annam in 1885. The pacification program, as it was called, like its British counterpart in Burma, reached its height in 1895 but extended until 1913. In one especially brutal campaign from 1909 to 1913, the French tracked down resistance leaders like De Tham ("the tiger of Yen Tre"), killing them one by one. Peasants sheltered the leaders of the resistance movement, among them the Vietnamese scholar-gentry class. Before 1900 the mandarins were under the illusion that although French occupation of their lands might mean loss of political control, the Vietnamese would retain cultural and spiritual independence. But a new generation of mandarins was aware of the pervasive educational and cultural impact of colonial rule; they feared *mat nuoc* (losing one's country) and were taken aback by the attitudes of the collaborator mandarins and the royal family, who had fallen prey to French temptations and imitated their ways. The mandarin class could thus be divided into three groups: those who had collaborated with the French, those who retreated to the villages in a kind of passive noncooperation, and those who battled to bring new meaning and ethnic salvation (*cuu quoc*) to their country.[3]

Two major events in Asia changed the direction of the Vietnamese opposition to French rule from an urge to restore monarchy and the status quo ante to a demand for popular democracy either through a constitutional monarchy or republicanism. One was Japan's spectacular rise as an industrially and militarily strong nation. The other was the 1899 Boxer Uprising against Western presence and domination of China, followed by China's reform movement and overthrow of the decadent Qing monarchy. The reform movement in China was led by Kang Youwei and Liang Qichao. The latter's writings inspired the Vietnamese and led them to read and absorb Chinese translations of great Western political philosophers, nota-

bly Locke, Rousseau, and Montesquieu. Numerous Vietnamese intellectuals were also influenced by Sun Yatsen and his revolutionary leadership
in overthrowing an autocratic, decadent monarchy in China and introduc-
ing a republican government with individual rights to freedom.

PHAN BOI CHAU AND PHAN CHAU TRINH

The happenings in East Asia had a direct impact on two Vietnamese
anticolonialist leaders, Phan Boi Chau (1867–1940) and Phan Chau Trinh
(1871–1926). A member of a scholar-gentry family, Phan Boi Chau passed
the regional examination in 1900 and soon became familiar with Liang
Qichao's writings. In 1902 he published the book *Ryukyu's Bitter Tears*,
which used the transfer of sovereignty of the Ryukyu Islands to the
Japanese as a metaphor for the Vietnamese loss of freedom under the
French. Two years later, Phan Boi Chau and some of his pupils and
associates founded the Duy Tan Hoi (Reformation Society) to foster revolutionary monarchism based on the model of Japan, whose emperor had
allowed the development of a constitutional government in response to
the challenges of the West. Supported by Prince Cuong De, the group
decided to obtain outside assistance to achieve its nationalistic ends. In
1905 Phan Boi Chau made a secret trip to Japan, where he met Liang
Qichao and, through him, Sun Yatsen and other Chinese revolutionaries
from whom he learned the techniques of starting a revolution. Liang also
introduced Phan Boi Chau to the Japanese leaders, who promised liberal
scholarships to Vietnamese students but no military assistance to overthrow the French rule. Soon afterwards, Phan published *The History of the
Loss of Vietnam*, which went through five editions in China and which
circulated clandestinely throughout Vietnam. The book had tremendous
impact both among scholars and common people in Vietnam because of
its nontraditional style and translation into *quoc-ngu*, romanized Vietnamese. Influenced by Phan's work, scores of Vietnamese students enrolled in
Japanese institutions, including military academies.

Meanwhile, Phan Boi Chau had made Canton his base for revolutionary
activity in Vietnam, establishing for the purpose the Viet Nam Quang
Phuc Hoi (Association for the Restoration of Vietnam) in 1913. In 1914 a
resolution to organize a "restoration army" was passed. Phan Boi Chau
was thereupon put behind bars by the governor general of Canton at the
instigation of the French colonial government. In 1917 the restoration army
attempted an uprising on the Vietnam border but failed miserably. Later
in the same year, Sun Yatsen's exertions resulted in the release of Phan
Boi Chau.

Phan Boi Chau spent the next few years in Canton and Shanghai. He
was responsible for getting forty Vietnamese admitted to the Whampoa

Military Academy, where Chinese nationalists and Communists worked together. Despite the nationalist-Communist honeymoon phase (1924–1927) of politics, Phan Boi Chau got into trouble with the Communists. In 1925, at Ho Chi Minh's instance, Phan Boi Chau was seized in Shanghai and "sold" to the French concession there for 100,000 piasters.[4] Phan Boi Chau was brought to Hanoi and sentenced to death, though later, because of widespread public protests and the somewhat liberal policy of the new Socialist governor general, Alexandre Varenne, the sentence was commuted to life. The great patriot languished and died in 1940.

For Phan Chau Trinh, however, monarchy as an institution had become outdated. He was a firm believer in democracy and an advocate of a Western-style republican constitution. He led a tax-resistance movement in 1908, was arrested, and was later deported to French prisons, where he remained until 1925. A few months after his release, he managed to reach Saigon, where he perceived that politics had changed so much during his long absence that he could not take part in the nationalist movement even if he wanted to. His death on March 24, 1926, however, unwittingly fueled the nationalist movement. Nguyen An Ninh, a reformer and editor of *La Cloche Fêlée,* wrote a eulogistic obituary for which he was arrested and his paper censored. The arrest provoked strikes among students and bank and postal employees. Several hundred students were expelled from colleges and universities for defying the ban on wearing bands mourning the passing of a great patriot.

BEGINNINGS OF THE MODERN NATIONALIST MOVEMENT

In the second decade of the twentieth century, the purpose and leadership of the nationalist movement gradually changed as the results of French education began to show. Many young individuals from well-to-do families who had been trained in Vietnam and France became nationalist leaders. Large numbers of Vietnamese youths went to China after the revolution of 1911. In 1913 these expatriates instigated small uprisings in Tongking and Cochin China. They had short-lived success despite the assistance of Emperor Duy Tan (1907–1916). In 1916 a more serious revolt was severely suppressed by the French authorities, sending Duy Tan and his father, Than Thai, the former emperor, into exile. That, in a sense, marked an end to the conservative, restorative, monarchical phase of the nationalist movement. After the exile of Duy Tan, no Vietnamese nationalist presented restoration of the Nguyen monarchy as a feasible alternative to French rule. After 1916 the alternatives were clearly populist, republican, or revolutionary. The immediate inspiration was provided by the Chinese Republic, established after the overthrow of the Qing dynasty in 1911.

Such a change favoring a wider, popular base for the nationalist movement was also helped by the events of World War I. Many of the more than 100,000 Vietnamese soldiers and workers who saw wartime service in France returned home full of new aspirations for freedom that were, in the French view, subversive ideas. Some of them joined the nationalists in making modest demands for participation in the councils and for greater accommodation in civil service positions. These were the moderates in politics, who were further inspired by pronouncements of Western leaders, such as those of U.S. President Woodrow Wilson, whose Fourteen Points included the right of self-determination of nations. Even a would-be radical revolutionary like Ho Chi Minh was apparently so impressed by the promise of self-determination that he attempted to seek a meeting with the Western leaders gathered at the Versailles conference. In the aftermath of the war, frustrated nationalists, who were fascinated with the success of the Russian Revolution, turned to Marxism as a means of liberating their homeland from colonial rule.

Many Vietnamese Communist and non-Communist youths received their initial, intellectual, organizational, and revolutionary training across the frontier in China. Although a good number of non-Communist leaders had been educated in French schools in Vietnam and France, almost all the Communist leaders (with the major exception of Ho Chi Minh) were trained in China. The exploits of the Kuomintang (KMT) as well as of Communist leaders in China inspired the Vietnamese nationalists. A distant but nevertheless potent source of inspiration was India, where a virulent and popular mass movement had been launched by Mahatma Gandhi, challenging the continuation of British rule on the subcontinent. A Vietnamese nationalist, Duong Van Gieu, met Jawaharlal Nehru at the Brussels meeting of the League Against Imperialism and for National Independence in 1927 and attended the meeting of the Indian National Congress the following year.

The 1920s proved to be a decade of tremendous political, intellectual, and ideological ferment over most of Southeast Asia. In Vietnam, a new class of educated young people had replaced the old mandarin class. The French themselves sought to create a new type of Vietnamese, "yellow gentlemen," who would accept French beliefs, standards of deportment, and values. The colonial educational system mirrored metropolitan models for reasons of both pride and pragmatism. The needs of colonial administration as well as those of the new economy, particularly of the French enterprises, required large numbers of French-speaking, indigenous, subordinate staff. The Vietnamese did not, however, limit themselves to such a rudimentary level of education, mastering as well the French writings included in the political and economic fields.

The new Vietnamese elite consisted of government employees, professionals, French-trained college and university students, educated landowners, and businesspeople. They were articulate enough to inspire the support of noncommissioned army officers and skilled workers. Vietnamese intellectuals quickly and clearly saw the contradiction in the French profession of the hallowed principles of equality, liberty, and fraternity and their practice of denial of fundamental freedoms in an atmosphere of official repression. They would soon demand important positions in high administration as well as legislation equating the Vietnamese status with that of French settlers. Above all, they demanded freedom of speech, association, and press.

The educated Vietnamese, particularly those schooled in France, perceived the difference between metropolitan France, where even the colonials could enjoy the democratic freedoms, and Vietnam, where they were denied such rights. They also noted that the colonial civil service, which was far inferior to that in France, was marked by unequal pay and unequal standards of eligibility for the Vietnamese, who were discriminated against irrespective of their competence. Vietnamese businesspeople rankled against the government regulations that favored French-owned enterprises over indigenous ones. The lack of representative institutions inhibited the efforts of the intelligentsia and business class to voice their grievances or make suggestions for improvement. The new elite produced a leadership that would articulate the problems of the semiliterates and skilled workers and organize the economically dissatisfied peasantry, and, in so doing, promote nationalism among the masses.

THE VNQDD

The most prominent of the non-Marxist organizations of the 1920s was the Viet Nam Quoc Dan Dang (Vietnamese Nationalist Party, or VNQDD) founded in Hanoi in 1927. Its organization modeled after the Chinese Kuomintang, it adopted Sun Yatsen's principles of nationalism, democracy, and people's livelihood and committed itself to overthrowing the French colonial rule with the KMT's help. A preparatory conference of the VNQDD had invited Phan Boi Chau to lead the new party. His arrest and absence put Nguyen Thai Hoc, a twenty-three-year-old teacher and revolutionary, at the head of the party.

The VNQDD was dominated by its leftist wing, which used terrorism as a political weapon. A number of such "terrorists" infiltrated the Vietnamese units in the army, inspiring and provoking them to oppose their French commanders. Contemporaneous with rise of the VNQDD was the growth of a number of Marxist groups—Communists and Trotskyites. They would be brought together in 1930 in Hong Kong by the most dynamic of their leaders, Ho Chi Minh. Even so, at that point the VNQDD held far greater appeal among the masses than did the Communists.

THE UPRISINGS OF 1930–1931

On February 9, 1929, Bazin, director of employee recruitment for rubber plantations, was killed by a Vietnamese youth, possibly at Communist instigation. The French authorities suspected the VNQDD and immediately imprisoned several VNQDD supporters and launched a thorough but clandestine investigation of the VNQDD's underground activities. Fearing that French retaliatory action could destroy the VNQDD, its leader, Nguyen Thai Hoc, ordered preparations for nationwide insurrection on February 10, 1930. When, at the last minute, the date was changed to February 15, chaos broke out. The military garrison at Yen Bay, unaware of the postponement, led its own uprising on February 10, killing French officers. Although the VNQDD expected the Yen Bay uprising to spark a nationwide revolution, only sporadic peasant uprisings in certain provinces took place. The French police easily suppressed the disturbances and conclusively destroyed the effectiveness of the VNQDD, many of whose members fled northward to China. Others were arrested and executed. The VNQDD underwent gradual attrition in Yunnan, where for some time it faced competition from another non-Marxist Vietnamese organization, namely, Phan Boi Chau's Association for the Restoration of Vietnam. At the end of World War II, a remnant of the VNQDD would be brought by Chiang Kaishek's troops to Vietnam to fish in the troubled waters of Vietnamese politics. The French destruction of the VNQDD accounted for the lack of strong and effective non-Communist leadership among the Vietnamese nationalist ranks in the post-1930 period, opening immediate opportunity for the Communists and virtually guaranteeing their ultimate control of the movement. The leader of the Vietnamese Communist movement was Ho Chi Minh.

HO CHI MINH

Ho Chi Minh was born to a modest mandarin family in 1890 in Kim Lien village in Nghe An province. His original name was Nguyen Sinh Cung, which he changed several times both out of fancy as well as to conceal his real identity.[5] Such aliases included Nguyen Tan Tranh (Nguyen Who Will Succeed), Nguyen Ai Quoc (Nguyen the Patriot), and Ho Chi Minh (He Who Is Enlightened). His father, Nguyen Sinh Huy, was a scholar and a revolutionary who had passed the civil service examination and held the mandarin's title of *pho bang*. Ho's schooling was very sporadic, though records indicate his enrollment at Quoc Hoc (National Studies) College in Hué.

Ho Chi Minh left Vietnam as a cabin boy on the merchant vessel *Amiral LaTouche Treville* in 1913. After many odd jobs in England and France as a kitchen aide, photographic retoucher, and painter of French-made "Chinese antiquities," Ho established his reputation as a good pamphleteer in leftist circles in Paris. He utilized his stay in London (1913–1917), most of it at the Carleton Hotel as a helper to the famous French chef Escoffier, studying English but also learning his activist ropes as a member of the Overseas Workers' Union, a secret anticolonial body, mostly under Chinese leadership.

In 1919 Ho Chi Minh appeared outside the Versailles peace conference intending to present to the statesmen assembled there his eight-point program potentially leading to the right of self-determination for his country. His demands were a general amnesty for Vietnamese political prisoners, equal rights for French and Vietnamese, abolition of the criminal court misused as an instrument for persecution of Vietnamese patriots, freedom of the press and of thought, freedom of association and of assembly, freedom of movement and of travel abroad, freedom to go to school and to open technical and vocational schools for the Vietnamese, substitution of the system of law for that of decrees, and appointment of a Vietnamese representative in Paris to settle questions concerning Vietnamese people's interests.[6]

Ho Chi Minh soon discovered that the doctrine of self-determination Wilson propounded was to be applied only to East European nations created by the breakup of the Austro-Hungarian Empire. His disillusionment led him directly to the Marxist fold. As Ho himself averred, until then he understood "neither what was a party, a trade union, nor what was Socialism nor Communism."[7] Afterwards, he became very active in the French Socialist Party, attending its congress in 1920 and voting with the majority for the Third International and for changing the party's name to the French Communist Party. It was after reading Lenin's *Theses on the National and Colonial Questions* that Ho felt drawn to communism. To quote Ho: "At first, patriotism, not yet Communism, led me to have confidence in Lenin and in the Third International."[8] One can reasonably assume that it was the French intransigence that pushed many frustrated Vietnamese nationalists into the Communist fold and that most of them, like Ho Chi Minh, remained nationalist first and Communist second.

In 1923 the French Communist Party sent Ho Chi Minh to the Soviet Union for further training at the newly opened University for the Toilers of the East. Ho also represented the French Communist Party at the Peasants' International (or Krestintern) meeting in October 1923. He was elected a member of the executive committee of the Peasants' International for the next eighteen months. In June through July 1924, Ho was a delegate to the Fifth Congress of the Communist International. His performance there caught the attention of the Soviet hierarchy, and later in the year he was sent to Canton, ostensibly as a translator to assist Mikhail Borodin, adviser to the KMT, but really to organize the Communist movement in Vietnam.

A year later, Ho Chi Minh formed Thanh Nien (Association of Vietnamese Revolutionary Youth) in Canton, which had attracted numerous fugitive revolutionaries from Vietnam. Although many of them already belonged to other existing nationalist associations or groups, Ho managed to persuade some of the younger activists, including many members of the Hanoi Students' Movement, to join his organization. For six months, Ho taught his followers Marxist revolutionary techniques. The movement was progressing slowly, the major problem being paucity of funds. In order to further finance the movement, some Thanh Nien members resorted to robbery and violence. Ho Chi Minh himself betrayed his early youth idol, the great nationalist Phan Boi Chau, to the French for a reward of 100,000 piasters, a sum he used for developing the Thanh Nien organization. Many years later, Ho's action was explained away by his associates on grounds that Phan Boi Chau was a spent force, that he was too old to lead the movement, that his arrest could only help the nationalist movement better through the wave of protest and hostility against the French that his arrest would surely arouse in Vietnam. All these were, indeed, unacceptable rationalizations of a dastardly and unpardonable act on Ho Chi Minh's part. Cooperation between the nationalist groups and the Thanh Nien ceased thereafter.

Over the period of the next two years, Ho Chi Minh trained about 250 men, got some of them enrolled in Whampoa Military Academy, and sent others to the Soviet Union for studies in Marxism. Most of these young men later made up the leadership of the Indochina Communist Party and the Democratic Republic of Vietnam. One of the trainees Ho sent to Whampoa was Pham Van Dong, who had been expelled by the French from Vietnam and who was later to rise to be Ho's righthand man and prime minister of Vietnam. In 1927, conflicts between the Chinese KMT and the Soviets obliged many Comintern members in China, among them Ho Chi Minh, to leave for Moscow. Because of these developments, the Communist movement among the Vietnamese was driven off the course the Comintern had charted.

Two years later, the Comintern sent Ho Chi Minh to Bangkok, where the Comintern South Seas Bureau had been established. Ho worked there among the Vietnamese immigrants for a time, trying to win converts to communism. By that time, the Thanh Nien and the small number of Communists in Vietnam itself were divided into several groups. In 1930

Ho fused the three prominent Vietnamese Communist factions in Hong Kong into a single Vietnamese Communist Party. The name was quickly and significantly changed to the Indochina Communist Party (ICP), although there were hardly any Communists then in Laos and Cambodia. Because he was so successful, Ho was appointed head of the Far Eastern Bureau of the Comintern. By 1931 the ICP claimed 1,500 members besides 100,000 peasants affiliated in peasant organizations.

Undeterred by the VNQDD failure and, in fact, to offset the VNQDD's relative popularity among the masses, the ICP decided to exploit the prevalent peasant unrest brought on by successive crop failures and the economic depression. Strikes in plantations and factories were organized beginning May Day 1930, and "soviets" were established in the provinces of Nghe An and Ha Tinh. Although Ho Chi Minh did not favor an immediate major uprising, advocated by the majority of the hard-liners in his party, he relented. The ICP met the same fate as the VNQDD at the hands of the French police. Hundreds were killed, many more arrested. Ho fled to Hong Kong, where he was arrested by the British police on June 30 of the following year. He was later admitted to a Hong Kong hospital for tuberculosis. In 1933 Ho suddenly disappeared and for the next eight years remained practically incommunicado. Except perhaps for a few senior members of the Comintern, no one knew Ho's whereabouts. During Ho's absence, the French Communist Party acted as the intermediary between Moscow and the Vietnamese Communists.

The two uprisings—the VNQDD's and the ICP's—had a tremendous impact on the Vietnamese masses, whose resentment against French rule multiplied manifold. According to Vietnamese nationalists, more than 10,000 of their compatriots had been executed, tortured to death, or killed with bombs or bayonets, grenades or guns during the two violent uprisings. The bombing of unarmed marchers at Vinh, which took several hundred lives, was unconscionable, as were the several hundred guillotinings without trials. Some French legionnaires were known to have rounded up suspected villagers and shot nine out of ten before interrogating the sole survivor. Prisoners were brutalized in the worst imaginable manner, having parts of their bodies cut off and being left to die. Many Communists were interned in the crowded dungeon cells on the Poulo Condore Island, their ideological beliefs and zest for independence hardened further as a reaction to the brutal treatment there.

The two uprisings also affected public opinion in France, leading some liberal colonialists to advocate reforms in Indochina. In September 1932, Prince Bao Dai was brought back from France at the age of eighteen to head a reformed monarchy with a moderate nationalist, Pham Quynh, as his chief of cabinet. That was an opportunity for nationalists like Ngo Dinh Diem, Bao Dai's new minister of the interior and chief of the reform commission, to push the reformist movement ahead. Diem came from an illustrious Catholic family with excellent connections. He was given to understand by Governor General Pierre Pasquier that the newly constituted emperor's council would have genuine authority to carry out reforms. In a few months, he was to realize that the French colonials, not for the first nor for the last time, could not be trusted. The disillusioned Diem left Bao Dai's cabinet and went into virtual political retirement, whereas the frustrated young emperor sought solace in the life of a playboy monarch, spending more time on the beaches of southern France than in Vietnam, a failing Diem never forgave him.

The VNQDD apparatus had been crushed by the French repression, but the ICP was soon able to reassemble its party machinery, thanks to its superior organization and party discipline. Its greater fortune lay also in the politics of the period of détente (1936–1939) in France, when the Popular Front recognized the ICP. In the early months of 1936, the Popular Front released all political prisoners, including Communists. The other Vietnamese parties remained without a coherent program or organization, but the ICP took advantage of the political situation to organize a broad Democratic National Front, under the leadership of Pham Van Dong and Vo Nguyen Giap, aimed at uniting all social classes and political groups— with the exception of their staunch enemies, the Trotskyites. With the outbreak of war, the Popular Front government fell in France, the honeymoon with Communists ended, and the ICP was banned. Most of its cadres went underground; some fled to China.

BIRTH OF THE VIET MINH

In August 1940, following the lead of the collaborationist Vichy government in France, the governor general of Indochina signed a general accord with Japan, which allowed the French administration to continue in Indochina in return for placing the military facilities and economic resources (rice, coal, rubber, and other raw materials) at Japan's disposal. Toward the end of 1941, the Japanese used Indochina for consolidating their land and sea forces to launch massive attacks against Malaya, Hong Kong, the Philippines, and Indonesia. The Japanese interned the French in March 1945, just before the war ended. The subservience of the French and their humiliation at the hands of an Asian nation completely obliterated the image of European colonial invincibility. Never again were the Vietnamese to regard the French with awe. When the French returned in September 1945 at the behest of the Allies, many, particularly those who had spent a lifetime in Vietnam, were shocked at the new attitude of insouciance, self-confidence, and challenge among their Vietnamese subjects.

During the war, the Soviet Union and nationalist China joined the Anglo-American forces in a common struggle against the Japanese, a situation making for strange political bedfellows. Ho Chi Minh was released from a Chinese prison at Chiang Kaishek's orders to enable him to lead a resistance movement in Vietnam against the Japanese-dominated Vichy government. Military and other supplies were made available to him by the U.S. Office of Strategic Services.

Meanwhile, the ICP's central committee met in southern China in May 1941 and decided to subordinate its plans for agrarian reform and class revolution to the immediate goal of independence and freedom for all Vietnamese. A new organization, the Viet Minh (short for the Viet Nam Doc Lap Dong Minh Hoi, the Vietnam Independence League), was launched in September 1941 to bring all Vietnamese, irrespective of their party or ideological affiliation, into a common front to fight for independence. Salvation associations called *cuu quoc* were to be organized throughout the country for popular participation in politics. The Viet Minh, though led by Communists, chose to seek a broader political base of patriotism and nationalism. They had a two-stage plan that called for a nationalist uprising to be followed by a Communist revolution.

It was easier for the Vietnamese Communists to play down their doctrinaire loyalties during World War II and make it appear to the nationalists that they placed the nationalist and democratic interests above those of communism. This was because of the alliance between the Soviet Union and Western powers. Parenthetically, it may be observed that to the Vietnamese, the doctrine of capitalism had manifested itself as the control of the economy by white foreigners. Democracy had represented to them a vague idea that looked attractive but that, whenever it was tried, had been easily suppressed by the French. Thus capitalism had come to be equated with French interests whereas the democratic forces had shown themselves too weak to stand up to French repressive policies. A nationalist movement led by anticapitalist Communists who could harass the French through their underground, terrorist, revolutionary techniques therefore won favor with a large number of people yearning for the country's liberation. Further, despite the early intervention on the part of the Soviet Union in the 1920s and 1930s through Ho Chi Minh, the Communists escaped the foreign label during World War II because of the peculiar international situation in which the Soviet Union was one of the Allies. The Communist-led Viet Minh thus gained acceptance by the Vietnamese people as the viable representatives of nationalism.

Despite such a nationalist stance, the Viet Minh was not readily acceptable to many of the non-Communist Vietnamese nationalists. Nor did the Kuomintang believe its claims of being a nationalist organization. During 1941–1942, the KMT rejected the Viet Minh's proposals to join forces against Japan. So distrustful was the nationalist Chinese government of the Viet Minh that toward the end of 1941 it arrested its leader, Ho Chi Minh (then still known as Nguyen Ai Quoc), and detained him in a prison in South China until the end of the following year.

The Chinese government called a meeting in South China in October 1942 to which all Vietnamese organizations functioning in exile in that part of the country were invited. Some Viet Minh leaders (but not Ho Chi Minh) were allowed to attend. At this meeting, a new organization named Viet Nam Cach Minh Dong Minh Hoi (Vietnam Revolutionary League) was created by bringing together ten different Vietnamese parties and groups, including the Viet Minh, in the hope that it would organize within Vietnam an effective opposition to the Japanese. The Dong Minh Hoi failed utterly in its mission. At the end of 1942, in the hope that his organizational abilities would make Vietnamese resistance to Japan possible, the Chinese government resolved to release Ho Chi Minh and make him head of Dong Minh Hoi. Though Ho entered Vietnam in that capacity, he quickly gave up the Dong Minh Hoi and instead mobilized the Viet Minh to provide effective assistance to the Chinese forces struggling against the Japanese. Dong Minh Hoi thereafter retained an insignificant existence mostly in South China, whereas the Viet Minh became the principal organization of Vietnamese resistance against the Japanese and (after 1945) the French.

The Viet Minh employed guerrilla strategies from the very beginning. In December 1944, with thirty-four men, Vo Nguyen Giap formed the first platoon of a guerrilla force. Its weaponry was limited to one light machine gun, seventeen rifles, fourteen flintstock rifles, two revolvers, and a modest amount of ammunition. Within a decade, in time for the battle of Dien Bien Phu, this platoon would grow into a well-trained and well-equipped army of six divisions.

The psychological and military guerrilla strategy used in this early period was similar to that used later to defeat the Americans. The Viet Minh would select for attack small isolated outposts of the French, keeping in mind exactly how many men and weapons awaited them. They would always make surprise attacks with superior numbers and in places where they were sure of success. They were eventually able to arm their increasingly growing army with weapons captured from the enemy. Such a strategy wore out the French and later on, the Americans, who were unfamiliar with the Vietnamese mountainous areas and marshy terrains and who were untrained and incapable of dealing successfully with guerrilla warfare.

By September 1944, the Viet Minh had an army of 5,000 men and the three mountainous provinces of Cao Bang, Langson, and Bac Kan under their control. Ho Chi Minh could clearly see that the day of his country's independence was not far away. From the jungles of northern Vietnam, he wrote:

> Zero hour is near. Germany is almost beaten, and her defeat will lead to Japan's. Then the Americans and the Chinese will move into Indochina while the Gaullists rise against the Japanese. The latter may well topple the French Fascists prior to this and set up a military government. . . . Indochina will reduce to anarchy. We shall not need even to seize power, for there will be no power. . . . Our impending uprising will be carried out in highly favour- able conditions, without parallel in the history of our country.[9]

Ho's crystal-gazing powers were later proved substantially right. In March 1945 the Japanese took over the direct control of administration, interning French officials. During those critical months, the Viet Minh received tremendous public support, the situation ironically helped by a gross human tragedy. A terrible famine stalked north Vietnam, killing 2 million out of an estimated population of 8 million. Neither the Japanese admin- istration nor the restored French officials in south Vietnam took steps to rush rice to Tongking. Much of the relief was organized instead by the Viet Minh. Taking advantage of the situation, the Viet Minh quickly established guerrilla bases and administration over three more provinces.

In the meantime, the Japanese had asked Emperor Bao Dai to abrogate the 1884 protectorate treaty with France and declare Vietnam independent. A puppet cabinet was appointed under Tran Truong Kim, a respected old scholar, as prime minister. The Japanese promised to transfer all general government services to the Bao Dai government by August 15. The Japanese also asked the kings of Laos and Cambodia to declare their independence.

ESTABLISHMENT OF THE DRV

When Japan surrendered to the Allies on August 7, 1945, the Viet Minh emerged from the sidelines to the center of politics. A national congress of the Viet Minh met at once and elected a national liberation committee, which was like a provisional government, headed by Ho Chi Minh. A ten- point plan approved by the congress was to seize power, gain indepen- dence for the Democratic Republic of Vietnam (DRV), develop the army, abolish inequitable taxes, promulgate democratic rights, redistribute com- munal lands, and maintain good relations with the Allies. There was no mention of any major agrarian reform or nationalization of any kind of property. It was a nationalist, not a Communist, program. On August 25, after the Viet Minh took over Hanoi, Bao Dai abdicated, handing over the sword and seal—the signs of sovereignty—to the provisional government and thus providing the new administration with legitimacy. He was made supreme counselor of state. A week later, on September 2, 1945, an enthusiastic crowd of .5 million in Hanoi heard Ho Chi Minh proclaim the birth of the Democratic Republic of Vietnam. On that occasion, Ho Chi Minh read out his declaration of independence, which contained passages lifted directly out of the American Declaration. It was a nationalist victory but with a strong base of power for the Communists inasmuch as ten members out of the fifteen in the new cabinet were Communists, though they did not openly admit their ideological affiliation. Ho Chi Minh himself successfully strove to project the image of a nationalist leader. In order to give his government a nationalist appearance, Ho invited Ngo Dinh Diem, among others, from his hideout in Tongking. Diem was not the only one to refuse to join a Communist-dominated government. The nationalist ranks were thus divided soon after the birth of the DRV.

The new republic was not recognized by any country. The Allies, meeting at Potsdam, had decided to reestablish the status quo ante and to that end asked nationalist China to occupy Vietnam north of the 16th parallel and Britain south of it. France maintained that the future of Indochina was an exclusively French concern. The Chinese forces arrived in north Vietnam in early September; the British troops under General Douglas Gracey arrived in Saigon on September 12. Gracey immediately released the French from prison and put them in charge of the administration of south Vietnam. Liberated France was, ironically enough, planning to reassert its colonial rights in Indochina despite an impassioned appeal to General Charles de Gaulle from Emperor Bao Dai:

> You would understand better if you could see what is happening here, if you could feel the desire for independence which is in everyone's heart and which no human force can any longer restrain. Even if you come to re-establish a French administration here, it will no longer be obeyed: each village will be a nest of resistance, each former collaborator an enemy, and your officials and colonists will themselves ask to leave this atmosphere which they will be unable to breathe.[10]

The Viet Minh could not easily establish themselves in the north because of the presence of the Chinese troops and the members of the VNQDD and the Dong Minh Hoi, who had accompanied them to Tong-king. By September 16, Hanoi was divided, the central and southeast suburbs under Viet Minh control and the northeastern parts held by the pro-Chinese nationalists, who also controlled several provinces. In south Vietnam, the Viet Minh, organized as the Committee of the South, acted swiftly against the Trotskyites Cao Dai and Hoa Hao. The French treated south Vietnam as a separate unit, much to the consternation of the DRV leaders, who maintained that Vietnam was a single entity. After the French took over the south, the Viet Minh continued the pressure on the government through guerrilla warfare, but their advances were not spectacular until at least a year later.

Ho Chi Minh, therefore, took several measures. First, on November 11, 1945, to the surprise of the non-Communists, he announced the dissolution of the Indochina Communist Party; it was clandestinely replaced by the newly formed Association of Marxist Studies.[11] Second, he offered the VNQDD seventy seats in the upcoming "free" elections to the National Assembly in January 1946. Power was ostensibly shared in a new cabinet composed of Viet Minh, Dong Minh Hoi, VNQDD, and others. On March 6, along with the vice-president (a Dong Minh Hoi representative) and minister of foreign affairs (a VNQDD member), Ho Chi Minh signed an agreement with the French allowing a limited number of French troops to enter north Vietnam to replace the Chinese in exchange for French recognition of the DRV as a "free state having its own government, its own parliament and its own finances, and forming part of the Indochinese Federation and the French Union." France also agreed to sponsor a referendum to determine whether Cochin China should join the union and to withdraw its troops gradually from all of Vietnam. The agreement was to be followed by negotiations for the resolution of other outstanding issues.

Why did Ho Chi Minh agree to the return of the French to Hanoi? It was principally to get rid of the Chinese troops, who had rampaged the countryside in a campaign of loot, plunder, and rape. With their withdrawal, the power of the VNQDD and the Dong Minh Hoi could then be easily broken. Finally, he felt that it would be easier to oust a distant power like France than the closer, traditionally dominant China. On this matter, Ho is reported to have remarked to a friend, in his customary earthy fashion: "It is better to sniff the French dung for a while than to eat China's all our lives."[12] Besides, he knew he could always blame the agreement itself on his VNQDD and Dong Minh Hoi colleagues—and he did.

THE FIRST INDOCHINA WAR

Meanwhile, the French attempted to strengthen their military and political position. Having no desire to give up its sovereignty, France hesitated, hedged, and finally reneged on most of the assurances. It is possible that the French were reluctant to share power and eventually to relinquish it because the Viet Minh was led by the Communists. Ho Chi Minh tried to convince them that he and his associates were primarily nationalist but to no avail. He also pointed out that the Americans were about to grant independence to the Philippines and that the British were planning to transfer power in India, but the French were hardly ready to give up their empire in any part of the world.

Negotiations between the French and the DRV continued through most of that year, neither side yielding ground and both sides preparing themselves for what seemed like inevitable open warfare. In November a French attempt to take over the customs department in Haiphong met with Vietnamese resistance. The French demanded that the Vietnamese lay down their arms. When the Vietnamese refused, the French used their cruiser *Suffren* to bomb the Vietnamese quarter of Haiphong on November 23, 1946, killing over 6,000 civilians in a matter of hours. Negotiations failed and the Viet Minh attacked the French troops stationed in Hanoi on December 19, 1946. That became a signal for the outbreak of general hostilities between the Viet Minh and France. The DRV leadership and its army of 40,000 trained troops withdrew confidently to the same limestone caves in northwest Tongking from which they had descended only seventeen months earlier. The First Indochina War (1946–1954) had broken out all over Vietnam, and the French had to face the Viet Minh at once on scores of fronts.

The French intransigence had led to the popularity of the Viet Minh, although its Communist nature was known to many Vietnamese nationalists. Having officially dissolved the party in November 1945, the Communists maintained that they were first and last nationalists. The devotion and dedication of the Viet Minh cadres to the cause of independence and their ascetic way of life had won over large segments of the population, whose only other alternative was the French-backed, largely self-serving and servile nationalist coalition. Besides, time seemed to be on the side of the Viet Minh. As Milton Osborne observes, after decades of disorientation, the people were predisposed to change.[13] The old feudal values of the mandarinate had been shattered as had the impression of French invincibility. The new leaders had demonstrated their willingness and ability to work with the peasants to alleviate the problems that had been pressing upon the rural population for generations. During its brief tenure in office, the DRV had grappled with the famine in the north, mobilizing the people to cultivate quick-growing crops on every spare inch of available space. The Viet Minh had also held relatively fair and free elections in Annam and Tongking and won handsomely. It was true, however, that the Communists among the Viet Minh had employed terror tactics against non-Communists within the Viet Minh and even murdered most of the prominent opponents. Quite a few people were turned away from the Viet Minh because of such excesses. Yet the vast majority, at least in Tongking, seemed to approve of the DRV government's actions, and indeed they resented the restoration of French rule at any cost.

On March 8, 1949, France announced the Elysée agreements between French president Vincent Auriol and Emperor Bao Dai under which Vietnam, along with Laos and Cambodia, would be an associate state within the French union. It made very little difference in practice because the major instruments of power were still under French control. Even nationalists like Ngo Dinh Diem refused to cooperate with the new government. France had shown some softness in policy because of the tremendous losses in men, money, and materiel caused by the "dirty war," as it was called in France. The war annually killed as many officers as were produced by Saint-Cyr, France's military academy. Their reluctance to transfer real power was partly because of their lingering concept of national glory, partly because it would set a chain of events in their other colonies, and importantly because of the substantial economic interests, particularly in rubber and rice. But as long as the French showed no genuine desire to part with power, their political moves were not going to gain any appreciable measure of endorsement from the Vietnamese masses.

The year 1949 must be considered crucial to the Vietnamese freedom struggle. The establishment of the Communist regime in China in October 1949 altered the complexion of the Vietnamese movement. Almost immediately, the Communist elements in the Viet Minh asserted themselves, openly admitting their affiliation with international communism. In August 1949, when the Communist victory in China appeared imminent, Ho Chi Minh told an American journalist that "it changed the center of gravity of power in Asia," but that "Vietnam is relying as always, on its own strength to win its independence."[14] Similar discretion was not demonstrated by his colleagues, some of whom took measures to strengthen control over the non-Communist elements within the Viet Minh. In November 1949, some of them attended the famous Beijing meeting of the World Federation of Trade Unions of Asia and Australia, at which China's Liu Shaoqi exhorted the colonial countries to adopt the Chinese path in their "struggle for national independence and people's democracy."[15] The Vietnamese Communists returned from China with directives from their Chinese counterparts as to how to conduct their fight for freedom from French rule. In December the moment of gloating glory came for these extreme elements in the Viet Minh when the Chinese Communists reached the Vietnamese frontier and unfurled the red flag at the international bridge linking Mon Kay and Tunghing.

From that point on, despite Ho Chi Minh's protestations and even genuine reservations, the Viet Minh subordinated nationalism to international communism. The shift did not necessarily benefit Ho Chi Minh's movement; if in the earlier years the French had played into his hands and helped him secure sympathy from former colonial peoples, the Viet Minh now played into French hands. At a time when the French were stalemated in Indochina, weakened militarily and economically, with little prospect of extensive foreign support, the Viet Minh made them a present of large-scale U.S. aid against the Vietnamese nationalist movement—not to maintain French colonial rule, which the United States had no particular reason to uphold, but to fight communism. The Indochina War thereafter became part of the worldwide struggle between Communist and "free world" forces.

In January 1950, with the recognition of the DRV by the Soviet Union and China, the cold war lines were clearly drawn. Bao Dai's Vietnam became an outpost of the Western bloc, protecting all of Southeast Asia against eventual expansion by China. U.S. Secretary of State Dean Acheson declared that Soviet recognition should remove "any illusions as to the 'nationalist' nature of Ho Chi Minh's aims and reveals Ho in his true colors as the mortal enemy of native independence in Indochina."[16] The United States recognized the Bao Dai regime in the hope that the Elysée agreement would form the "basis for the progressive realization of the legitimate aspirations of the Vietnamese people." France was already receiving U.S. help indirectly under the Marshall Plan, thus allowing France to release francs for military expenses in Indochina. But from early 1950, with the signing of a Mutual Assistance Program, U.S. aid to the French effort in Indochina was to be direct. It amounted to $3 billion by 1954. The Indochina situation was becoming internationalized, and for the first time the cold war seemed to extend into Asia.

It is difficult to get through the maze of propaganda and identify the real reasons for the Viet Minh's military success and the French defeats. Both sides made blunders costing heavy casualties, the French generals hardly knowing how to fight a nonconventional guerrilla war and the Viet Minh forces lacking experience in pitched battles. After the cease-fire in Korea in 1953, the Communist countries concentrated on Indochina. Large amounts of Soviet and Chinese ammunition and weapons came across the northern borders to strengthen the Viet Minh supply position. By early 1954, the French forces were thoroughly demoralized, particularly by the public opinion at home, which overwhelmingly pressed for ending the war. Cabinets fell rapidly until the prime minister of the twentieth government to hold office since the end of World War II, Pierre Mendès-France, who became premier on June 17, 1954, vowed to resign his office if a settlement in Indochina were not reached by July 20, 1954.[17]

DIEN BIEN PHU

The last French commander, Henri Navarre, the fifth commander in as many years, pledged "to break up and destroy regular enemy forces in Indochina." For years, French military officials had consoled themselves that the ill-clad, "cowardly" Viet Minh succeeded because of their hit-and-run tactics and that in a pitched battle of the conventional type, which the French armies were trained to fight, the Viet Minh would be crushed. The battle of Dien Bien Phu was contrived not so much by General Giap as by General Navarre. His plan was to lure the core of the Viet Minh forces into a set-piece battle in the remote valley of Dien Bien Phu, close to the Laotian border, deemed strategically very important. He expected the Viet Minh to pass through the valley in early 1954 for a second attack on Laos. With their air superiority and better firepower, the French expected an easy victory and large-scale destruction of Vietnamese forces, which had no aircraft, no tanks, and hardly any means of transport fit for mountain warfare. A major defeat of Giap's forces there would be crippling to the Viet Minh's military effort. The French general had, however, underestimated the Viet Minh's ability to transport large cannon on human backs and ordinary bicycles and to position them in the surrounding hills, besieging the French troops. Logistically, the valley of Dien Bien Phu was the most indefensible site, leaving the French troops directly within the long range of Viet Minh artillery fire. The only way to supply the French troops was by air, which was also made extremely hazardous by the Viet Minh guns directed at the airplanes.

In April and early May 1954, the use of nuclear weapons seemed to the U.S. Secretary of State John Foster Dulles to be the only way to save the beleaguered French garrison from total extermination by the Viet Minh. But the United States would act only jointly with Great Britain, and the latter firmly refused to go along and thereby open the prospect of a third world war, the action probably bringing massive Soviet retaliation. The situation enabled General Giap to register his greatest triumph at Dien Bien Phu on May 7, the eve of the Geneva conference on Indochina. The losses on both sides were colossal. Of the 15,000 French troops, 1,500 were killed and 4,000 wounded, and of the 51,000 Viet Minh troops, 8,000 died and 15,000 were wounded. The Viet Minh's victory completely demoralized the French troops in Vietnam and the French politicians and diplomats at Geneva.

THE GENEVA SETTLEMENT OF 1954

The Geneva agreements of July 21, 1954, temporarily divided Vietnam along the 17th parallel into two zones; the question of reunification was to be decided by a Vietnam-wide election in 1956. The Viet Minh accepted the settlement most reluctantly under pressure from their Communist allies, the Soviet Union and China, who were at the time espousing a global policy of peaceful coexistence with capitalist powers. China had another reason of its own: its historical policy of discouraging political consolidation among its neighboring countries. The Soviet Union was possibly concerned that in the event that an agreement were not reached by the deadline set by Premier Mendès-France, the French might resume fighting, and the United States might enter the fray directly on the French side. To the United States, it appeared like the Viet Minh would soon take over the southern part of Vietnam. It refused to sign the declaration of the Geneva conference and proceeded to support the government of South Vietnam, of which Ngo Dinh Diem had been appointed premier on June 16.

The Viet Minh or Communist leaders had urged a division of Vietnam at least along the 14th parallel and wanted the proposed elections for the reunification of the country to take place no later than six months from the signing of the agreements. If negotiations are to some a continuation of war by other means, to the Vietnamese Communists they represented a big power game that had snatched a sure political victory from their hands. The Geneva conference sounded the death knell of French colonialism in Southeast Asia without, however, assuring freedom to Vietnam as one nation and without guaranteeing continued peace to an already war-weary land.

CHAPTER 5

Roots of the
Second Indochina War

 The Geneva conference that ended the First Indochina War (1946–1954) divided Vietnam at the 17th parallel. It created two zones for the rival military forces to regroup and withdraw to the respective zones. The partition was to be temporary, for two years, at the end of which elections were to be held to reunify the country. The implementation of the Geneva agreements, including the elections, was to be supervised by an International Control Commission under Indian chairmanship, with pro-West Canada and Communist Poland as members.[1] The success of the commission's work depended, indeed, on the cooperation of the governments of North and South Vietnam. Great Britain and the Soviet Union acted as cochairs of the Geneva conference to whom the International Control Commission reported periodically.

SOUTH VIETNAM AFTER THE GENEVA CONFERENCE

U.S. Reaction to the Geneva Agreements

The United States and the new government of South Vietnam had refused to sign the Geneva agreements, though at Geneva the United States said that it would "not use force to disturb the Geneva settlement"; that instead it would seek "to achieve unity through free elections, supervised by the United Nations to ensure that they are conducted freely."[2] U.S. actions in the next two years completely contradicted these statements and were primarily responsible for the unfortunate events of the next two decades in Vietnam. The United States, in effect, encouraged the Diem government to turn the southern zone into an independent state and convert the provisional demarcation line at the 17th parallel into an international border. Further, Saigon refused to cooperate with the International

Control Commission in the planning of the elections scheduled for 1956. Those elections were never held.

U.S. policy toward Vietnam was principally governed by the doctrine of containment of communism almost consistently from the early 1950s to at least the end of the following decade. Within days of the Geneva settlement, U.S. Secretary of State John Foster Dulles pursued the "united action" strategy in a new fashion by getting Britain and France, among others, to sign a pact that would in essence counter the spirit of the Geneva accords. Dulles's efforts resulted in the Manila Pact on September 8, 1954, creating the Southeast Asia Treaty Organization (SEATO). Its name belied its membership; it included only three Asian members—Pakistan, Thailand, and the Philippines—in addition to the United States, the United Kingdom, France, Australia, and New Zealand. The major nonaligned powers of south and Southeast Asia—India, Burma, Cambodia, and Indonesia—opposed the pact. SEATO did not include Laos, Cambodia, and South Vietnam, as this would have directly violated the Geneva agreements; SEATO's Article 5, however, included these areas as "protocol" countries to be defended by SEATO powers, thereby legitimizing later U.S. involvement in the Vietnam conflict.

SEATO represented a resumption of the cold war in Southeast Asia. It conflicted with the purposes and goals of the Geneva accords, which, in turn, reflected the five principles of peaceful coexistence contained in the April 1954 Sino-Indian agreement on Tibet.[3] It was no surprise that SEATO could enlist only three Asian members, others following India's lead in staunchly opposing any military pacts that were likely to perpetuate Western military or "neocolonial" presence in Southeast Asia on the pretext of containing China. The Manila Pact and, specifically, U.S. policy in Vietnam in the years following Geneva aggravated tensions and frustrated the Vietnamese people's yearning for a peaceful reunification of their country. Writing a decade later, a critic of U.S. policy observed:

> In these two years can be found the roots of the critical political military situation as it has existed in Vietnam since 1960. In 1954 and 1955 the United States could still have charted a different course. But once it chose the direction it did in 1954 and proceeded in that direction through 1956, it became a captive of its policy and committed to its continuation.[4]

The Rise of Ngo Dinh Diem

While the Geneva conference was in session, on June 16, the French government, along with Emperor Bao Dai, announced appointment of Ngo Dinh Diem as premier of the "state" of Vietnam. Diem was a "mixture of monk and mandarin" who hailed from a prestigious Catholic family from Phu Cam in central Vietnam that had converted to Christianity in the seventeenth century. Members of his family had served as mandarins. Diem's father, Ngo Dinh Kha, was counsellor to Emperor Than Thai, deposed by the French in 1907. Extremely bright in his studies, Diem, like his older brother, Khoi, had been promoted by the French in the 1920s to the high office of provincial governor. An anti-Communist nationalist, Diem was by no means a collaborator with the colonial regime. In 1933 the French showed readiness to restore some of the long lost authority of the imperial council and advised the eighteen-year-old Emperor Bao Dai to appoint Ngo Dinh Diem his minister of the interior. Diem sought and received assurances from the French that the council would have genuine authority to institute administrative reforms. Disillusioned because the council did not have the promised authority, he resigned his post within three months, much to the consternation of the French, who took reprisals against his family and threatened to arrest him. Bao Dai quickly lost, if he ever had any, interest in administration. He spent the next two decades largely ignoring his imperial obligations.

Diem remained in contact with the other non-Communist nationalists on an individual basis over the next decade but was not active in the nationalist movement. His reputation as a nationalist and a good administrator, however, was regarded important enough for Ho Chi Minh to invite him to join his government in 1945. Diem refused because of the Viet Minh's heinous acts toward his family and hundreds of other innocent people. In August 1950 Diem left Vietnam for the United States, where he lived until 1953, mostly at Maryknoll Seminaries in Lakewood, New Jersey, and Ossining, New York. During that period he acted as a spokesman for the Vietnamese nationalist movement, giving lectures and meeting a number of prominent politicians, including Senators John F. Kennedy and Mike Mansfield and Justice William O. Douglas. In May 1953 Diem spent time in the Benedictine monastery of St. André les Bruges in Belgium. Around the time of the Geneva conference on Indochina, he and his brother Luyen were in Paris hobnobbing with French politicians. At that point the French government and Bao Dai, independently of the United States, chose Diem to head the government of the "state of Vietnam."

With the partition of the country in July 1954, Diem faced numerous challenges to his authority. For the most part, South Vietnam was under the irregular control of three religio-military sects: Cao Dai and Hoa Hao, each with private armies estimated at fifty thousand men, and the Binh Xuyen, which held vice concessions in gambling houses, narcotic dens, night clubs, and brothels and virtually controlled Saigon's police force. With admirable ability, Diem succeeded in crushing the sects and eliminating all extralegal challenges to his government within the first six months of his administration. His handling of the problem of rehabilitation of nearly 1 million refugees, mostly Catholics from North Vietnam, won

Diem international acclaim, notably in the United States. In order to secure his position, Diem held a referendum on October 23, 1955; he received an embarrassing 99 percent of the vote, resulting in the removal of Bao Dai and making Diem president of the newly proclaimed Republic of Vietnam. Diem then announced his plans for election of a "national" assembly on March 4, 1956, which would draw up a constitution for the new republic. He repeatedly repudiated any obligations arising out of the Geneva agreements, including the crucial provision for Vietnam-wide elections for reunification of the country. Recognized by the United States and thirty-five other countries of the Western bloc, the Republic of Vietnam by late 1955 became, for all purposes, an independent member of the international community. From a situation of total collapse of governmental authority at the time of the country's partition in mid-1954, Diem had miraculously emerged as the central authority in South Vietnam.

U.S. Support for Diem

In all these moves, the United States supported Diem to the hilt, parading him as an intense anti-French, anti-Communist, nationalist leader of spotless honesty and integrity. The Americans held Diem as a "nationalist alternative" to Communist Ho Chi Minh. But Diem had been out of Vietnam for so long before 1954 that he had no idea of his people's aspirations in a period of fast-paced political upheaval. His political style, moreover, was as paternalistic and aloof as that of the outdated mandarins, and he increasingly withdrew to the shelter of his "Forbidden Palace," depending for information and guidance on a close coterie of "court" sycophants and even more so on members of his extended family. Diem's popular base was slim, made up mainly of the refugee Catholics who constituted a minority of 10 percent. Most of the southern Buddhist population were hostile to the refugees because of both their religion and their northern origin.

With the advantage of historical hindsight, one can blame South Vietnam's many problems on the United States' unfortunate decision to give its full support to Diem. In 1954, despite the general misgivings about Diem's popularity, the influential Senator Mike Mansfield recommended that if the Diem government collapsed, "the United States should consider an immediate suspension of all aid to Vietnam . . . except that of a humanitarian nature."[5] The U.S. Department of State interpreted this to mean that all aid should be given to the Diem government to prevent its fall. On November 3, 1954, President Dwight Eisenhower's special representative, General J. Lawton Collins, announced in Saigon that the United States would give "every possible aid to the Government of Diem and to his government only."[6] On February 19, 1955, Eisenhower formally offered the Diem government unconditional support against its Communist as well as non-Communist foes.[7]

Diem did not have the aura of prestige, sacrifice, and struggle against colonialism to match Ho Chi Minh's reputation. Despite his ruthlessness and atheism, Ho Chi Minh gave the impression of mildness and asceticism and was always dressed in simple fatigues and rubber sandals. A fervent Catholic with a monastic background, Diem seemed more a sectarian than a national leader and wore sharkskin and Irish linen suits. Both were bachelors. Having no family ties whatsoever, Ho Chi Minh stood above suspicion of nepotism. He had a reputation for honesty and sincerity and had gained the trust of the masses. Instead of living in the former governor general's palace in Hanoi, Ho preferred to live in the guest house and keep his same, simple habits. For the avuncular Ho Chi Minh, the nation became his family.

In contrast, Diem had close ties to his extended family, almost equating it with the state by giving family members powerful positions: His brother Nhu and Nhu's wife became Diem's closest advisers. The megalomaniac Nhu was in a perpetual drugged fog (perhaps without Diem's knowledge) and espoused an obtuse philosophy of "personalism." Madame Nhu, who had recently converted from Buddhism to Catholicism, ardently championed her new faith and advocated puritanism in public life. Her extremist policies on religious and secular matters alike alienated large segments of the predominantly Buddhist population. Diem's elder brother, Thuc, was archbishop of Hué, the highest Catholic official in the land; another brother controlled central Vietnam as a virtual personal fiefdom; and yet another brother was ambassador to Great Britain. As the president's family became more and more entangled in governmental affairs, Diem became increasingly isolated from the Vietnamese people. Consequently, he became a prisoner of his family, with access only to such information as they (notably the Nhus) made available. Under their influence, Diem suppressed newspapers, enforced strict censorship, exiled men by administrative fiat, and suspended court judgments. A Western commentator lamented that instead of confronting the totalitarian north with the evidences of freedom, the South Vietnamese government "slipped into an inefficient dictatorship."[8]

Communist Rule in North Vietnam

Initially, Hanoi also had to grapple with a host of problems that engendered considerable discontent among the people of North Vietnam. The Democratic Republic of Vietnam embarked upon its promised land redistribution in the already congested and overfragmented Red River Delta, where agriculture had suffered dismally in the final phase of the fighting immediately before the Geneva settlement. Famine could not be relieved by imports of grain because of lack of foreign exchange. The French had removed most of the machinery from the coal mines, which had been North Vietnam's principal earners of foreign exchange. Furthermore, the DRV launched a crash program of building roads and railroads leading to China by using forced labor on a massive scale. All these factors—combined with the most potent of them, religion—helped to swell the flood of refugees from the north to the south. The DRV's efforts to stem the migration had very little effect, particularly upon the Catholics, who had been told in their parishes that God had moved south, where the government was headed by one of their Catholic brethren. At least 1 million people, mostly Catholics, migrated from North to South Vietnam from 1954 to 1955, but over 800,000 Catholics still remained in North Vietnam.

In 1956 the land reform campaign, which had been given up in 1955, was resumed with dubious results. Many Communist Party cadres exploited the new land laws as weapons to settle scores with their old enemies or to secure material advantages for themselves. According to the critics of the DRV, land reform became a major terror campaign, taking hundreds of thousands, perhaps as many as .5 million lives. The figures may have been exaggerated, though the fact of large-scale peasant discontent and repression was incontestable.

The DRV quickly adopted a socialist system on the Soviet model. In 1955 the State Planning Committee was established, but it was not before 1961 that the First Five-Year Development Plan was launched. The core of the new economic system in the DRV was to be the agrarian cooperative. The basic philosophy seemed to be that the society could move directly to socialism without any transitional capitalist stage. This was because there were few, if any, major Vietnamese-owned capitalist enterprises to be nationalized. Collectivization of agriculture proceeded by definite stages. By the early 1960s, thousands of cooperatives consolidating the traditionally fragmented, small units of land were created. Most of the cooperatives, however, were not large enough to generate adequate money or manpower for large-scale irrigation projects. In fact, in the initial years the government had to assist each cooperative with a substantial subsidy. By the late 1960s, the small cooperatives were consolidated into "high-level" collectives, providing for common ownership of all means of production and distribution and giving a share to farmers in proportion to their contribution. The high-level collectives controlled far more land, money, and manpower than before, enabling substantial improvement in the irrigational infrastructure. The government established production targets as well as prices for purchase and sale of agricultural products.

Despite such far-reaching, intensive measures, the internal saving capacity of each collective remained very low. Later, the government estimated such reinvestment funds to be capable of expanding the cultivable area in each collective by no more than about 2.5 acres. Nor were they enough to buy some basic machinery to improve farming in each collective. Except for the half decade after the partition of the country in 1954, the extraordinary political and military situation in which the DRV was involved until 1975 inhibited any sustained effort to implement agricultural reforms in North Vietnam.

Paralleling the creation of agrarian collectives was the reorganization of business enterprises—large, medium, and small, in industry, forestry, fishing, construction, transport and communications, and the service sector. The DRV converted some private enterprises into state-private partnerships virtually controlled by the government. During the decade of the Second Indochina War (1964 to 1975), consumerism in North Vietnam declined to among the lowest levels in the world, the diplomatic staff in Hanoi reported mostly empty shelves in the capital's stores. Thus a whole generation of North Vietnamese, political and military leaders included, learned to live on bare necessities. No wonder that when the North Vietnamese troops and cadres marched into Saigon in April 1975, they went on a mad spree, wildly buying up—or more often looting—U.S.-made consumer goods.

In terms of political stability, however, North Vietnam contrasted sharply with South Vietnam. The state was headed by a legendary hero, Ho Chi Minh, who was known for his qualities of determination, sacrifice, austerity, and whole-hearted devotion to the cause of his country's liberation, reconstruction, and reunification. Ho had endeared himself to the masses through his simple habits. As an old Bolshevik, Ho also commanded respect in the Communist world. Ho's cabinet comrades followed his example, inspiring the common cadres to dedicate themselves to the achievement of socioeconomic goals. Their firm commitment to the reunification of the country gave them the support of the majority of the people, both in the North and in the South. As Eisenhower observed in his memoirs: "I have never talked or corresponded with a person knowledgeable in Indochinese affairs who did not agree that had elections been held at the time of fighting, 80 percent of the population would have voted for the communist Ho Chi Minh as their leader rather than Chief of State Bao Dai."[9] That was in 1954.

UNREST IN SOUTH VIETNAM

Diem's Oppressive Policies

The problem of "subversion" in South Vietnam was principally of Diem's making. After the suppression of the Cao Dai, Hoa Hao, and Binh

Xuyen sects, Diem could have liberalized politics and turned to the much-needed alleviation of social and economic problems. Instead, in 1957 he unleashed a campaign to denounce and purge Communists, using emergency powers and vague definitions of espionage and treason to carry out arbitrary arrests of Communists and non-Communists alike. His brother Nhu's security apparatus included a secret police force trained by experts from Michigan State University. It terrorized all opponents and herded them into prison camps, several thousand alleged Communists being placed into concentration camps like Phu Loi, where such atrocities as massive poisoning were reported. Dissident nationalists, whose numbers increased rapidly, were soon branded Communist traitors, and a censorship was clamped down on the press more severe than at the worst time of the French colonial rule. The repressive policies were based from May 1959 on the infamous 10–59 law creating special military tribunals that delivered summary judgments within three days after the accused were cited for "provoking economic disturbances" or "disrupting the security of the state" and gave out death sentences with no chance for appeal.

As for the rural areas, Diem did introduce some land reform. But his policies were ill conceived and ill implemented—and therefore disastrous in their effect. He sought to rehabilitate refugees and the landless poor by expropriating and redistributing landholdings beyond the high ceiling of 247 acres, which made very little land available for redistribution. Diem also abrogated a major land distribution program that had been undertaken during the First Indochina War, when over 1.2 million acres of rice fields had been redistributed to the peasants. The Diem government confirmed only about 15 percent of such distributions. Because most of the requisitioned land, primarily in the Mekong Delta, was now given to "foreign" landlords—supporters of Diem from central Vietnam and prominent Catholic refugees from North Vietnam—large numbers of peasants long established in the Mekong Delta became hostile to the government.

Diem's land reform program allowed for 20 percent of the rice land to pass from large to small farmers; in reality, only 10 percent of all tenant farmers benefited. As much as 47 percent of the land remained concentrated in the hands of 2 percent of the landowners; 15 percent of the landlords owned 75 percent of all land. The peasant discontent was further fueled by increased land rents and bribes to officials, together amounting to 45 to 50 percent of the crop. The few farmers who benefited from Diem's program were more often than not northern Catholic refugees, a situation that invited the charge of favoritism and thereby further deepened peasant alienation in South Vietnam. There were even widespread allegations that the Diem family had enriched itself by manipulating land transfers.

To add insult to injury, in June 1956 the Diem government replaced village notables with its own appointees, again northern Catholic "outsiders," summarily terminating the 2,000-year-old Vietnamese tradition of village autonomy. They were unable to contain or resolve the discontent much less inspire confidence and trust among the peasantry.

By 1960 Diem, the all-knowing Mandarin, had alienated all major sections of the South Vietnamese population. The intellectual elite was rendered politically mute, labor unions impotent, Buddhists distrustful, Montagnards suspicious. Loyal opposition in the form of organized parties was stifled out of existence, Diem's policies virtually assuring that political challenges to him would have to be extralegal and violent. Ultimately, these emerged from diverse sources in South Vietnam: the armed forces, the religious sects, intellectuals, Communists, and even the peasantry.

Birth of the National Liberation Front

It is against such a backdrop of large-scale urban and rural discontent caused by the government's policies of alienation and repression, nepotism and corruption, family rule and religious insensitiveness that the birth of the Mat Tran Dan Toc Giai Phong (National Liberation Front, or NLF) in late 1960 must be viewed. The NLF was a grassroots organization that consisted of various elements within South Vietnamese society. For most of the NLF's fifteen-year existence, the common factor binding its components was not communism but nationalism, a determination to overthrow the regime in Saigon and to set up one that would end foreign intervention and guarantee a minimum of democratic liberties. Despite its considerable non-Communist membership and a non-Communist Saigon lawyer, Nguyen Huu Tho, as chairman, the real authority and leadership increasingly lay in its Communist constituents—the People's Revolutionary Party and the National Liberation Army, who took their direction (if not direct orders) from the Politburo in North Vietnam. The NLF's objectives did include reunification of the country but not necessarily under the hegemony of the north.

The origin of the National Liberation Front lay in the Saigon-Cholon Committee for Peace, formed in August 1954 to protest the Diem government's shooting at a rally of peaceful demonstrators asking for immediate release of political prisoners under terms of the Geneva agreements. It consisted of Saigon intellectuals and left-wing progressives (not necessarily Communists). Its ranks swelled as Diem refused to implement the provisions of the Geneva settlement in regard to the reunification of the country. Although its protests were peaceful and followed the proper legal channels, the NLF suffered more than other groups after 1957, when Nhu's security setup turned South Vietnam into a quasi police state. As the governmental repression became unbearably severe, particularly after the passing of the 10–59 law, the dissidents adopted violence to fight back.

Eager to take part in armed attacks, the Communist (former Viet Minh) cadres left behind in 1954 in the south hoped to take advantage of the situation. They were discouraged by their comrades in the north on the grounds that the conditions were not yet ripe for such a stage of the struggle. Hanoi warned the southern cadres: "To ignore the balance of forces and rashly call for a general uprising is to commit the error of speculative adventurism, leading to premature violence and driving us into a very dangerous position." Despite such inhibiting instructions, the southern Communists joined the militants in a number of attacks against government officials in the countryside.

A number of events during 1959–1960 culminated in the establishment of the NLF. In 1959 two significant revolts among tribal groups—the Kar in January and the Hre in July—took place. In March 1960, Nguyen Huu Tho, president of the Saigon-Cholon Committee for Peace, urged his fellow compatriots in eastern Cochin China to resist. In May some army units in coastal Quang Ngai province revolted, and in November three crack paratrooper battalions and a marine unit under Lieutenant Colonel Vuong Van Dong attempted a coup. It was against such a background that various movements and political parties—Armed Propaganda Groups of the People's Self-Defense Forces, the Associates of Ex-Resistance Members, the Saigon-Cholon Committee, the Democratic Party, and others—coalesced into a national movement, creating the NLF as an organizational framework within which a general political military struggle could take place.

For quite some time, Hanoi had been under pressure from the southern Communist militants to support their movement. They criticized the north's weak protest of the nonobservance of the 1956 general elections and Hanoi's relatively passive reaction to Diem's repression during 1957–1959. In early 1959 Le Duan, secretary general of the Lao Dong (Workers') Party—the name of the Vietnamese Communist Party since its resurrection by Ho Chi Minh in 1951—traveled to the south and later reported to the party that if the southern Communists did not join the other opponents of the Diem regime they would lose credibility with the people.

Despite misgivings on the correct timing of the insurrection, the northern leadership finally conceded. On May 13, 1959, the Fifteenth Plenum of the Lao Dong Party's central committee meeting in Hanoi decided that the time had come to initiate a struggle against the government of South Vietnam. The party leaders' goal was to create a unified Vietnam by any means. The following year, in September, the Third Congress of the party authorized support for an antigovernment revolutionary organization in the south. By December the NLF was established in South Vietnam. The creation of the People's Revolutionary Party (PRP) on January 1, 1962, within the NLF represented Hanoi's attempt to direct the southern insurgency via northern Communists, such as Nguyen Don, the director of

Military Region Five (the northernmost third of South Vietnam) and alternate members of the Lao Dong central committee. The PRP only had the appearance of an independent existence; actually it was nothing but an extension of the Lao Dong Party.

Roots of the Insurrection

How far was the opposition in South Vietnam to Diem's rule an indigenously inspired movement and what was the degree of Hanoi's involvement in it? A few dates are significant though not conclusive in this respect. Until July 1956, Hanoi had hoped that the reunification of the country would be accomplished through elections. Thereafter, until early 1959, North Vietnam was compelled by considerations of Sino-Soviet global policies of peaceful coexistence to refrain from resorting to a violent alternative for achieving the country's reunification. During this period, the North Vietnamese hoped that the Diem regime would disintegrate in the south because of its own weakness. The first rumblings of the Sino-Soviet dispute leading to China's decision to oust Soviet technicians and reject Soviet aid in 1959 may have led to alterations in Hanoi's posture in regard to the south. Throughout the Second Indochina War, the Communists claimed that the war in the south was entirely a southern affair, the assistance from North Vietnam being no more than moral, ideological, and diplomatic. In contrast was the official view of the South Vietnamese government and of the United States in regard to the "insurgency," as summarized by Douglas Pike:

The National Liberation Front was not simply another indigenous covert group, or even a coalition of such groups. It was an organized effort, endowed with ample cadres and funds, crashing out of the jungle to flatten the [government of South Vietnam]. . . . A revolutionary organization must build; it begins with persons suffering genuine grievances, who are slowly organized and whose militancy gradually increases until a critical mass is reached and the revolution explodes. Exactly the reverse was the case with the NLF. It sprang full-blown into existence and then was fleshed out. The grievances were developed or manufactured almost as a necessary afterthought. The creation of the NLF was an accomplishment of such skill, precision, and refinement that when one thinks of who the master planner must have been, only one name comes: Vietnam's organizational genius, Ho Chi Minh.[10]

Even if the southern movement received organizational and material assistance from the north, its initial stimulus was undoubtedly southern. It is true that there was a core of Communist cadres at its center. When the Viet Minh regroupment was carried out in terms of the Geneva accords between 1954 and 1955, a network of 5,000 to 10,000 cadres was left in the south, with instructions to blend into the new environment and agitate for elections. The Viet Minh also left behind large caches of weapons. But of these, 90 percent had been liquidated by the "extreme manhunt" carried out by Diem's government between 1955 and 1957. The southern movement undoubtedly began as a response to Diem's mopping-up campaign of 1957 and basically involved southerners. As George McTurnan Kahin and John Lewis observed:

> The insurrection is Southern rooted; it arose at Southern initiative in response to Southern demands. The Liberation Front gave political articulation and leadership to the widespread reaction against the harshness and heavy-handedness of Diem's government. It gained drive under the stimulus of Southern Vietminh veterans who felt betrayed by the Geneva conference and abandoned by Hanoi. . . . Contrary to U.S. policy assumptions, all available evidence shows that the revival of the civil war in the South in 1958 was undertaken by Southerners at their own—not Hanoi's—initiative.[11]

According to a Rand Corporation study, between 1956 and the launching of the NLF, approximately 30,000 northern agents, regroupees, were sent to South Vietnam. Although the regroupees did have an influence on the NLF, particularly in terms of military strategy and political goals, they could not have dictated their demands because of the local conditions and the NLF's heavy reliance on the grassroots structure. Geographically, the resistance forces were isolated from the north, making communication and transportation extremely difficult. In fact, the early NLF successes were without aid from North Vietnam. From the very beginning, the main military activity occurred in the deep south; the first "liberated" area was the Ca Mau Peninsula. Most weapons the NLF used were those captured from their enemy; approximately 80 percent of their weapons were of U.S. manufacture. It was only after the massive infusion of U.S. troops and weapons in South Vietnam from the mid-1960s that North Vietnam used the Ho Chi Minh Trail through Laos and Cambodia to supply the south with North Vietnamese manpower and materiel manufactured in Communist countries.

The NLF was originally intended to be a political rather than a military movement. Its initial doctrine was that of *khoi nghia*, or the general uprising. It would inspire the Vietnamese in the nation's 2,500 villages to such a pitch that at some precise moment there would come a spontaneous uprising, and the people, led of course by the NLF, would seize power. This was constantly drummed into the minds of the peasants by NLF cadres working in villages. The NLF's organizational structure therefore relied heavily on the participation of individuals, associations, and, in the countryside, entire villages. By 1963 the NLF became a gigantic organization composed of various departments such as the Farmers' Liberation Association, the Women's Liberation Association, and the Youth Liberation Association. The front's central committee in charge of political and military strategy consisted of representatives of such diverse elements as the political parties of South Vietnam, including the Democratic Party, the Radical Socialist Party and, indeed, the People's Revolutionary Party.

As noted before, the NLF had given primacy to the political struggle, armed resistance being secondary. After mid-1963, however, the armed struggle gained precedence over the political aspect of the movement. Several factors were responsible for the shift in policy. First was the increasing use of sophisticated combat weaponry by the Army of the Republic of Vietnam (ARVN) against the NLF. The latter, therefore, augmented its guerrilla units and military capabilities. Their success against the ARVN supported the argument for larger, more numerous, and better-equipped guerrilla units that would bring a quicker ultimate victory. A second factor for the policy shift was that the northern cadres reinterpreted the revolutionary doctrine, placing greater stress on the armed struggle. Therefore, politically as well as militarily, the management of the NLF after 1963 passed on increasingly to the Hanoi-trained Communists of the People's Revolutionary Party, the arm of the Lao Dong Party in South Vietnam. The DRV's assistance to the NLF in the form of military training, arms supplies, and manpower were stepped up phenomenally after 1964 in direct correlation to the U.S. commitment of troops, money, and materiel. The Americans, for their part, claimed that their increased involvement was a direct response to the level of insurgency in the south, which they alleged was entirely inspired, directed, manned, and supported by the north. The United States also believed that the Vietnam conflict was a test case of a theory of revolutionary warfare centrally directed from Moscow and Beijing. It was an attitude consistent with the policy of containment the United States followed in Indochina for a quarter of a century.

The Buddhist Crisis

Ironically, Diem's downfall was brought about by non-Communist elements in South Vietnam. Two military coup attempts in November 1960 and February 1962 had failed. The most serious challenge was posed in spring and summer 1963 by religious malcontents. The movement, led by Buddhist monks and nuns, drew its strength not from the abstractions of Communist ideology, which could only be antithetical to Buddhism, but from the wave of social discontent silently sweeping the population.

Traditionally, the Vietnamese had not perceived religion and politics as separate entities. Their religion was a blend of Confucianism, Taoism, Buddhism, and animism. As in most of Asia, religion provided "the authority for, and the confirmation of, an entire way of life—an agriculture, social structure, and a political system."[12] It is well said that the "Vietnamese are Confucians in peacetime, Buddhists in times of trouble."[13] Buddhism had always stressed a morality that lay "beyond loyalty to existing authorities," and the Buddhist bonzes in the past had provided an intellectual and moral leadership to oppose an oppressive regime.

During the French rule, the Buddhist monks had by and large remained apolitical. They had been allowed internal autonomy in the running of the monasteries and freedom to celebrate the numerous Buddhist holidays. Unlike the Catholics, the Buddhists did not have a well-organized "church" hierarchy; each pagoda was, for most purposes, an independent entity. With Diem's overtly pro-Catholic policies, however, the Buddhists felt threatened enough to organize themselves and form the General Buddhist Association in 1955. In 1963 in direct response to the religious crisis, the Unified Buddhist Church was born. Its political arm, styled the Buddhist Institute for Secular Affairs, continued to operate even after Diem's downfall, until it was replaced by the Vietnam Buddhist Force in April 1966. The position of the Buddhist associations vis-à-vis communism and Communist regimes was one of absolute neutrality, neither praise nor condemnation. In fact, they did not take sides in the ongoing conflict in South Vietnam until the government blatantly acted against the Buddhists in 1963.

Even more than President Diem, one of his brothers, the Catholic Archbishop Ngo Dinh Thuc, deliberately antagonized the Buddhists. Since the exodus of nearly 1 million Catholics from North to South Vietnam in 1954, the government had favored the Christian minority, not only through programs of rehabilitation of refugees but by giving preferred government positions to them. They certainly held more posts in civil as well as military services than their numbers, estimated at 2,200,000 (10 percent of the population), warranted. During the French rule, the Catholics had got used to receiving preferential treatment. A higher percentage of them spoke and read French than any other community; they were more sophisticated and better organized through their churches. They had shown inveterate hostility toward the Communists and the Viet Minh before 1954 and the Viet Cong after 1960. As such, they were the natural allies of the pro-West, anti-Communist Diem regime. Because the Catholics were coreligionists of the family in power, even greater advantages flowed to them. A French Catholic publication, *Informations Catholiques Internationales*, averred in March 1963 that it was because of Archbishop Ngo Dinh Thuc's efforts that the missionaries had found it easy to baptize entire villages collectively. With official help the archbishop built a spectacular center called Our Lady of La Vang, 20 miles south of the 17th parallel. Government officials, irrespective of their faith, were compelled to donate funds to the center. For example, the police sold lottery tickets in support of the center, forcing drivers to buy them in lieu of payment for traffic offenses.

If the people in South Vietnam were looking for some divine indication that Diem had forfeited his mandate to rule the country, a clear sign appeared in spring 1963. On May 7 Archbishop Ngo Dinh Thuc forbade the display of Buddhist flags in Hué to commemorate the birth of the Buddha and banned the general festivities as well. As a result, 3,000 would-be celebrants stormed a radio station and demanded that they be allowed to broadcast a program in honor of the Buddha. What the crowd received in response was tear gas and shooting in which nine people lost their lives.

To protest the government's action, the Buddhists launched a series of self-immolations, beginning with Thich Quang Duc, a venerable monk who doused himself with gasoline and set himself on fire in full view of the public. A few weeks later, the celebrated Vietnamese novelist Nhat Linh, who was to be tried for opposition to the Diem government, committed suicide by taking poison. Such acts of supreme sacrifice reflected the general frustration, bringing masses of people closer as equals against a common tyranny. The self-immolations continued as the government refused to negotiate. Madame Nhu publicly ridiculed the sacrifices as a "barbecue of bonzes"; her husband, Ngo Dinh Nhu, ordered the police to raid the pagodas. The press and television coverage brought the magnitude of the government's injustice and callousness as well as the sacrifices of the Buddhist bonzes to an international audience. The Confucians had theorized on a possible rebellion against those who had lost the mandate of heaven; the Buddhists now provided an emotional and spiritual platform to bring down an oppressive government.

U.S. Policy and Diem's Assassination

The Buddhist crisis exposed the excesses of Diem's rule to the world. It also changed the official U.S. view of the merits of his administration. So far, the United States had been totally impervious to Vietnamese opposition to Diem, viewing the conflict exclusively as an extension of the clash between the forces of freedom and Communist totalitarianism. The United States had perceived the problem as being more military than political. In the Diem era, 75 percent of U.S. economic aid provided to South Vietnam was used to bolster the country's military budget. Not until 1961 was U.S. influence brought to bear on the Diem government to redress socioeconomic imbalances that would improve the hopes of the masses for a better future. Such a belated change in policy yielded no positive results; it only helped to estrange the relationship between the United States and the Diem administration. The misplaced emphasis on military outlay is best indicated in the construction of a 20-mile highway between Bien Hoa and Saigon. Used mostly for military purposes, the highway absorbed more U.S. funds than all the aid provided for social welfare and education programs in South Vietnam between 1954 and 1961. Even in late 1961, despite the evidence to the contrary generated by its own agencies, the U.S. perceived the conflict in South Vietnam mainly in terms of aggression by North Vietnam. A white paper entitled *A Threat to the Peace* bluntly stated:

> The determined and ruthless campaign of propaganda, infiltration, and subversion by the Communist regime in North Viet-Nam to destroy the Republic of Viet-Nam and subjugate its people is a threat to the peace. The independence and territorial integrity of that free country is of major and serious concern not only to the people of Viet-Nam and their immediate neighbors but also to all other free nations.[14]

Yet only a month before the publication of this document, a government report of October 5, 1961, had placed the Viet Cong strength at less than 17,000 men, adding that 80 to 90 percent of them were southerners. It had added that the Viet Cong were hardly dependent upon outside assistance.[15]

The U.S. military commitment to Vietnam was raised sharply thereafter. During the Kennedy administration alone, the number of U.S. military "advisers" went up from several hundred to 16,500. Socioeconomic reforms and nation-building were indeed considered important objectives but were subordinated to the immediate task of liquidating the "subversion." From mid-1963, however, U.S. support of Diem rapidly declined because of the latter's intransigence toward the Buddhist majority. The Ngo brothers wanted U.S. aid, equipment, and troops but not advice on how to handle the Buddhist question, which they regarded as a purely domestic matter.[16] Consequently, the United States did not discourage the generals who decided to overthrow the government and assassinate President Diem and his brother Nhu on November 1, 1963.

The liquidation of the Diem regime did not solve any of South Vietnam's basic problems. The political instability worsened, with several generals playing musical chairs for power. All of them were pro-U.S. and dependent upon the United States to keep them in power. With the exception of General Duong Van (also known as Big) Minh, who was inclined to establish a "neutral" government with NLF participation, they were all thoroughly anti-Communist, believing that the conflict was first and last a Communist conspiracy hatched in Hanoi. Throughout the decade, from

Diem's assassination to the withdrawal of U.S. forces from Vietnam in 1973, the United States continued to give priority to the pursuit of the war effort. After 1966, believing that major socioeconomic reforms would have to await a successful conclusion of the war, the United States only half-heartedly insisted on democratic trappings like elections.

CHAPTER 6

The Indochina
Imbroglio

The coups and countercoups producing revolving-door governments in South Vietnam resulted in further alienation of the government from the people. That was part of the reason the war was going badly for South Vietnam. In April 1964 the U.S. Department of Defense estimated that the South Vietnamese government controlled 34 percent of the villages as against the NLF's control of 42 percent, with the loyalties of the remaining villages still contested. The Strategic Hamlet Program had collapsed. The northern Communists were not long in taking advantage of the deteriorating situation in the south. In order to step up the level of guerrilla warfare to the stage of attacking towns and larger army units, Hanoi began to infiltrate large tactical units along the Ho Chi Minh Trail through Laos and Cambodia into South Vietnam. The United States was frustrated that its plans to withdraw troops from South Vietnam had to be abandoned in a year of U.S. presidential elections. The United States was looking for a pretext to invade the north so as to halt the deteriorating situation in the south. The excuse was provided by the Gulf of Tongking incident.

In a dramatic nationwide television broadcast on August 2, 1964, at 11:30 P.M., President Lyndon Johnson charged that the U.S.S. *Maddox* and *Turner Joy* had been wantonly attacked by North Vietnamese torpedo boats and that U.S. aircraft had retaliated by bombing strategic North Vietnamese targets. Three days later, an emotionally charged U.S. Congress passed the much-heralded Gulf of Tongking Resolution authorizing the president to take "all necessary measures to repel any armed attacks against the forces of the United States and to prevent further aggression."[1] In the ensuing years this blanket authority was to draw the United States far more deeply into the quagmire of war than the legislators had envisaged. Armed with that authority and without further reference to Congress, Johnson sent a force of ultimately .5 million to Vietnam to fight in an undeclared war. The resolution remained in force for six years, until its repeal in the face of mounting antiwar sentiment in the country. As the *Pentagon Papers* revealed in 1968, Captain John Herrick, the local U.S. commander in the South China Sea, had informed Washington that there was no direct, visual evidence of any North Vietnamese torpedo attack and that the sonar operators may have mistaken "freak atmospheric conditions" for torpedoes.

Nonetheless, with such sweeping congressional authorization and a national consensus behind him, Johnson exercised no restraint in escalating the war. After the NLF's attacks on the U.S. air base at Pleiku on February 7, 1965, the U.S. bombing of North Vietnamese military installations and staging areas was undertaken on a regular basis as part of Operation Rolling Thunder. The operation's objectives were to cripple the DRV's economy, reduce the flow of troops and supplies to the south, and force the North Vietnamese to agree to a negotiated settlement. Such bombing, however, had very little effect on the progress of the war and soon became almost an end in itself. North Vietnam offered very few bombing targets of real strategic value because its economy was largely agrarian, most of its sophisticated military equipment coming from Soviet and Chinese sources. For one-third of the year, during the monsoon season, poor weather conditions obscured the landscape and inhibited the efficacy of strategic bombing. Moreover, the NLF's dependence on North Vietnamese supplies was not absolute; most of the NLF's ammunition was, in fact, obtained by capturing South Vietnamese and U.S. arms depots. The bombing in the north united the people there and made them even more determined to fight.

Between 1965 and 1966 the South Vietnamese government became relatively stable. Or at least the premiership of Nguyen Cao Ky, the flamboyant air force marshal, and the presidency of General Nguyen Van Thieu lent the semblance of stability. Ky remained in the government as vice-president and a real power at least until the Communist Tet offensive of 1968, when a number of his powerful allies in the armed forces were killed off. Thereafter, until 1975, the U.S. government's policy was to strengthen the Thieu government. During the Ky-Thieu and later Thieu regimes, the people continued to distrust the government, criticizing it in private for its acts of crass corruption and nepotism.

By spring 1965, U.S. forces in South Vietnam numbered 45,500; in the next twenty-four months the numbers would rise to a staggering .5 million.[2] Corresponding U.S. estimates of "Viet Cong," which was Ngo Dinh Diem's appellation for Vietnamese Communists, were 160,000 in spring 1965 and 250,000 two years later. The U.S. military strategy was to "search and destroy" the enemy in the South through a variety of means, including bombing, chemical defoliation, psychological warfare, and counterinsurgency operations. The criterion of success was not how much territory was conquered or brought under control but how many Viet Cong were killed. Unit commanders were consequently compelled to justify previous requests for aerial support by altering figures of enemy casualties, even if these were not matched by counts of actual bodies or captured weapons. Discrepancies in the body count were explained away by the Viet Cong "practice" of not leaving the dead behind. Weapons counts were manipulated by adding caches previously captured but not reported.

The United States gave massive economic and military aid to the Saigon government, whose armed forces numbered nearly 1 million by the end of the 1960s. The inevitable consequence of such a policy coupled with growing U.S. military presence was the militarization of South Vietnamese society. The dominance of the armed forces was evident everywhere. The opportunities for graft and corruption available to military officials in a U.S.-funded war were unlimited and debilitating to the larger society. Black marketing of basic necessities, smuggling of foreign goods, pilferage from U.S. and South Vietnamese military bases, foreign exchange racketeering, and substandard performance in military construction jobs became rampant. A class of nouveau riche emerged that completely undermined the old social system in which bureaucrat-intellectuals and monks had commanded general respect.

The war's effects on the common people were disastrous. Millions of desperate refugees from the countryside flocked to the cities. Many youths either volunteered or were forced by the NLF to join its military forces. Others were drafted by the ARVN. Still others escaped NLF recruitment or deserted the ARVN by dissolving into the burgeoning population of Saigon-Cholon. U.S. aid to South Vietnam did not improve the lot of the people there. A substantial portion of the funds went not into agricultural or industrial development but into the creation of services for the Americans. Some of the aid did go to increasing the fighting efficiency of the South Vietnamese troops, but a substantial portion simply lined the pockets of the generals. A large part of the economy consisted of a support population of secretaries, translators, interpreters, maids, shoeshine boys, and prostitutes, none of whom contributed to the economic production of goods. Agriculture suffered because of bombing raids, defoliation, the paucity of manpower, and the general lack of incentive. Many of the unfortunate migrants in cities remained unemployed, found themselves in the army, or became beggars, pimps, mafia underlings, or members of street gangs. Much of the population came to depend on the continued presence of U.S. troops and the money they spent. Tempted by the lures of city life and fast money or simply out of economic necessity, young girls migrated to Saigon or to the periphery of U.S. military bases to become prostitutes. According to a 1975 World Health Organization estimate, Saigon alone had about 400,000 prostitutes, making that city, in the words of Senator William Fulbright, a huge brothel. The city's population expanded from the prewar 2 million to over 7 million, placing an unbearable strain on the city's infrastructure.

By August 1971 there were 335,000 civilian dead, 740,000 wounded, 5 million refugees in Vietnam, and 1 million refugees in Laos. By 1975 there were an additional 4 to 5 million refugees (two-thirds of the country's total population) in Cambodia alone. As of December 31, 1971, the U.S. armed forces reported 45,627 killed and 302,896 wounded; the South Vietnamese army had lost 137,000, with three times that number wounded. According to U.S. estimates, the NLF lost 788,000, which, in the words of U.S. Secretary of Defense Robert McNamara, included "unarmed parties and bystanders."[3] By 1971 the United States had spent over $150 billion, averaging more than $190,000 per NLF member killed. An MIT study pointed out that the costs of the war, including future payments to veterans, equalled the entire gross national product of the U.S. in 1971—over $750 billion.

U.S. DISENGAGEMENT

As early as 1967, a number of high U.S. government officials were aware of the futility of the war in Vietnam, though they were then in a minority. The U.S. mentality refused to accept defeat or acknowledge that sophisticated weaponry that gave the United States tremendous land, water, and air superiority was ineffective in the face of the poorly clad, poorly fed, and poorly equipped Viet Cong, who were determined to sweep their land clean of foreign intruders once and for all regardless of the costs. It took a long time for the U.S. generals trained in conventional warfare to understand the sociopolitical implications of a guerrilla warfare and the frustrating inability to crush what might be called a people's war.

Among the U.S. officials who began questioning the purposes of the war and America's role in it was Defense Secretary McNamara. McNamara resigned in March 1968. His successor, Clark Clifford, soon had similar reservations:

> I was convinced that the military course we were pursuing was not only endless, but hopeless. A further substantial increase in U.S. forces would only increase the devastation and the Americanization of the war and thus leave us even further from our goal of peace that would permit the people of South Vietnam to fashion their own political and economic institutions.[4]

Such discordant voices in the U.S. administration had been preceded by nationwide student protest. By 1968, an election year, the anti–Vietnam

War movement had widened to include most intellectuals and created a severe rift in the Democratic Party's ranks. After the war's initial benefits to the U.S. economy, deterioration had set in. Recession, growing unemployment, and a declining dollar boosted public clamor to end the "dirty war." Both sides in the Vietnamese War kept an eye on the U.S. political situation. North Vietnam and the NLF's decision to launch a major offensive on all the main cities and towns of South Vietnam around the time of the Tet festival (January 1968) must have been taken with a view to exploit U.S. electoral politics. The attack would be followed by negotiations in which the Americans would be at a distinct disadvantage.

The Tet offensive produced a military stalemate, though it did have a tremendous impact on U.S. politics. The NLF was not successful in holding any of the cities and towns except Hué and that for only a short period. The NLF's expectation that the Tet offensive would inspire major popular uprisings in its favor all over urban Vietnam did not materialize. Its losses were heavy—about 40,000 killed and many more wounded. The effect on U.S. and South Vietnamese forces was disastrous. In Washington a major debate on the potential costs of continuing the war took place based on the assumption that only a quarter of North Vietnam's forces were involved in the Tet offensive. From that point on, the United States seemed resolved to disengage from Vietnam "with honor." Bombing and other forms of warfare would be continued to secure the best terms in the ensuing negotiations. An immediate result of all this was President Johnson's decision not to seek office again. By the end of the year, the former cold-war hero Richard Nixon was elected to the presidency on a platform of "ending the war and winning the peace" in Vietnam.

From 1969 to the signing of the Paris accords in January 1973, the United States followed, albeit with some modifications, the "two tracks plan"[5] of Henry Kissinger, Nixon's national security adviser and, later, U.S. secretary of state. According to Kissinger's plan, the United States and the DRV would negotiate a military settlement of the war whereas the Saigon government would seek a political accommodation with the NLF. Although U.S. forces would gradually be withdrawn, a greatly expanded ARVN—armed and supplied by the United States—would bear the brunt of the fighting. The process was dubbed "Vietnamization." The ARVN soon had more than 1 million troops, including eighteen- and nineteen-year-old draftees taken from the poor peasant population, large numbers of city-dwellers avoiding the draft through bribery or influence. The greater flow of U.S. monetary aid only worsened the social situation.

On the larger plane, Nixon promulgated a new doctrine in May 1969 to limit the U.S. role in subsequent Vietnam-type situations. In the face of future aggression that did not involve one of the nuclear powers, the United States would "provide elements of military strength and economic resources approximate to our size and our interests" and would consider the "defense and progress of other countries" as "first, their responsibility and second, a regional responsibility."[6] The new policy was also based on rapprochement with China, which seemed eager to use its newfound friendship with the United States against the Soviet Union. During Nixon's visit to Beijing in February 1972, the Chinese, in secret agreements, allegedly promised not to attack Taiwan precipitately and to tolerate a U.S. presence in Vietnam on the same reduced level as in South Korea. As mentioned before, Beijing's interest in leaving Vietnam divided fitted into the traditional Chinese policy of weakening its neighbors, whether Communist or not.

The "gradual" withdrawal of U.S. troops did not occur without further bloodshed. Efforts to make the operation compatible with the achievement of peace with honor involved resumption of more saturation bombing of North Vietnam (which had been halted by President Johnson) and of the countryside in South Vietnam and the mining of Haiphong Harbor to prevent Soviet supplies from reaching North Vietnam. From 1970 to 1973, the Vietnamese conflict truly became an Indochinese war. Its implications were grave. The bombing of Laos and Cambodia was undertaken to strike at Communist bases and supply routes from North to South Vietnam passing through those countries. The large-scale invasion of Cambodia in 1970 was aimed at capturing the alleged underground headquarters of the Central Office of South Vietnam (COSVN). (It was not found.) A large number of peasants were killed in these operations, and millions of refugees from the countryside flocked into Cambodia's capital of Phnom Penh, contributing to the swelling of its population from .5 million to 4 million— half the country's entire population. The bombing during Nixon's first two years in office surpassed the total tonnage the United States dropped in Europe and the Pacific during World War II. In May 1972 the daily costs of bombing were estimated at $20 million dollars.

CAMBODIA SINCE GENEVA

Cambodia was the most successful of the three Indochinese states in achieving a national integration and preserving its independence despite the wars raging around it. The success could, in large measure, be attributed to the magnetic, complex personality of Norodom Sihanouk, who was the country's king at the time of the French withdrawal in July 1954. In March 1955 he abdicated the throne and the position of head of state in favor of his father so as to free himself actively to participate in the country's politics and lead its government until his sudden overthrow in 1970. Immensely powerful and popular, Sihanouk kept his small country from becoming seriously enmeshed in the neighboring conflict.

Cambodia's foreign policy during the Sihanouk era amounted to a struggle to survive as an independent state hemmed in between two potentially hostile neighbors, Thailand and Vietnam. At the Afro-Asian Conference at Bandung in April 1955, thanks to Nehru's mediation, Sihanouk received from China and the DRV adequate assurances of noninterference in the affairs of his country. Thereafter, Sihanouk adopted neutrality in foreign affairs as a "dictate of necessity."[7] Until the early 1960s, he alternated between pro-West and pro-Communist policies. By the middle of the decade, however, he became convinced that the future lay with China as the regional power, the United States' interest in the region and ability to control it being limited and transient. Sihanouk also decided that the North Vietnamese and the NLF represented the winning side in the Vietnam conflict and were therefore potential neighbors of Cambodia. Consequently, friendship with the Chinese and the Vietnamese Communists became the anchors of Cambodia's foreign policy, though the Cambodian leadership trusted neither side. Sihanouk was suspicious of the Vietnamese for their traditional expansionism at Cambodia's expense. Further, he distrusted Communists in general, as they might well see a feudal prince as a logical candidate for political liquidation. Yet Sihanouk knew that friendship with China could be used as a lever against the Vietnamese, who were historically suspicious of their northern neighbors. Sihanouk thus followed the Kautilyan foreign policy dictate of befriending one's enemy's enemy.

CAMBODIA'S NEUTRALITY

Intent upon safeguarding its national integrity, Cambodia nervously watched its borders. In 1964–1965, exasperated by frequent frontier incursions by U.S. and South Vietnamese forces in pursuit of guerrillas, Sihanouk severed diplomatic relations with the United States. In the following years, however, the Communist use of Cambodian territory increased. The U.S. bombing of North Vietnam and of the Ho Chi Minh Trail passing through southeast Laos had made it necessary for North Vietnam to seek alternate routes of supply. The Ho Chi Minh Trail was extended to northeast Cambodia, which lay beyond the bombing zone. More significantly, the Communists used the facilities of the new port of Sihanoukville to bring in supplies and materiel from North Vietnam and China. These would be transported by profit-seeking Chinese entrepreneurs in Phnom Penh to the eastern provinces, where the Communists had built underground storage facilities. As the war expanded, the Communists occupied larger chunks of Cambodian territory, allegedly using them as sanctuaries for about 20 percent of their forces.

There is no doubt that the Communists badly needed the sanctuaries and would hold them with or without Sihanouk's consent. Recognizing the "inevitable," the Cambodian prince strove to keep Communist occupation to a limited area by obtaining Communist promises of self-restraint. To maintain some degree of control over the Vietnamese Communists, Sihanouk allowed the NLF to maintain a legation in Phnom Penh.

The Communists abandoned such restraints toward the end of 1968. The area of the sanctuaries under Communist use and control increased. Well-staffed hospitals, extensive training camps, and ammunition-manufacturing facilities replaced the rudimentary structures of the earlier days. The Communists established an almost complete administration in the area, even collecting taxes and growing crops. By the beginning of 1969, varied accounts, Cambodian and American, placed the estimates of Communist troops in the sanctuaries at 40,000 to 50,000. U.S. intelligence further claimed that the headquarters of the guerrilla movement, COSVN, was itself based well within Cambodia's borders.

THE KHMER ROUGE

Of immediate concern for Sihanouk's government was the increase in the activities of the Khmer Rouge, the Cambodian Communists. In 1954, because of Sino-Soviet pressures at Geneva, the Viet Minh had abandoned the cause of the Khmer Rouge, agreeing that it be disbanded and that its cadres retreat to Hanoi. Consequently, about 5,000 Khmer Rouge, later labeled the Hanoi Khmers, withdrew to North Vietnam. A few radicals, known as the Khmer Viet Minh, were decimated by Sihanouk's government. The radical ranks were later reinforced by younger and newer leaders like Ieng Sary, Khieu Samphan, Hou Yuon, and Saloth Sar (later known as Pol Pot),[8] mostly trained in law or economics. In contrast to the Hanoi-based Khmer Rouge, many of whose members were married to Vietnamese women, the new breed of Cambodian Communists (also known as Khmer Rouge) were nationalist Communists, fiercely anti-Hanoi and independent of the Indochina Communist Party. The new Khmer Rouge never forgot nor forgave the Vietnamese Communists for their "betrayal" in 1954.[9] In the late 1960s, contrary to Hanoi's wishes, the new Khmer Rouge conducted maquis-type operations against Sihanouk's government.

Sihanouk was not privy to the internal dispute between the Khmer Rouge and the Vietnamese Communists. In January 1970 he went abroad, ostensibly for medical treatment of chronic obesity but really to try to bring diplomatic pressure on Hanoi to restrain the Khmer Rouge. During his absence in March 1970, his prime minister, General Lon Nol (who was pro-U.S. and anti–Khmer Rouge), staged a coup deposing him. Sihanouk learned of the coup while he was on his way home via Moscow. Accepting asylum in China, he headed the Cambodian government-in-exile. In a book written from exile, he blamed the CIA for his ouster.[10] Some time between 1970 and 1975, the Khmer Rouge made Sihanouk (in Beijing, but still popular in Cambodia) the nominal head of the Khmer Rouge; the prince seemed to have no choice but to accept the role.

Meanwhile, the United States withheld support from the Lon Nol regime for a "respectable" period of five weeks. Thereafter, the Nixon administration stood solidly behind the Lon Nol government with plenty of military assistance to fight the Khmer Rouge, who had, by April 27, 1970, blocked five out of the seven approach roads to the capital. Washington used its new leverage with Phnom Penh for enlarging the Vietnam conflict. In a gross reversal of his policy of withdrawal from Vietnam, Nixon decided on April 30 to invade Cambodia and capture the COSVN, which the United States believed to be the headquarters of the Communist military operations in South Vietnam. The official explanation was that one such decisive victory would tilt the balance and compel Hanoi and the NLF to agree to a political settlement at the Paris talks.

The United States' action did indeed fuel a civil war in Cambodia, a land that had so far been an oasis of peace in the midst of the holocaust in Laos and Vietnam. As for the military value of the adventure, it was very limited; large caches of ammunition were found but not the COSVN itself.

THE PARIS ACCORDS OF 1973

On January 27, 1973, the DRV, the Provisional Revolutionary Government (PRG), South Vietnam, and the United States finally signed the Paris accords bringing about a cease-fire in Vietnam, Cambodia, and Laos. The agreement provided for withdrawal of all U.S. troops, the return of prisoners of war to the parties concerned, and a cease-fire without demarcation lines. For the South, there was to be a democratic solution: The PRG and the Thieu government were to resolve their conflicts through mutual consultation. A Council of Reconciliation and Concord was to be set up to organize elections in the South, after which a tripartite coalition government of Thieu, the PRG, and neutralists would be created. Reunification of Vietnam could be considered through subsequent consultations between the North and the South. With regard to Laos and Cambodia, the Paris accords confirmed the provisions of the Geneva agreements of 1954 and 1962. An unwritten clause of the accords was an alleged U.S. undertaking to pay $3.2 billion toward the reconstruction of North Vietnam, ravaged by U.S. bombing. The sum was never paid. The North Vietnamese march into Saigon in April 1975 had, in Washington's view, absolved the United States of that promise.

Although the accords earned a Nobel Peace Prize jointly for Le Duc Tho, chief North Vietnamese negotiator (who did not accept it), and Henry Kissinger, they did not bring lasting peace to the states of Indochina. The three Vietnamese parties to the accords viewed the agreement as a temporary truce, giving all of them time to prepare for the final phase of the conflict. The accords had implicitly allowed the DRV to station about 140,000 troops in the South until a political solution was reached. The cease-fire left South Vietnam with pockets of territory under the PRG rule. The withdrawal of U.S. forces meant the South was exposed to an eventual invasion by the North.

COMMUNIST VICTORY IN VIETNAM AND CAMBODIA

Not long after signing the peace accords, the three Vietnamese parties— the PRG, DRV, and Thieu—again took up their conflict. Thieu demanded immediate withdrawal of DRV troops as a prerequisite to elections, though neither the DRV nor the PRG had ever acknowledged the presence of North Vietnamese troops in the South. Thieu also hampered the PRG candidates' freedom of movement to campaign. With Thieu mounting a new offensive against the PRG-held areas, war was resumed by the end of the year. The level of military operations was, on the whole, low-key on all sides, however, because of the reduced levels of external support from the United States, China, and the Soviet Union. In March 1975 the DRV suddenly launched a major offensive that ended in the capture of Saigon on April 30. The DRV's gamble was perhaps predicated on the military weakness of the Thieu government caused by reduced U.S. aid and the perception that the Ford administration would be incapable of any retaliation because of the post-Watergate U.S. political environment and the dwindling U.S. commitment to the conflict. The gamble paid off. Thieu's order to his army in the central highlands to make a "tactical retreat" led to their resounding defeat. Thieu resigned on April 21 and left the country. A government established under the neutralist General Duong Van Minh surrendered to the Communist forces on April 30. It was a victory for the bulk of the Vietnamese people, who had fought long for this moment. In recognition of Ho Chi Minh's contribution to the movement, Saigon was renamed Ho Chi Minh City.

Meanwhile, in Cambodia, the Khmer Rouge had continued its guerrilla operations against the Lon Nol regime. The Khmer Rouge ranks were not, however, united. In the early 1970s, Hanoi had sent to Cambodia about 5,000 Khmer Rouge who had lived in North Vietnam since 1954. These "Hanoi Khmers," as they were disparagingly called by the indigenous Khmer Rouge under Pol Pot's leadership, were expected to control the latter, inhibiting their independence and frustrating the Cambodian goal of thwarting long-term North Vietnamese ambitions to dominate all of Indochina. After the Paris accords of January 1973, open conflict developed, the Pol Pot group purging or killing large numbers of the Hanoi Khmers. The Khmer Rouge did not comply with Hanoi's urging to lay down arms as stipulated in the Paris peace accords. Although Hanoi cut off all further military assistance, the Khmer Rouge continued with the offensive, toppling the Lon Nol regime a fortnight before the North Vietnamese capture of Saigon.

REASONS FOR THE U.S. FAILURE IN VIETNAM

The U.S. debacle in Vietnam can be attributed primarily to the incorrect diagnosis of the reasons for the insurrection. The conflict was not as much pro-Communist as it was anti-Diem and later anti-Ky and anti-Thieu, all of whom failed to initiate and implement the much-needed political and socioeconomic reforms. Beginning as it did with the southern initiative, the movement was manned and supported mainly by southerners and not by Hanoi, as Washington had wrongly perceived. The conflict called for a political rather than a military solution, possibly to satisfy a widespread urge to reunify the country.

The infusion of massive U.S. military aid had the effect of fueling inflation. The economic aid was not substantial. Moreover, as much as 40 percent of the economic aid, according to a *New York Times* estimate, was swallowed by corrupt contractors, high administrators, generals, business intermediaries, and government officials. U.S. supplies meant for the war effort were pilfered on a gigantic scale. As a former premier, Nguyen Cao Ky, wrote in 1976: "In Qui Nhon market, you could buy anything from army rations and clothing to washing machines and grenades . . . and if you wanted to buy a tank or a helicopter it would be arranged."[11]

The infusion of U.S. military manpower had an even worse effect. The specter of alien forces on Vietnamese soil revived anticolonial, nationalist sentiment. The Second Indochina War was as much directed against the U.S. presence as was the first against the French colonial rule. The Vietnamese rightly perceived that it was because of U.S. support that several corrupt, self-serving military dictatorships had survived in Saigon for a decade and in Cambodia for half a decade, contributing to social and moral decay, spiraling inflation, and devastation of the countryside. After 1964 large numbers of non-Communist university students and faculty and professionals joined the NLF because, like their predecessors at the turn of the previous century, they seemed to feel they were on the verge of losing their country. In the early years after the Geneva settlement of 1954, the United States failed to insist on socioeconomic reforms or liberalization of the political process—and thus failed to create among the

South Vietnamese people either a feeling that they had some stake in the country's independence or a desire to support the central government. The shortcomings of the Diem regime were basic; the momentum lost was never regained. The postponement of sociopolitical reforms until the end of the military conflict and the characterization of that conflict as one between Communists and anti-Communists contributed to U.S. ineffectiveness and to South Vietnam's ruin.

CHAPTER 7

The New Vietnam

Vietnam suffered immensely in the period following World War II, undergoing continual conflict from 1940 to 1975, with only a brief respite of peace following the Geneva agreements of 1954. Millions of Vietnamese children grew up in that period carrying memories of bloodshed, terror, bombing, and dislocation. Vietnam occupied the front page of newspapers and figured prominently in other media consistently for years, probably more than any other single country or event during that time. The Vietnamese conflict divided public opinion all over the globe, particularly in the United States, whose social, political, and economic fabric was torn by the long "undeclared" war. The spectacle of a small country with far less sophisticated weaponry than its opponents immobilizing an advanced, militarily well-equipped nation put in doubt the very basis of strategic defense in the modern world.

The loss in human lives was staggering. Eight million tons of bombs, four times the tonnage used in World War II, had been rained on a tiny country. Ten million gallons of a chemical, Agent Orange, had been sprayed in order to destroy the canopy of its lush forests. The United States spent nearly $150 billion and lost 57,000 lives (with several times that number maimed or disabled for life); the figures for the Vietnamese on both sides of the conflict were unavailable but casualties were roughly estimated at over 2 million. The disruption of normal life was spread over many years for some but lasted at least a decade for the nearly 5 million refugees from the countryside who flocked to major cities for protection.[1] Saigon became a cesspool of vice where a large segment of the noncombatant population busied itself in corruption of diverse sorts. Human morality and values seemed to lay in irreparable ruin all over South Vietnam. It was, therefore, a great relief for millions of people to see the end of the Vietnamese conflict in 1975. The end of the war and the reunification of Vietnam a year later were hoped to usher in an era of peace and reconstruction to a war-ravaged country.

The Communist leadership in Vietnam has not shown itself as adept at peace and reconstruction as it was at war and revolution. The bleak economic situation in Vietnam in the decade following the end of the war in 1975 may, in some substantial measure, be attributable to the particular conditions in the previous decade. The continued failure of the Vietnamese government to improve the economic condition of the common citizen is related to several other factors, including leadership. The socioeconomic legacy of a long and devastating war; the special character of the U.S.-subsidized, war-oriented economy of South Vietnam; a succession of natural disasters such as droughts and floods between 1976 and 1978; wars with China and occupation of Cambodia; and the absence of expected foreign assistance all may be responsible for the failure of plans to stabilize the economy and fulfill the wants of a people whose primary consumer needs had been denied for decades.

In the short run, the leadership appeared divided between those who stood for ideological purity and insisted upon the immediate transformation of the South Vietnamese economy to socialism and those pragmatists and moderates who saw no alternative to making concessions and offering capitalistic incentives, especially to encourage agricultural production in the South. Economic policies therefore vacillated from liberalism in 1975–1976 to rigidity during 1976–1979, to make way again for limited private trade and manufacturing and practical incentives to farmers. For the morale of revolutionary cadres, the impact of such a policy of postponing the creation of a Communist society was indeed grave.

The war's adverse effect on the economy of North Vietnam and on the society and economy of South Vietnam were incalculable. The war in the countryside had turned South Vietnam, formerly a leading exporter of rice, into an importer of grain to feed a large population that could not attend to agriculture, had been conscripted into the army, or had simply fled to urban centers. Nevertheless, the war created a false sense of prosperous economy, particularly in Saigon and around the U.S. military bases. The vast array of imported consumer goods, including shiny automobiles, stereo systems, and electrical appliances, was subsidized by the United States. The large amounts of external funds pumped into the economy resulted in a galloping inflation, impoverishing the middle class and people with fixed incomes. The only people who seemed to prosper in the U.S.-sponsored "free enterprise" system were smugglers, black marketeers, building contractors, and intermediaries of all sorts, not to mention pimps and prostitutes.

During the Second Indochina War (1964–1975), the southern economy had thus become almost parasitical, dependent on external financing and on purchases by the U.S. armed forces of South Vietnamese goods and services. More than 50 percent of the gross national product was generated by a service sector almost completely dependent upon a U.S.-funded war and in which imports (equal to 25 percent of the GNP in 1971) were twelve times the exports. The industry accounting for 8 percent of the GNP was 85 percent dependent upon foreign countries for raw materials and absolutely dependent on foreign machines and fuel. Consequently, with the beginning of the withdrawal of U.S. forces in 1971, the service sector suffered grievously, bringing the rate of growth of the GNP in the following four years to about 1 percent per annum, while the population increased by about 3 percent. The subsequent debacle of the Saigon government burst the economic bubble completely.

The economic situation in North Vietnam, too, was critical. The losses there due to U.S. "strategic" bombing from 1965 to 1972 were staggering. A United Nations mission visiting Vietnam in 1976 reported that the entire North Vietnamese economic infrastructure had been blasted out of existence during those seven years. Railroads had been thrown out of commission for long stretches on various lines, most of the bridges on the Hanoi-Langson and Hanoi-Vinh lines having been blown up. Tongking's dike system, built over two millennia, suffered grievously, with 183 dams and canals and 884 water installations in need of major repairs. Twenty-nine of the thirty provincial capitals and thousands of villages were damaged, some of them completely destroyed.

Hanoi had, however, taken advantage of the time—about twenty-eight months—that elapsed between the cessation of U.S. bombing of North Vietnam and the Communist takeover of Saigon to restore its infrastructure, including Tongking's intricate and vital dike system. By mid-1975, the government had repaired or rebuilt the numerous cement and glass enterprises as well as dockyards in the Haiphong industrial sector, the chemical enterprises in Viet Tri and the steel complex in the Thai Nguyen industrial center. Roads and bridges had also become serviceable again.

The ecological balance in the South had been damaged the most. The report of the UN Commission to Vietnam pointed out that chemical warfare had created a large number of "blank zones" in the countryside. The U.S. armed forces had engaged in large-scale defoliation because the thick foliage helped the guerrillas to hide and also obstructed the U.S. aircraft landing. The defoliation operations were undertaken, however, in the name of a "food denial program" against the guerrillas. By 1969 more than 5 million acres of land had been sprayed with herbicides, mostly Agent Orange against forest vegetation and Agent Blue (which had arsenic in its composition) against rice and other food crops. The ruinous impact of these chemicals on the productive abilities of the soil was incalculable. The removal of the jungle canopy increased the exposure of the soil to sunlight, which altered the soil's properties. The rate of soil erosion increased with rapid exhaustion of humus. It was estimated that an equivalent of three decades of South Vietnam's timber supply had been destroyed, and that it would take anywhere from five years for the fruit trees to a century or so for the rare timber trees to become productive again.[2]

POSTWAR ECONOMIC MEASURES

After the Communist victory in 1975, the new government took up the task of reconstruction at all levels: economic, social, political, ideological. The problems it found were truly stupendous. Huynh Kim Khanh summarized the gamut of socioeconomic woes of the new Vietnam thus:

> The legacy of the U.S.-Thieu regime was an economic and social malaise of unknown proportions: an economy that was on the verge of bankruptcy; a threatening famine in the northern provinces of Central Vietnam; more than three million unemployed people, excluding an army of a half-million prostitutes about to be out of work; six to seven million refugees who had been forced by wartime activities to flee their native villages into the cities, etc.[3]

Moreover, fleeing officials and bankers had stolen most of the country's foreign exchange reserves. The new government also had to do something about the former employees of the deposed government of South Vietnam, which included 1.1 million regular troops in addition to .5 million paramilitary forces, 125,000 police and 350,000 civil service officials, very few of whom could be relied upon for their loyalties to the Communist regime. Given the ideological context, reconstruction in the South meant not only rehabilitation of urban refugees but relocation and "reeducation" of several million individuals, practically one-third to one-half the population of South Vietnam. Another important aspect of the relocation was the large number of handicapped persons from out of an estimated 2.2 million war casualties, some of whom could not be expected to contribute to the rebuilding of the economy at full strength and who, in fact, might need state assistance of some kind for periods of time.

The new government's short-term strategy was twofold: to convert the economy from "free enterprise" to socialist and to integrate the South Vietnamese economy with its northern counterpart. Its immediate tasks included efforts to restore the industrial capacity of the Saigon-Cholon area and to relocate a large number of its population to the countryside for resumption of agricultural activity. The government planned an immediate additional employment for over 1 million people in agriculture and allied occupations by bringing more than 1.2 million acres of fallow land in the Mekong Delta under cultivation. The new slogan in mid-1975 was: "Break with the past, return to the countryside to work for production." As in postrevolutionary China, the new program had its sadistic overtones in compelling the city-bred, soft-lived intellectuals, civil service officials, and vast numbers of army officials of the former government to work with their hands like the rest of the proletariat in a "reeducation" program. Whereas the early Maoists in China had distrusted technology, claiming it would be deleterious to socialist values, the Vietnamese had only financial constraints in the use of technology. They perceived no contradiction between the building of a modern economy and the building of a socialist society, not unlike the thinking of the post-Maoist leadership in China.

Other short-term measures announced by the government were largely in the area of banking and currency reform. Thus private banks and other financial and lending institutions were abolished in August 1975. A month later, all individuals and organizations were required to exchange old dong notes at the rate of 500 to 1 for new notes issued by the National Bank of Vietnam. Limits were announced for categories of individuals and organizations in terms of how much of the old money could be exchanged; the surplus funds were to be deposited in savings accounts. Any large withdrawals had to be sanctioned by the government. The new government thus created at one stroke a large amount of surplus capital for reinvestment. The sectors of the society most affected by the new measures were the so-called comprador-bourgeois class, mostly merchants, importers, and intermediaries who had become wealthy by dealing solely with the U.S. and South Vietnamese governments.

Because the new government was socialist and revolutionary, it predictably announced a number of anticapitalist, anti-West measures. Immediately after the takeover of Saigon, the government declared a policy of nationalization of foreign enterprises. It refused to honor the fallen South Vietnamese government's debt obligations. The government nationalized all manufacturing and industrial activity even though the prospects of success were not very bright because of the lack of raw materials, fuel, and, above all, U.S.-made spare parts. Only retail trading remained in private hands.

After the initial demonstration of revolutionary zeal, the government bowed to the tactical needs of foreign exchange and capital. In 1977 Vietnam announced a number of measures calculated to woo foreign capital. In a reversal of its previous policy, it accepted responsibility for the South Vietnamese government's debt obligations to Japan and France. Ideological purity was clearly abandoned in favor of pragmatism. The government welcomed outside investment of finance and technology on a joint-venture or production-sharing basis, Vietnam supplying the labor, allowing remission of profits, and assuring that the new joint enterprises would not be expropriated. A little earlier, Vietnam had joined the International Monetary Fund, unlike most Communist countries (with the

significant exceptions of Yugoslavia and Romania), which had either refused to join the international body or withdrawn from it. Vietnam also
joined the World Bank and the Asian Development Bank yet remained
only an observer of the Moscow-dominated Comecon International Investment Bank. All these steps softened the attitude of some countries,
particularly members of the European Economic Community, Sweden,
and Japan, who signed economic assistance agreements with Vietnam.
Vietnam also made specific efforts to attract capital from non-Communist
countries for oil exploration and the mining of tin, tungsten, apatite,
phosphate, and anthracite coal.

FIVE-YEAR PLANS AND ECONOMIC POLICY

Economic planning in Communist Vietnam has been the responsibility
of the party, whereas implementation of the plans is left to the government.
Crucial to the understanding of the Vietnamese economic policies are the
deliberations of the Fourth National Party Congress (December 1976), the
Fifth Congress (March 1982), and the Sixth Congress (December 1986).
The party's goal has indeed been to take the country through a period of
"transition to socialism." This would be achieved in three stages. The first
would conclude with the Second Five-Year Plan in 1980; the second would
cover "socialist industrialization" through five successive five-year plans
till 2005; the third would extend till 2010 and would be devoted to
"perfecting" the transition to socialism.

Second Five-Year Plan

At the Fourth Party Congress in December 1976, the Vietnamese Communist Party adopted an ambitious Second Five-Year Plan (1976–1980).
Because of the war, the DRV's economic planning had practically been in
abeyance since 1965; the Second Five-Year Plan constituted a hurried
revision of a plan originally formulated only for North Vietnam in 1974
and now expanded to include projects for South Vietnam. The process of
formulation of an integrated plan for all of Vietnam took some time. When
the plan was finally announced in December 1976, there were only four
instead of five years to meet its targets.

The objectives of the Second Five-Year Plan were twofold: to build a
material and technological base for the new socialist state and to raise
the standard of living of the population. To this end, the plan proposed
a threefold program: reorganization of production in the South along the
lines of collectives in North Vietnam, reallocation of labor, and implementation of a "correct investment" policy through better economic
management.

Of the projected outlay of $7.5 billion, at least half the sum was expected to come from outside donors. The Soviet Union promised $2.7 billion and East European countries $700 million. China was expected to contribute $600 million. Vietnam also expected aid from friendly Western countries. More importantly, Hanoi still believed the United States would fulfill a "promise" made at the time of the Paris peace accords to give Vietnam $3.2 billion in reconstruction aid. By the forcible capture of South Vietnam in April 1975, the North Vietnamese had, in the official U.S. view, violated those accords and absolved the United States of its "promise." Vietnam, however, continued to hope that some U.S. assistance would be forthcoming, particularly after the advent of the Carter administration and as a reward for Hanoi's efforts in investigating the whereabouts of U.S. troops missing in action (MIAs). The U.S. aid never materialized. Assistance from socialist countries also dropped below expectations or, as in China's case, dried up altogether, making Vietnam's foreign exchange problems acute and the prospects of the plan's implementation bleak.

The Second Five-Year Plan proposed major agricultural and industrial projects involving large-scale demographic changes. Out of the total planned expenditure of $25 billion, $7.5 billion were marked for agriculture, $8.75 billion for industry, and an equal amount for transportation and services.[4] The plan stressed the primary sector of the economy, though it also aimed at laying the groundwork for heavy industry. Thus 30 percent of the total outlay was earmarked for agriculture in the expectation by 1980 of a food production of 21 million tons, with an annual surplus of 3 million tons of rice for export.

Most of this agricultural development was to take place in the South by reclaiming 6.4 million acres of land, mainly in the Mekong Delta. The government envisaged large-scale collectivization of agriculture through the creation of some 250 giant collectives, one in each district of South Vietnam, each employing about 100,000 persons. The Hanoi government claimed to have set up 137 such collectives in South Vietnam by 1978, before the march into Cambodia. Their establishment "released" some 4 million people, who were then settled in the new economic zones (NEZs) in both parts of Vietnam. Half the population of the Saigon-Cholon area as well as the Hanoi-Haiphong regions were relocated to the NEZs near the Cambodian border. Urban people moving into the NEZs were given the necessary tool and grain supplies to last six months, with the stipulation that they develop a tract of land and bring it under cultivation.

Vietnam's economic plan thus involved demographic relocation on a gigantic scale similar to that in the Soviet Union and China after their respective revolutions. The Vietnamese government also announced plans that would relocate about 10 million people from the country's overcrowded areas to the mountainous border zones in the north and west over the subsequent twenty years. From the Red River Delta and the central coast alone, about 4 million would be resettled in the mountainous zone, Mekong Delta, eastern coast, and offshore islands, particularly the Spratlys. As economic units, the NEZs would develop centers of light industry, helping to produce articles of consumption not only for the domestic population but also to help exports. In previously sparsely populated regions, the NEZs would be used to bring new areas under cultivation.

The concept of organizing territory into NEZs had already been adopted in North Vietnam in 1970 to create twenty-three NEZs in fourteen provinces. But in South Vietnam the NEZs were not set up purely for socioeconomic reasons. In the view of one critic, they were forms of population control that facilitated the work of the internal security police and served the strategic purpose of peopling the underpopulated border areas.

The plans for industry and commerce in South Vietnam matched the pattern earlier implemented in North Vietnam during the First Five-Year Plan. That plan had aimed at denuding the South of all Western—specifically, U.S.—influence and transforming its economy into a socialist one. Despite such a proclaimed goal, the government in effect allowed private enterprises to continue in a new form: All were newly designated as state-private partnerships. The previous owners, except those who had flagrantly sided with the former South Vietnamese government, were compensated with government bonds and were reemployed by the government to manage the new partnerships. Although some of the richest smugglers and black marketeers were apprehended and holdings of large landowners confiscated, most small businesses continued under private ownership. Later, in March 1978, the government took over the retail trade partly by compensating the owners and rehiring many of them as managers of what now became government-owned consumer goods stores. Another major economic measure integrated the currencies of North and South Vietnam in May 1978 with the issue of a new currency that became legal tender throughout the country.

Transport and communications were allocated the same high-priority investment as industry. This was indeed necessary because the transportation systems had been severely damaged by U.S. and South Vietnamese bombing both in the North and the South. The Second Five-Year Plan called for repairs to all arterial highways, bridges, and ports, particularly Haiphong, which had been the North's principal port for international trade and had been badly damaged by U.S. bombing and mining in late 1972. The wartime road network was to be adapted to peacetime activities, and new major roads were to be built connecting the North and South to supplement the old coastal highway.

Failure of the Second Five-Year Plan

Vietnam's wars with Cambodia and China in 1978–1979 (see Chapter 8) cost Vietnam dearly. The continued occupation of Cambodia by Vietnamese forces and the state of military preparedness on the Sino-Vietnamese border limited the funds that could be more fruitfully spent on developmental programs. In 1979 the government decided to decentralize industry as part of the national defense strategy, and in the following year it formally stepped up the defense expenditure to absorb almost half of the nation's budget. The government altered its priorities on a number of major policy decisions, adversely affecting, for example, the plans for further development of the NEZs and population resettlement schemes.

The conflicts with Cambodia and China were not the only reasons for the failure of the Second Five-Year Plan. The plan had run into major problems almost from the very start. It stands to the credit of the Vietnamese leadership that it openly admitted the plan's gross failure and assessed the reasons for its poor performance. The Central Committee's Sixth Plenum in September 1979 and the Ninth Plenum in December 1980 provided a thorough critique. The committee cited paucity of funds, internal and external (particularly caused by U.S. and Chinese boycotts), as one factor. The Hanoi-based government's lack of appreciation of the socioeconomic structure of pre-1975 South Vietnam and the forced pace of changes was given as another. The committee also blamed many loyalists of the former anti-Communist regimes for actively "sabotaging" the state plans. Fourth, the party cadre and officials, who had served the country efficiently and selflessly during the critical war years, were now accused of maldistribution of goods, bureaucratic bottlenecks, and widespread corruption. Finally, the report noted that three successive years of bad weather, floods, and drought had severely curtailed agricultural output.

In terms of funds, no more than two-thirds of the total planned investment actually became available; loans and grants from abroad fell far below expectations. China granted only loans from 1976, and even those were completely cut off in 1978. The United States did not contribute to reconstruction; the U.S. embargo on trade with Vietnam continued. Even Soviet economic aid was reduced, presumably because it was contributing heavily toward defense expenditures—an estimated $3 million a day toward Vietnam's military commitments in Cambodia. As for aid from Western countries, three-fourths of the promised amount was held back after early 1979 because of resentment over Vietnam's march into Cambodia.

Economic assistance from the Soviet Union nevertheless played a major role in Vietnamese planned expenditure. Soviet technical assistance was crucial in agriculture, public health, transport and communications, geological explorations, and energy. The treaty of friendship and cooperation signed in November 1978 called for economic cooperation between the Soviet Union and Vietnam for ten years. Another agreement signed in July 1980 provided for offshore drilling for oil. Because of successive crop failures, some of the Soviet economic aid had to be diverted to finance about 10 to 15 percent of Vietnam's food grain requirements. On the fifth anniversary of the Soviet-Vietnamese friendship treaty, Tran Quynh, vice-chairman of the Vietnamese Council of State, wrote in Nhan Dan that Soviet aid had been further stepped up "to counter attempts by Vietnam's enemies to paralyze the nation's economy." He indicated that the Soviet Union was supplying 100 percent of Vietnam's fuel and lubricant imports, 100 percent of its communications systems and military equipment and weaponry, and more than 90 percent of its fertilizers and metallurgical products. In partial repayment of loans and grants, Vietnam had to supply the Soviet Union with natural resources and labor, sending more than 100,000 workers to the Soviet Union for several years.

Vietnam's foreign exchange predicament was further compounded by its export trade, which lagged far behind the plan's projections of an annual increase of 10 percent. Vietnam's exports in 1980 were only about 15 percent of its imports. Vietnam's principal export was coal, responsible for 95 percent of the total; other major imports have included wheat, wheat flour, fertilizers, machinery, and oil, and most of its trade has been with the Soviet Union and East European countries. Because of its trade deficit, Vietnam has had to send several thousand workers to the Eastern European countries (in addition to those to the Soviet Union) to earn Soviet bloc currency to repay the loans and to offset the unfavorable balance of trade.

The State Planning Committee report submitted by Vice-Premier Nguyen Lam in December 1980 revealed that food production had not kept pace with the increase in population, that severe shortages of raw materials and energy had crippled industry to about half its capacity, and that per capita income had actually declined since the Second Five-Year Plan was announced. National income had increased by 9 percent in 1976 and by only 2 percent in 1977. In the remaining years of the plan, national income actually declined because of the inclement weather that reduced agricultural output and the costly wars with Cambodia and China during 1978–1979. The report stated that during the plan period, agricultural output increased only by 18.7 percent and industrial production by 17.3 percent against a projected growth of 50 percent in agriculture and industry. Total area under cultivation increased by 4.4 million acres, that under irrigation by 1.5 million acres. Mechanized plowing through use of tractors increased by 37 percent. There was all-around progress in the production of coal, construction materials, and industries. In no area, however, were the planned targets reached. Thus in 1980 the harvest reached about 12 million tons against a target of 21 million. Because of severe food shortages between 1977 and 1980, rice was rationed to a level matching the lowest point of supply in North Vietnam during the war. About 3 million tons of rice had to be imported annually between 1977 and 1980. A population growth rate of 2.5 percent and the meager increases in national income since the reunification of Vietnam meant a lower standard of living.

Another reason for the plan's failure was the inordinate hurry on the government's part to unite the two halves of the country and transform it into a socialist state. North Vietnam, which did not have enough qualified management personnel and technicians, took upon itself to administer a country suddenly doubled in size, refusing to put trained South Vietnamese into administrative positions of trust, technical know-how, and responsibility. The short-sightedness of not fully integrating the South was the key to the failure of the Second Five-Year Plan. The strategies and plans, originally devised for North Vietnam, had merely been extended to the South. The distinct character of the South and its special problems of transition from a U.S.-subsidized capitalistic economy to a socialist economy were not adequately taken into consideration.

Economic Liberalization and the Third Five-Year Plan (1981–1985)

Aware of the reasons for the failure of the second plan, the Central Committee's Sixth Plenum decided in September 1979 to decelerate the collectivization and cooperativization of agriculture in South Vietnam both because of social resistance to such a process and, more importantly, because it had failed to yield results. After 1979 the government instructed that family farms that were run efficiently should be left alone. Others that had been converted into cooperatives were not to be precipitately taken over by state enterprises. All control stations established to check the movement of goods between rural areas and urban centers—which had virtually become bureaucratic bottlenecks and hunting grounds for pilferers, profiteers, bribe takers, and black marketeers—were abolished. The party agreed that in some fields of industry and trade private management would be more capable than government control in meeting consumer needs. It acknowledged that there were severe problems in the public-sector undertakings: poor management skills, inadequate technological know-how, and insufficient worker enthusiasm. The party therefore resolved to rescind the government orders nationalizing private business and trade and to restore small-scale enterprises and retail trade to the private sector. Additionally, the party unhesitatingly adopted the capitalist practice of increasing productivity through manipulation of economic incentives. Workers were given bonuses and other rewards to improve production and to raise their morale.

Despite such clear directives, the plan failed in its last year, 1980, to move the country economically forward. As the Ninth Plenum observed in December 1980, the failure came about because of bureaucratic reluctance to implement "capitalist" directives, for fear that the creation of a socialist state would thereby be jeopardized. The Ninth Plenum endorsed the Sixth Plenum's resolutions on flexible application of policies. Moreover, it resolved to decentralize management from the central to the local level, clearly defining the rights of major industrial and economic establishments to take their own decisions in most matters, including wage schemes, bonuses, and worker welfare. The pragmatic liberalization implicit in the decisions of the two plenums countered the overly rigid and dogmatic tenor of the Fourth Congress of the Party (1976), thereby providing a better base for the Third Five-Year Plan.

The third plan was neither formally drawn up nor officially presented to the National Assembly for adoption. As such, the several resolutions approved at the Fifth National Party Congress in March 1982 provided details of the Third Five-Year Plan. The new plan did not officially abandon the goal of transforming the economy of the South along socialist lines. It did, however, urge slowing down the pace of such a transformation by the temporary retention of private capitalist activities. This was particularly so in the field of agriculture through the development of a "family economy" by allowing the peasants to utilize such economic resources, including land, as were not being used by the agricultural cooperatives. Moreover, peasant families were encouraged to sign contracts with the collectives to farm land owned by the latter and agree to deliver to the state certain assigned quotas of grain or produce. In case of deficit, the peasant families could make up in the following year; in case of surplus, the peasant families could sell it on the open market or to the state for a price to be mutually settled.

By the middle year of the plan, the government reported that at least half of the peasants' total income and one-third to half of the foodstuff came from the "family economy." The new policy brought into the economy large numbers of peasants in the South who had refused to cooperate with the government and boycotted the agricultural cooperatives. It is important to note that unlike the peasants in North Vietnam, who were mostly tenants, the South Vietnamese peasants were mainly freeholders who cherished their property rights and refused to join the cooperatives. The effect of the new policy on agricultural production was, however, modest; the total food production was reported to have increased by 19.5 percent from 1980 to 1984, an average increase of about 5 percent but far above the annual 2.3 percent increase in population. This was partly because the state investment in agriculture remained low, at 18 percent in 1982, for example, as against 53 percent in industry. By the end of the third plan, the average annual per capita food consumption still hovered around 660 pounds.

Such emphasis on agriculture did not mean gross neglect of industry. In the short run, the further development of small-scale industry in the private sector was encouraged to meet domestic demand for consumer goods and to help exports. It was also expected that such a development would create a stronger base for heavy industry. Still, the process of transforming medium-scale enterprises into state-private joint enterprises, which had been taken up in the Second Five-Year Plan, was accelerated. Toward the end of the third five-year period, the Sixth Plenum of the Fifth Congress of the Vietnam Communist Party in July 1984 conceded that the state was not yet capable of shouldering the responsibility for trade, wholesale or retail. It advocated decentralization of planning and special training of government officials and party cadres in management of trade and industry. A year later the Eighth Plenum decided in favor of production autonomy at both the factory level and at the level of the individual farm.

Fourth Five-Year Plan (1986–1990)

The policy objectives of the fourth economic plan were outlined at the Sixth Congress of the Vietnam Communist Party meeting in December 1986: "Economic plans and policies must be governed by the following guiding principle: all existing productive capabilities must be liberated, all potentialities of the country exploited, international assistance put to effective use with a view to vigorously developing the productive forces along with building and strengthening the socialist production relations."[5] Despite such liberal wording, the party resolved to "concentrate the country's human energy and material wealth" on successfully implementing the three major comprehensive programs on "grain and foodstuffs, consumer goods and export goods." Accordingly, grain production was targeted to reach 22 to 23 million tons annually by the end of the fourth plan to provide per capita food at 733 to 766 pounds. The plan encouraged Vietnam's essentially rice-consuming population to include corn, sweet potatoes, white potatoes, and manioc in their diet. Moreover, the plan aimed at increasing short-term commercial crops such as beans, peanuts, and seeds conducive to the production of edible oils and long-term commercial crops like coffee, tea, pepper, and coconuts. Fisheries and forestry were also to be developed.

There is no doubt that such an exclusive emphasis on agriculture and consumer goods was the party's acknowledgment of gross dissatisfaction among the people, who had waited for decades for the minimum improvement in their standards of living. Some ill-conceived economic measures, particularly monetary reform, had sent the economy into an unprecedented inflationary spiral in the mid-1980s. Thus Vietnam devalued the dong from 1.20 to the dollar to 15 dongs to the dollar. It also replaced the old ten-dong note with a new one-dong note. In the second half of 1985, inflation hit 50 percent and in 1986 shot up by 500 to 700 percent, making the commoner's already miserable life even more unbearable. At the Sixth Party Congress in December 1986, Vo Van Kiet, vice-chairman of the Council of Ministers and a member of the reformers' group, attacked the governmental agencies responsible for the failure to ensure inputs of chemical fertilizers and pesticides. He also criticized the state pricing system for underproduction of commercial crops such as coffee, tea, rubber, jute, sugar, and groundnuts.

The lack of emphasis on heavy industry during the fourth plan was also the consequence of Vietnam's continuing shortage of foreign exchange. The new strategy seemed to be self-reliance in the production of consumer goods for the domestic market, protection of domestic production through a ban on imports of consumer items, and utilization of the scarce foreign exchange to import raw materials for the production of consumer goods both for the domestic market and for exports. Exports were targeted to increase by 70 percent above the goals of the previous plan. An important component of such exports would be provided by processed agricultural goods, marine products, and handicrafts.

Relatively speaking, industry has on the whole done better than agriculture in Vietnam since 1975. The invasion and occupation of Cambodia, the war with China, and the loss of business talent through the exodus of ethnic Chinese have been detrimental to a speedy industrial development. The wars demanded the diversion of economic resources to the armed forces; the occupation of Cambodia estranged Vietnam's relations with the Western powers and Japan, inhibiting foreign investment in Vietnam. These factors so affected industry that production in many sectors was appreciably below the 1975–1976 levels. The third plan had largely restored the economy in most sectors to the levels of 1975, taking the country ahead through significant production achievements in only a few areas. These were in the processing of sugar and the manufacture of chemical fertilizers and pesticides. The production of coal remained fairly steady at about 5 million tons, accounting for nearly two-thirds of the country's energy consumption. Electric energy production, however, steadily improved from 3.8 billion kWh to 5.4 billion in 1985, though at 50 percent below what the industry required in terms of the plan. Vietnam expects its energy situation to improve dramatically when the three megaprojects supported by the Soviet Union at Pha Lai (Hai Hung province), Tri An

(Dong Nai province), and Hoa Binh (Ha Son Binh province), together aiming at 2,700 megawatts, are completed.

GOVERNMENT AND POLITICS IN THE NEW VIETNAM

Reunification

After the Communist takeover of South Vietnam, it was expected that some decent interval would be allowed before the political, economic, and administrative integration of the two halves of the country would begin because of traditional southern fears of the North's domination. Indeed the DRV gave such assurances to the NLF during the protracted war in the South. In the wake of its victory, however, the northern leadership was overwhelmed by the counterargument that reunification and integration would be difficult if it were delayed. The South's economic and political interests would become well grounded if given the time, and the corrupt, capitalist way of life to which the southerners were accustomed during the war would have a deleterious effect on the North. Therefore, within a few months of the "fall" of Saigon, the leaders of the North and the South decided on political and administrative integration within a year. On April 26, 1976, the first anniversary of the northern victory, elections were held for the national assembly for all of Vietnam. By July 1976 the two Vietnams were formally unified, the DRV dissolved, and the Socialist Republic of Vietnam (SRV) proclaimed with Hanoi as its capital. The NLF was also disbanded, its numerous mass associations absorbed by its counterparts in North Vietnam. The Lao Dong Party was also disbanded, as was the People's Revolutionary Party of the South. The two were combined into the Vietnamese Communist Party (VCP) in December 1976. Thus the year 1976 represented the culmination of the decades-long dream of the Vietnamese to end the artificial divisions of their country under the French and, since 1954, under the Geneva agreements and to unite under a common political banner.

The Leadership of the Party and the Government

The party and governmental structure of the Democratic Republic of Vietnam was now extended to the Socialist Republic of Vietnam. Later, in 1980, a new constitution was adopted. As in all Communist countries, two parallel hierarchies from the highest down to the lowest levels of the party and government exist in Vietnam, the party's Politburo having primacy over the government, though there is considerable overlap in their respective compositions. The party itself had grown from about 1,000 members in 1941 to 5,000 in 1945 to a massive 500,000 in 1953. After the partition in 1954, the party's membership was kept relatively stable, though several million people were later involved in the long war aimed at the reunification of the country. The link between the party and the general public involved in the "people's war" was provided by numerous mass associations organized mostly on a functional basis: for workers, peasants, students, artists, women, and so on. At present, such links are provided by organizations such as the Vietnam Fatherland Front, the Vietnam General Confederation of Trade Unions, the Red Scarf Teenagers' Organization, and the Ho Chi Minh Communist Youth League. They also serve as recruiting grounds for the party cadres.

The Vietnamese Communist Party and its precursor, the Indochina Communist Party, record only six congress meetings in their combined history of six decades. Following the founding of the ICP in 1930, the First National Party Congress met secretly in Macao in 1935; the second met in Tuyen Quang in the north Vietnamese highlands in 1951; the third met in Hanoi in 1960; the fourth in 1976; the fifth in 1982; and the sixth in 1986. The infrequent party congresses are noted for some momentous decisions at crucial points in the party's or country's history. They are too unwieldy for articulate deliberation: The Sixth Congress had 1,129 delegates.

The National Party congress elects the party's Central Committee, which theoretically holds office for five years. In 1991 it had 124 full members and 49 alternate members who met twice a year to endorse the decisions made by its subcommittees. The Politburo stands at the apex of the party structure. Its thirteen full members and one alternate member represent the topmost leadership of the party. Serving the Politburo are the Party Secretariat, a Central Control Commission, and a Central Military Party Committee. Since 1986, the Secretariat has had thirteen members, five of them, including the most powerful of them all, the general secretary, holding concurrent membership in the Politburo. The Central Control Commission and the Central Military Party Committee are appointed by the Central Committee of the party but work under the direction of the Politburo. Numerous departments, paralleling the ministries of the government, work under the Secretariat's direction.

According to the constitution of 1980, the highest legislative, representative body with power to amend the constitution is the National Assembly. Although legally supreme, the National Assembly acts at the direction of the Politburo, implementing the latter's resolutions by enacting laws. The National Assembly's membership has remained a little below 500; only those approved by the party are allowed to run for election to the assembly.

Below the National Assembly is the Council of State, Vietnam's "collective presidency," which acts as the standing committee of the assembly. It has a chair, several vice-chairs, a general secretary, and about seven members. Its term, like that of the National Assembly, runs for five years. The Council of Ministers is the highest executive and administrative body and is elected by the National Assembly or, when the latter is not in session, by the Council of State. The Council of Ministers elects its own standing committee of ten to thirteen members, a close body coordinating all administrative activities. Each minister is assisted by two to twelve vice-ministers. In 1991 there were twenty-three ministers, each one with two or more subdivisions under a vice-minister.

The Vietnamese Communist leadership has been a remarkable, relatively stable gerontocracy. The average age of the members of the Politburo is a little over seventy. Barring a few purges and deaths, the leadership remained the same for four or five decades. Ho Chi Minh, Pham Van Dong, Vo Nguyen Giap, and Truong Chinh officiated at the birth of the Viet Minh in 1941, and in 1946 the Central Committee of the Viet Minh was expanded to include Le Duan, Pham Hung, and Nguyen Chi Thanh. Differences, ideological or otherwise, were not allowed to surface, so there were few changes in leadership—with some major exceptions: During the war, there were in fact two principal factions led respectively by the strategist Vo Nguyen Giap and the ideologue Truong Chinh. There were also those who were influenced by the Sino-Soviet rivalry. In 1956 the party took note of the failure of the land reform movement and removed Truong Chinh from the post of general secretary, though he was allowed to remain a member of the Politburo. The post of general secretary remained vacant until 1960, when Le Duan, considered a southerner, was appointed to it to emphasize the party's decision to launch the movement that would end with the reunification of the country. Ho Chi Minh (until his death in 1969) and Le Duan (until 1976) successfully struck the middle path and closed the ranks in the name of the movement for the country's reunification.

After the passing of Ho Chi Minh, Le Duan held the reins of power (partly sharing it with Le Duc Tho after 1976) until his death in mid-1986. Born in 1908, the son of a successful member of the gentry, Le Duan finished high school, a substantial level of education in those days. He was a founding member (along with 210 others) at the birth of the Indochina Communist Party in Hong Kong in 1930. During World War II and the First Indochina War, he was assigned to the South, where he developed an effective party base—facilitating his election as general secretary of the party in 1960 when the movement for the liberation of the South was launched. Although he was born in central Vietnam, he was regarded as a southerner because of his work there, and he generally represented southern interests in the Politburo in the North. After Ho Chi Minh's death, Le Duan became the first among equals in a system of collective Politburo-level leadership mandated by Ho Chi Minh in his will.

In the aftermath of the war, the party's solidarity suffered. Since 1975 there have been at least three major purges of people within five categories: pro-Maoist elements; advocates of a softer approach toward China and the Khmer Rouge; critics of the management of the economy, particularly the collectivization program in South Vietnam; corrupt and inefficient party members; and, finally, the opponents of Le Duan and Le Duc Tho's leadership of the party.

At the party's Fourth Congress in 1976, four members of the Central Committee and a Politburo member, Hoang Van Hoan, former ambassador to China and Le Duan's adversary, were purged. Three years later, Hoang defected to China and openly condemned the "Le Duan clique." Also in 1976 Le Duan, under immense pressure from China to choose sides in the Sino-Soviet rivalry, opted in favor of the Soviet Union. The decision led to a purge of several pro-Chinese members of the party. In 1980 a major cabinet shake-up involved nineteen changes, the most important of these being the replacement of Vo Nguyen Giap, defense minister since 1945 and legendary hero of Dien Bien Phu, with General Van Tien Dung, the commander of the Saigon offensive of 1975. Giap continued, however, to be a member of the Politburo and was later put in charge of the less powerful portfolio of family planning. Another change involved Foreign Minister Nguyen Dan Trinh, who was replaced by Nguyen Co Thach. Le Trong Tran, a general trained in the Soviet Union and East Germany and also foremost in the 1975 offensive, became chief of the general staff. Pham Hung, one of the principal leaders of South Vietnam, replaced Tran Quoc Hoan as minister of the interior. Lieutenant General Le Duc Anh, commander of the forces in Cambodia, became a member of the powerful and prestigious Political Committee in April 1982. The chairman of the Planning Commission was removed along with a number of officials in the economic ministries responsible for the lackluster performance of the economy. Such large-scale purges must have sent shivers down the spines of many leaders, some of whom moderated their stand to avoid being eased out. One such was Truong Chinh, who was made chair of the newly constituted Council of State in 1981.

At the time of the Fifth Congress of the VCP in 1982, .5 million members were purged. In order to replace their ranks, a recruitment drive enlisted as many as 325,000 new members, 90 percent of them under thirty years old and 70 percent of them war veterans. The soldiers of the revolution were now expected as party cadres and leaders to direct peacetime reconstruction. Despite such a policy of infusing fresh blood into the party, only the Central Committee was allowed to change, as one-third of its members were replaced by young people drawn from the armed forces. The Politburo's membership was still restricted to a gerontocracy.

In the 1980s, disillusionment with the leadership of Le Duan and Le Duc Tho steadily intensified, especially among the young, provincial-level party secretaries, who were frustrated with the massively troubled economy and the military stalemate in Cambodia that drained money and troops away from Vietnam. Considerable soul-searching took place, particularly during 1985–1987, on how best to grapple with inflation, shortages of critical goods, unemployment and, above all, corruption. For a while it looked as if the party were headed for a clear schism within the Politburo between economic reformers like Pham Hung, Nguyen Van Linh, and Vo Chi Cong and doctrinaire hard-liners like Truong Chinh, Le Duan, Pham Van Dong, and Le Duc Tho, who believed in the purity of socialist principles and the "correctness" of Marxism-Leninism under all circumstances. Within certain limits, the Vietnamese leadership had already compromised and liberated the economy from the old, strict controls. It had allowed personal incentives like cultivation of small garden plots by individuals and some amount of retail trading, particularly in the South. Reformers now advocated a system of production contracts, autonomy of state enterprises, and capitalistic modernization along the lines of the experimentation in China. The reformers, however, had to contend with a general preference for adherence to strict party discipline and avoidance of a crude struggle for power.

Such conservative sentiment and Le Duan's declining health intensified the movement for change in early 1986, leading to a purge of several high-level party and government officials who were directly responsible for the economic reverses under Le Duan. Among them was Vice-Premier To Huu, Vietnam's poet laureate, who was replaced by reformer Vo Chi Cong. Along with To, six other ministers in charge of finance and domestic and foreign trade and the governor general of the state bank were removed. They were replaced by those who had established reputations for being innovative and reformative at the provincial and planning-commission levels. In a countermove in May 1986, a triumvirate of three Politburo members, Truong Chinh, Pham Van Dong, and Le Duc Tho took over the duties of the ailing Le Duan, who continued to be the nominal general secretary of the party. Le Duan died on July 10, 1986, and was officially replaced as general secretary by Truong Chinh, who continued to hold the post of chairman of the Council of State as well.

By the end of the year, at the Sixth Congress of the VCP, the pendulum of power swung within the party to the other side. The critical economic situation, certainly exacerbated by the continuing military impasse in Cambodia, compelled drastic changes in the domestic power equation. Economic reformers and those in favor of a conciliatory approach to the Cambodian question pushed out the old guard. The former argued that in the new context of Mikhail Gorbachev's conciliatory policy toward China, the Cambodian question would have to be resolved on a political plane, particularly because China had cited it as one of the three preconditions for normalizing relations with the Soviet Union. The triumvirate of Truong Chinh (age seventy-nine), Pham Van Dong (eighty), and Le Duc Tho (seventy-five) was forced to resign from the Politburo, marking for the first time in decades a real shift of power within the Politburo. The reformer Nguyen Van Linh became general secretary; the revised roster in December 1986 was more heavily weighted in favor of the reformers. Renewal and renovation became the new rallying cry of the party, which seemed determined to root out corruption, streamline the administration, and genuinely liberalize the economy.

The old guard did not, however, give up the government posts: Pham Van Dong continued as prime minister and Truong Chinh as chair of the Council of State. In order to test the rival strengths of the two groups, the Council of State decided, on January 3, 1987, to hold elections to the 496-member National Assembly in April. The National Assembly would convene in June and elect the prime minister and the chair of the Council of State. The struggle for power and moves to arrive at a compromise between the hard-liners and reformers continued through the first half of 1987. One such compromise resulted in a major cabinet shake-up on February 17, 1987, when a hard-liner and number two in the Politburo, Pham Hung, was relieved of his charge of the Ministry of the Interior (though he continued to be a deputy prime minister). Also removed were eleven of a total of thirty-five ministers.

The elections of the highest officials by the new National Assembly in June 1987 clearly showed that Vietnam was still far from passing the power to a new and younger team or to the reformers who were willing to take risks in tackling Vietnam's massive economic problems. In a country where Confucian respect for seniority still persists, it was evidently impossible to ignore the older generation completely. Instead of choosing reformers like Foreign Minister Nguyen Co Thach and Vo Van Kiet, head of the State Planning Commission (both in their sixties), the National Assembly elected the seventy-five-year-old Pham Hung as prime minister (replacing Pham Van Dong, who had been in that post since 1955). The seventy-four-year-old moderate reformer Vo Chi Cong, who had pioneered pragmatic economic management in the 1970s, was appointed to the largely ceremonial post of chairman of the Council of State, replacing Truong Chinh. Even Vo Nguyen Giap, who had failed to get a seat in the National Assembly, was made one of the deputy prime ministers. Pham Hung served only nine months as prime minister. On his death in March 1988, Du Muoi, ranked fourth in the Politburo and sixty-eight years old, was named prime minister. Vietnam's party and governmental hierarchy thus continues to be a gerontocracy.

VIETNAM AS A MILITARY POWER

With a population of nearly 67 million, Vietnam does not figure among the ten most populous countries of the world. Yet in terms of its military strength and proven capability, Vietnam must be ranked among the top five in the world. Even before the reunification of Vietnam in 1976, North Vietnam had the best-trained army in all of Southeast Asia. At present its regular army numbers about 1.1 million, augmented from 600,000 in the wake of the border war with China and occupation of Cambodia, making it the fourth largest standing army in the world. Because of the naval craft and military equipment left behind by the United States, Vietnam ranked in the mid-1970s as the fifth largest navy in the world. Supplied by the Soviet Union with MiG planes and surface-to-air missiles (SAMs), Vietnam has a fairly respectable air capability. What is more important than all the weapons and numbers of armed personnel is the exceptionally high morale of the Vietnamese defense forces, who have tasted victory on the battlefield against a superpower. Hanoi represents the capital of a successful Communist revolution, potentially capable of becoming the point of inspiration, guidance, and assistance to Communist parties in the other countries of Southeast Asia. Does Vietnam have the economic capability and political ambition of supporting and leading Communist revolutionary movements in the neighboring countries? What would be a fair prognosis of Vietnam's international role in the next decade or so?

Vietnam's successful march into Cambodia in a seventeen-day war that established a pro-Hanoi government in Phnom Penh and the inconclusive war with China have confirmed the long-held view of military analysts of the high morale and efficiency of the Vietnamese military machine. In 1975, before the victory in Saigon, the North Vietnamese forces were estimated by the U.S. Defense Department at 583,000, the air and naval elements being responsible for only about 14,000 whereas the bulk belonged to the army. Estimates of the National Liberation Front forces varied by a wide margin; details of their integration into the reunified Vietnam's armed forces are lacking. The usually well-informed London-based International Institute for Strategic Studies (IISS) placed the total armed forces of Vietnam in 1988 at about 1 million, with strategic rear-force reserves of some additional 4 to 5 million.[6]

The army is organized into sixty-two infantry divisions plus two training divisions, one artillery division (ten regiments), ten armored regiments, fifteen independent infantry regiments, forty AA artillery regiments, twenty SAM regiments (each with eighteen SA-2 launchers), eight engineering divisions, and ten economic construction divisions. The army's equipment has been plentiful, varied, and substantial, thanks to Soviet supplies of heavy equipment, China's old supplies of light weapons, and a rich assortment of U.S. hardware that fell into Communist hands in April 1975. The air force numbered 12,000, consisting of four air divisions, and the navy's strength of 40,000 (including 27,000 naval infantry) is organized into four naval zones.

An extremely important factor in evaluating the military strength of any country, apart from assessing its manpower and equipment, is taking into account the proven fighting performance, discipline, and morale of its troops. The Vietnamese score high in all three categories, equalling the best anywhere in the world, with a record of successive victories sometimes achieved ahead of schedule. In terms of the present armed strength of Vietnam, however, one has to keep in mind that about 10,000 to 15,000 of its armed forces are stationed in Cambodia and 25,000 to 30,000 in Laos. Earlier, Vietnam planned to divert substantial numbers of its armed personnel to peacetime reconstruction tasks. Military involvement in Cambodia and on its own northern borders with China have compelled Vietnam to revise such plans.

CHAPTER 8

Vietnam's International Relations

 It is ironic that in the postunification period, Vietnam's principal problems in external relations lay with its Communist neighbors. Vietnam's march into Cambodia in late 1978 and its occupation of that country for slightly over a decade created one focal point. Another was the Sino-Soviet feud. The long war with the United States had given North Vietnam an excuse not to take sides in the conflict between the two Communist giants. In 1976, however, China compelled Vietnam to choose between the two, and Vietnam did so in favor of the Soviet Union. It is hard to say whether during the decade and a half after Vietnam's unification, considerations of regional leadership or partisanship in the global Sino-Soviet rivalry dominated its policies toward its neighbors, Cambodia and Laos. A more recent factor determining Vietnam's relations with Communist countries has been its reaction to the liberal policies of *glasnost* and *perestroika* adopted by the Soviet Union and enthusiastically embraced by Eastern European states. The Vietnamese leadership is still divided on the question whether to follow the East European example and liberalize the administration both economically and politically or to adopt the Chinese model and accept only economic liberalization, suppressing citizens' demands for democratic rights (as did China in Tiananmen Square in 1989).

With the dramatic Communist victories in South Vietnam and Cambodia in spring 1975 and the "silent Communist revolution" in Laos in December, it was widely believed that the Communists would regard the three victories as the culmination of the "liberation" movements in the Indochinese Peninsula and devote themselves to the tasks of domestic reconstruction. Even those anti-Communists who believed in the two-decade-old domino theory and saw its practical fulfillment in the "fall" of the three capitals in rapid succession regarded the phenomenon as appli-

117

cable only to the states of the Indochinese Peninsula because of their common history of French rule. The initial feeling of panic and grave apprehension among the states in the Association of Southeast Asian Nations (ASEAN) gave way to the reassurance that there would be more than a breathing spell before the new Communist states would be ready or willing actively to assist the fraternal Communist movements in the other states of Southeast Asia. Even in the non-Communist world, hardly anyone expected such fissures to develop among the new Communist states as would provoke large-scale interstate warfare culminating in the Vietnamese blitzkrieg in Cambodia at the turn of 1978 and the "punitive" Chinese march across the southern border into Vietnam in February and March 1979. Nor did anyone predict that the new government of Vietnam would create an atmosphere in which an estimated 1 million of its people, mostly of Chinese ethnic origin, would prefer to take the risks of a clandestine, financially costly departure by unsafe boats to indeterminate destinations than to remain in the country. The question of the boat people, as they were called, aroused global concerns and helped revive tensions in Southeast Asia.

Recent events have also brought to the fore the political interdependence of the three Indochinese states—Vietnam, Laos, and Cambodia. The emergence of Communist regimes in all three countries in the same year, 1975, was no coincidence. The Communist organization of Laos, the Pathet Lao, and a segment of the Khmer Rouge had both received assistance from Hanoi, perhaps with Hanoi's expectation that they would seek Vietnamese guidance and direction after coming to power. Events in Vietnam over the previous two decades had partly shaped and overshadowed the political developments in the two other Indochinese states. Was the Vietnamese occupation of Cambodia a part of a Vietnamese plan to create an Indochinese federation as a prelude to its domination of the entire Southeast Asian region? Is Vietnam militarily and economically capable of pursuing such alleged goals without external help and without provoking China more than it already has? If Southeast Asian nations have lived in the shadow of Communist China for a quarter century, they have been apprehensive of the rising power of Vietnam and its regional ambitions at least since 1975.

VIETNAM AND CAMBODIA

Historical Hatred

Vietnam's Southeast Asian neighbors, notably Cambodia, have reason to suspect Hanoi's expansionism. The Khmers, proud inheritors of a glorious legacy of empire once extending over the southern belt of mainland Southeast Asia, have historically hated the Vietnamese, who deprived them of the rich Mekong Basin in the eighteenth century and then shared with Thailand the suzerainty over what was left of the Khmer Empire. The French conquest of Vietnam and Cambodia did not obliterate such memories or fears of Vietnamese aggressiveness. The prospect of withdrawal of the French in 1954 revived Cambodian apprehensions. At the Geneva conference that year, the Cambodian delegation openly expressed its fears and suspicions of domination by the Viet Minh, which had already occupied portions of Cambodia in April 1954. Cambodian diplomacy during 1954–1955 was geared to enhancing the country's security against the Vietnamese through a military alliance with the United States. Such moves were aborted quickly after Prince Norodom Sihanouk received assurances of noninterference from North Vietnamese Premier Pham Van Dong. Tensions between Phnom Penh and Saigon continued even after a pro-U.S. government was established in Cambodia in 1970 under General Lon Nol. Thus in the wake of the "friendly" U.S.-Vietnamese invasion of their country in 1970, Cambodian officials turned their eyes away from the Cambodian massacre of thousands of Vietnamese civilians on the pretext that they were all Viet Cong. The hostility was mutual. The South Vietnamese forces treated Cambodia as a "military playground, with any Kampuchean fair game." According to William Shawcross, South Vietnamese air force pilots, "until then very lazy, actually paid bribes for the privilege" of flying bombing missions seven days a week over Cambodia.[1]

Cambodian suspicions of the Vietnamese were not limited to non-Communists or anti-Communists. As early as 1930, the Vietnamese Communists had betrayed their "imperialistic" ambitions. In January of that year, Ho Chi Minh succeeded in uniting the three Communist parties of Vietnam. In October the party was renamed the Indochina Communist Party to include Cambodia and Laos, probably for the Comintern's convenience in treating all of Indochina as a national section of the Communist International. Until 1951, when the ICP technically divided itself into three national parties for the practical reason of organizing better resistance against the French, there was no separate Cambodian Communist Party. The ICP early advocated a federation of Vietnam, Cambodia, and Laos after the liquidation of French rule, although subsequently the ICP did pass resolutions leaving it to each nation to decide whether or not to join such a federation. Nevertheless, the Cambodian Communists did not abandon their fear that Vietnam would—by virtue of its geographic size, population, educated work force, economic strength, and military prowess—some day compel Cambodia and Laos into such a composite polity under Vietnamese domination.

The Khmer Rouge

Differences between Khmer Rouge and Vietnamese Communists origi-
nated in 1954 at the Geneva conference on Indochina. Presumably under
the pressure of Moscow and Beijing, which were eager to arrive at a
settlement as part of their global policy of peaceful coexistence, the North
Vietnamese did not press the cause of Khmer Rouge but instead agreed
that it be disbanded and that its cadres retreat to Hanoi. The Khmer Rouge
never forgave the Vietnamese Communists for this "betrayal." Retreating
to North Vietnam, several thousand of them fought in the maquis against
Sihanouk's government in the 1960s. The North Vietnamese were quite
content with Sihanouk's cooperation in allowing the flow of men and
materiel along the Ho Chi Minh Trail across eastern Cambodia and from
the port of Sihanoukville (Kompong Som) into South Vietnam and, most
importantly, in permitting the establishment of extensive secret base camps
inside the Cambodian border for the Vietnamese NLF. By 1969 there were
an estimated 40,000 to 50,000 North Vietnamese and NLF troops in the
Cambodian sanctuaries.

It was certainly not the first time that a Communist state had, for tactical
reasons and out of its own national interest, sought and received assistance
from a non-Communist government at the expense of a "fraternal" Communist Party. It was, therefore, only natural that the Khmer Rouge's distrust of the North Vietnamese would continue even after a tactical alliance
among the four regional Communist groupings of Pathet Lao, Lao Dong,
NLF, and Khmer Rouge was established soon after Sihanouk's overthrow
in early 1970. At this point, Hanoi needed the Khmer Rouge's cooperation
in keeping the supply lines to the NLF open by harassing the troops of
Lon Nol, the United States, and South Vietnam in eastern Cambodia. The
tension between the Khmer Rouge and Vietnamese Communists was such
that the former insisted on having an upper hand in the operations without
Vietnamese assistance.[2] Even though the North Vietnamese were contributing substantially to the growth and training of the Khmer Rouge during
the early 1970s, they did not want the latter to develop independence and
the ability to frustrate long-term North Vietnamese ambitions to dominate
all of Indochina. In order to ensure a pro-Vietnamese position, the North
Vietnamese sent into Cambodia about 5,000 Khmer Rouge who had been
held in reserve in Hanoi ever since their withdrawal from Cambodia in
1954. These Hanoi Khmers, as they came to be called, clashed with the
homegrown Khmer Rouge under the leadership of Pol Pot and Khieu
Samphan. In 1973 many Hanoi Khmers were purged or killed by the Pol
Pot group.

By 1972 the Khmer Rouge numbered well over 50,000, mostly young
people, not necessarily Communist, with varying grievances against the

U.S.-backed Lon Nol regime. The evidence of their superior training, discipline, fighting power, and ability to handle Chinese, Soviet, and U.S. weapons supplied to them by the North Vietnamese was noted in skirmishes with Lon Nol's troops as well as in the successful maintenance of the supply lines to the NLF. In early 1973 the Khmer Rouge was confirmed in its suspicion of the North Vietnamese when the latter repeatedly pressured them to accept a cease-fire that was presumably the precondition for a U.S. grant of reconstruction aid to Hanoi. It was the general impression that the Khmer Rouge was Hanoi's puppet. Despite Hanoi's cutting off of military assistance and the U.S. saturation bombing, the Khmer Rouge continued the offensive that brought the downfall of the Lon Nol regime a full fortnight before Hanoi's victorious march into Saigon.[3]

The Khmer Rouge would not easily forget the North Vietnamese subordination of Khmer interests to their own in 1973 and 1954. Nor would they forget the timely, massive military assistance they received from Beijing starting in mid-1974. The Chinese leaders had attempted unsuccessfully to encourage a U.S. dialogue with Sihanouk, who since his ouster in 1970 had been in exile in Beijing. Finally, the Chinese threw in their lot with the Khmer Rouge, replacing the North Vietnamese as the principal suppliers to the Khmer Rouge of automatic weapons, ammunition, and mines. Such Chinese equipment was used in the final siege of Phnom Penh and its capitulation, achieved partly through mining the waterways and cutting off the capital's food supply.

Tension between the Khmer Rouge and the Vietnamese Communists continued after the overthrow of the Lon Nol regime in March 1975. Moreover, at least one of the four factions into which the Cambodian government was divided was clandestinely linked with Hanoi, whereas another advocated rapprochement with Vietnam on pragmatic grounds. The Phnom Penh government was a coalition, the core of which consisted of the Khmer Viet Minh and the student groups that had produced leaders like Pol Pot, Ieng Sary, and Khieu Samphan. They allied with moderates led by Sihanouk and other non-Communists who were intensely nationalist, suspicious of Vietnamese expansionism, and pro-Beijing and favored rapprochement with the United States. Foremost in their links with Vietnamese Communists were obviously the Hanoi Khmers led by Chea Sim, the minister of the interior. Last was a smaller group of "constructionists" who advocated accommodation with Vietnam for pragmatic reasons. Its leader, Heng Samrin, became the clandestine conduit of top secret decisions of the Phnom Penh government to Heng Samrin's allies in Hanoi.

Pol Pot's Regime—The Crisis Deepens

Through Premier Pol Pot's five-hour speech in September 1977, the Khmer Rouge told the world that Hanoi had all along harbored plans to compel Cambodia into an Indochinese federation as the first step toward its annexation. The Pol Pot regime was certainly justified in attempting every means to avert Cambodia's conversion to a Vietnamese satellite. But it should have been realistic enough to appreciate the immensely superior Vietnamese military machine and should therefore have acted in such a way so as not to give an excuse for the alleged Vietnamese expansionism to succeed. As it was, the Khmer Rouge launched the most brutal, insensate domestic programs, which had the effect of dislocating, decimating, and alienating the bulk of the Cambodian population to the shock and dismay of the entire civilized world. The excesses of the Pol Pot regime amounting to a gross genocide made any aggression by an external power to terminate the horrible condition prevalent under the Pol Pot regime look less culpable than otherwise. Further, it created a large exodus of Khmer people into Vietnamese sanctuaries in eastern Cambodia that spilled into Vietnam, where the Khmer refugees could be organized by the Vietnamese into an alternative rallying point for overthrowing the anti-Hanoi Pol Pot regime. And internationally, instead of playing the Vietnamese against the Chinese so as to maximize their own diplomatic maneuverability, the Phnom Penh government chose to adopt adventurist policies that were certain to provoke Vietnam to an eventual showdown. First, beginning in April 1977, they took the initiative to attack the border provinces, particularly the NEZ in Tay Ninh, with a view to bringing pressure on the Vietnamese to vacate the sanctuaries inside Cambodia. Second, they allied themselves with Vietnam's enemy, China, and invited several thousand Chinese military and technical personnel in what Vietnam called a bid to encircle it. Such policies, internal and international, could neither ensure Cambodia's domestic stability nor reduce its vulnerability to Vietnamese aggression. The Vietnamese march into Cambodia, at the back of the newly born Kampuchean United Front for National Salvation (KUFNS), occurred at a time when Vietnam could only have done so because of the Pol Pot government's ill-conceived and compelling tactics.

The new Cambodian leadership felt that its fears of Vietnamese expansionism had been confirmed by the Vietnamese refusal to quit the sanctuaries on Cambodian soil allowed them by Prince Sihanouk since the late 1960s. In addition, within two weeks of the Communist victory in Saigon, the Vietnamese government opened an old sore with Cambodia by claiming some islands in the Gulf of Thailand. That led to the first clash between the two Communist governments, and although Hanoi recognized Phnom Penh's claim to Puolo Wai, at the May 1976 bilateral meetings the Vietnamese questioned the entire maritime boundary with Cambodia that had supposedly been settled by the Brevie Line in 1939 during the French rule. The incident helped to strengthen Cambodia's apprehensions of Vietnamese expansionist aims. An attempted coup in September 1976, sparked in all likelihood by the government's domestic policy excesses, was alleged to be a Vietnamese plot to overthrow the government through Hanoi Khmer army units. The Pol Pot regime took advantage of the situation to liquidate the remnant of the Hanoi Khmers, which included five members of the twenty-member party Central Committee. The regime's attitude toward Vietnam hardened. The Phnom Penh government refused to hold talks with Vietnam until the latter completely moved out of all territories claimed by Cambodia.

The Khmer-Viet Conflict

Thereafter, Cambodia obviously decided that offense was the best form of defense, an attitude for which it did not initially receive the full support of its Chinese allies. Beginning in January 1977 and escalating their activities between April and September 1977, Cambodian forces moved into the old Vietnamese sanctuaries where an NEZ was being established. The attack would achieve the multiple purpose of weakening Vietnam's economy, keeping military pressure on it so as to secure the complete evacuation of the sanctuaries, and frustrating Vietnam's alleged plan to integrate Cambodia into a Vietnamese-dominated Indochinese federation.

If the Vietnamese indeed had any such plans, they were not in a hurry to implement them because of their preoccupation with problems of economy and domestic dissidence. Their policy of conciliation with Thailand since 1977 and their apparent readiness to endorse the ASEAN concept of a neutral zone in Southeast Asia free of any big-power influence were indicative of their desire to demonstrate even to their non-Communist neighbors that Vietnam sought peace and had no plans of military intervention in other states at least for several years.

If Vietnam wanted to live within its self-imposed constraints, China and Cambodia seemed determined not to allow it that kind of luxury. Since the conclusion of the Vietnam War, China had emphasized in its relations with Southeast Asian nations that the Soviet Union represented the "present strategic danger to Southeast Asia,"[4] and cautioned them to beware of "the tiger at the back door while repelling the wolf through the front door."[5] From mid-1977 therefore, by holding back further economic aid and building up Cambodia's military strength, China began to exert pressure on Vietnam to condemn Soviet hegemony. Thus between 1975 and 1978, China supplied Cambodia with 130-mm mortars, 107-mm bazookas, automatic rifles, transport vehicles, gasoline, and various small weapons, enough to equip thirty to forty regiments totaling about 200,000 troops. There is no way of knowing how much economic assistance was additionally provided by China beyond the initial gift of $1 billion made at the time of Sihanouk's return to Phnom Penh in 1975. An estimated

10,000 Chinese military and technical personnel were sent to Cambodia to improve its military preparedness. In the political circumstances of the time, such tactics could only have been directed against Vietnam, as China had bent over backward in the postwar period to become friendly with Thailand, the only other neighboring country that could be a threat to Cambodian security. Critical of these Sino-Cambodian measures, Vietnam alleged that they were designed to destroy the Vietnamese economy and encircle the country militarily.

An all-out war with Cambodia was not suited to Vietnam at that point for several additional reasons. Apart from the diplomatic damage it would cause by destroying its new image of sweet reasonableness Vietnam was attempting to create among its Southeast Asian neighbors, a belligerent act of those dimensions would certainly frustrate efforts to secure economic aid from other countries. Second, in the absence of a militarily strong anti–Pol Pot movement, sizable Vietnamese forces would be locked in direct combat with the Cambodian army, supported by China. The Vietnamese leadership therefore attempted to negotiate with the Khmers but to no avail. They then resorted to large-scale fighting for three months beginning in October 1977, with the limited purpose of securing a Khmer-Vietnamese border treaty. In January 1978 Vietnam proposed that both sides withdraw their troops to 5 miles from the existing border and submit themselves to an internationally supervised truce commission. In May 1978 Cambodia agreed to peace talks that would begin in 1979, after Vietnam had demonstrated its genuine desire not to integrate Cambodia into an Indochinese federation under Vietnamese control. Vietnam doubted the genuineness of the Cambodian offer, particularly because of the internationalization of the conflict, brought about by Beijing's overt and firm commitment to Phnom Penh and the general deterioration in Sino-Vietnamese relations.

VIETNAM-CHINA RELATIONS

Historical Backdrop

Vietnam-China relations are best understood in terms of the nations' rival long-term ambitions in Southeast Asia. Communist China has over the last four decades periodically published maps showing most of Southeast Asia as lying within China's sphere of influence. For its part, the Vietnamese Communists have at least since the establishment of the Indochina Communist Party in 1930 indicated their plans to dominate the territories formerly under French rule.

Vietnam's ambition for a regional leadership through assistance to Communist movements and domination of governments could be attributed to other than purely ideological reasons. Its desire to create a strong independent center of power is partly a quest for enhanced security born of a traditional fear of Chinese domination of Vietnam. Historically, Vietnam has been a fiercely freedom-loving country apprehensive of its northern neighbor's expansionism. The several revolts during the thousand-odd years of Chinese rule extending over the first millennium (111 B.C.–A.D. 939), the successful overthrow of the Chinese rule again in the fifteenth century (1407–1428), the readiness to sign an agreement to allow the return of the French only to get the Chinese occupation troops out in 1946, and the reluctant acceptance of the cease-fire along the 17th parallel in 1954 at Geneva all demonstrate Vietnam's intense distrust and suspicion of China under whatever government—imperial, nationalist, or Communist.

During the greater part of the three-decade-long struggle that ended in 1975, the Viet Minh and later the DRV and the NLF had to maintain cordial relations with China because of much-needed military assistance. Although no reliable figures on Chinese aid to North Vietnam exist—even official Chinese estimates vary from $14 billion to $21 billion—there is no doubt that Chinese economic and military assistance was crucial for the Communist success in South Vietnam. Despite such dependence, Hanoi retained its political autonomy; it refused, for instance, to enter into a formal military alliance with China and politely declined to "invite" Chinese volunteer forces to aid the Vietnamese liberation movement. Until 1965 there was greater consensus between Chinese and Vietnamese strategy and tactics, the Vietnamese being more appreciative of the Chinese than of the Soviets because of the former's support to wars of national liberation. Also, until that point, the Chinese aid to Vietnam was far more, almost double the amount proffered by the Soviet Union. The situation changed in early 1965 with the beginning of U.S. strategic bombing of North Vietnam, whose need for sophisticated defense equipment, including surface-to-air missiles, could be met by the Soviet Union rather than China. Thus far, the North Vietnamese had relied more on guerrilla warfare and much less on mobile warfare to carry on the struggle in the South. In mid-1965 the North Vietnamese strategists judged the time had come to switch to mobile warfare and in some instances even to positional warfare. Such an advanced war strategy was not condoned by the Chinese, who preferred a protracted war in which the Vietnamese would depend for indefinite periods of time on Chinese assistance in the form of small weapons. Lin Biao's celebrated doctrine of the "wars of national liberation" launched on September 3, 1965, emphasized a policy of self-reliance, an indirect exhortation to Vietnam to reduce its dependence on the Soviet Union.

During the years of the Cultural Revolution, the Chinese authorities acted deliberately to impede the flow of Soviet military aid to North Vietnam. For example, the Soviet Union was asked to pay in U.S. dollars the freight for transporting armaments by Chinese railroad wagons whose availability would be inordinately delayed. From 1967 until the end of the war, the Soviet Union consequently had to supply by sea both large and small weaponry, which included SAMs, MiG aircraft, bombers, helicopters, antiaircraft batteries, a radar defense system, and all kinds of transport vehicles. The annual Soviet military aid to North Vietnam soon surpassed the Chinese figure.

Vietnam and Sino-Soviet Rivalry

The more recent phase of Sino-Vietnamese differences began in 1971 with the Chinese and U.S. moves toward rapprochement. Hanoi regarded U.S. efforts to end the Vietnam conflict by asking China to stop its military aid to Vietnamese Communists and subsequent Chinese emphasis on a struggle against revisionism rather than Western imperialism as Beijing's game to subordinate Vietnamese interests to those of China. At the Geneva conference in 1954, at China's insistence, the North Vietnamese had reluctantly agreed to the partition of their country in the interests of the then global Communist policy of peaceful coexistence. By the early 1970s, the Vietnamese suspected that China did not want to see a strong, reunified Vietnam to emerge as a potential competitor for influence in Southeast Asia. Additionally, they found themselves on the opposite side of the Chinese in regard to the U.S. presence in Asia, which China regarded as a desirable counterbalance to Soviet ambitions in the area.

With the end of the war in South Vietnam, it was only a matter of time before the two halves of the country would unite to create a single state. China was certainly not happy at the prospect of the emergence of a strong state on its southern borders. It would certainly not be a spectator to Hanoi's suspected ambitions to dominate Laos and Cambodia and lend assistance to fraternal Communist parties in Southeast Asia, traditionally an area of China's political influence. In order to force Vietnam to reassume its historical role as China's "vassal" state, China threatened to stop its loans and grants to Vietnam if it did not join China in condemning Soviet hegemony. When the Vietnamese gently pointed out that the late Premier Zhou Enlai had made a commitment in June 1973 to continue economic and military aid at the then existing level for five years, the Chinese "explained" that a prior agreement between Zhou Enlai and Ho Chi Minh called for termination of aid after the Vietnamese War ended. China did not make an exception even on humanitarian grounds. Thus when Vietnam was hit by severe food shortages during 1976–1977 because of adverse weather conditions, China did not send any food grains across its southern borders. In contrast, the Soviet Union supplied 450,000 of the 1.6 million tons of food rushed to Vietnam by external agencies.

Vietnam alleged that China thereafter attempted to "contain" it by organizing a coalition with the United States, Thailand, and Cambodia as a counterweight to Vietnamese influence on mainland Southeast Asia. Until late 1977 China continued to apply pressure on Vietnam in an effort to obtain the latter's loyalties in its conflict with the Soviet Union. The steady deterioration of Sino-Vietnamese relations during that interregnum was aggravated by three specific issues: the offshore islands, Vietnamese of Chinese ethnic origin, and border claims. The real issues were political, centering on the question of political hegemony, in the short run over Indochina and eventually over all of Southeast Asia.

The Islands Issue

Soon after the Provisional Revolutionary Government assumed authority in Saigon it attempted to occupy the offshore Spratly Islands (located 280 miles northeast of the Cam Ranh Bay), thereby coming into conflict with the People's Republic of China. The Spratly and Paracel Islands had been the subject of rival claims between China and Vietnam in the nineteenth century. Apart from their strategic location in the South China Sea on the maritime artery between the Indian Ocean and the western Pacific, these uninhabited islands suddenly became valuable in the early 1970s in the eyes of China, the Philippines (which was interested only in the Spratly group), and South Vietnam because of some preliminary geological surveys indicating rich oil deposits. When the South Vietnamese government officially incorporated the Spratly Islands through a special decree in September 1973, and China contested its claim, the DRV and the NLF had maintained silence, although Hanoi had previously expressed territorial claims on the archipelago. Beijing took naval and air action in January 1974, but only to occupy the Paracel Islands, closer to Chinese naval bases than the Spratlys, 550 miles further south. Perhaps because the Spratlys were beyond the range of Chinese air support, China took no action to prevent South Vietnam from occupying those islands. But the Chinese boats for firing short-range missiles, located on the naval base of Yulin on the Hainan Islands, showed a clear superiority over South Vietnam's coastguard cutters, destroyer escorts, and patrol boats in the engagements of January 19–20, 1974. Beijing's occupation of the Paracel group was important because of the presence of a Chinese naval complex and sophisticated radar facilities on one of the islands since 1971.

Both the groups of islands—the Spratlys and the Paracels—continue to be an issue between Hanoi and Beijing.[6] Vietnam's interests in the Spratlys are both strategic and economic. Hanoi is eager to continue the offshore oil exploration begun under the previous government and has sought external financial and technical assistance from Norway and India, among other countries. There is no doubt the islands' worth is crucial for Vietnam's economic future and its plans for self-reliance in oil. Since 1975, however, Hanoi's efforts to negotiate with Beijing on the future of the islands have been fruitless, largely because of China's refusal even to answer Vietnamese communications on the subject. It is, therefore, left for China to reopen the dispute at its convenience.

The Ethnic Chinese Issue

The "overseas Chinese" in Vietnam were as much hated by the local people as they were elsewhere in Southeast Asia because of their superior economic standing. Their loyalty to Vietnam was always suspect. Their unruly and disruptive behavior during the years of the Cultural Revolution was least appreciated in Vietnam. After the Communist victory in Saigon, the large Chinese population, noted for its industry and wealth, received special attention from the new government. The community's cooperation was vital for keeping the economy going until the government gradually moved to eliminate the private sector. By 1977 such cooperation was not as badly needed. The Vietnamese Chinese were then grouped along with intellectuals, devout Buddhists, and Catholics as potential opposition to the spread of socialism. Although the Vietnamese Chinese were not specifically named as "capitalist" opponents of the new government, the frequent mention of the areas in which the Chinese predominantly lived as being the cesspools of black marketing and corruption was an indirect condemnation of the community. In the campaign for "ideological certification" of the "misfits," the Chinese were progressively moved to the NEZs in the countryside, which included the border province of Tay Ninh. There, the Chinese would also serve as a buffer between the Vietnamese and Cambodia.

The Vietnamese government came down most openly against the Chinese community in March 1978, not long after China began an initiative to win the loyalty and support of the overseas Chinese. Beijing's campaign was perhaps launched with the twin objective of drumming up support for itself vis-à-vis Taipei and for securing technical and financial assistance from the overseas Chinese in Southeast Asia and the United States to help China's program to modernize its economy. The vigor of the campaign unnerved many of the Southeast Asian states with large Chinese minorities because of its political implications. Was the Vietnamese government's action against the ethnic Chinese a reaction to China's new policy toward the overseas Chinese, or was it, as seems more likely, a response to China's decision to help Vietnam's enemy, the Pol Pot regime, in Cambodia? In any case, the Vietnamese government's policy toward the ethnic Chinese went far beyond mere verbal attacks. It resulted in the migration of a large number of them, providing the most visible and dramatic evidence of the growing gulf between Beijing and Hanoi.

In the name of official plans to carry out the rapid socialization of the economy, the Vietnamese government raided the Cholon area of Saigon where the Chinese lived and ordered their assets frozen. Of note was the official reclassification of the Vietnamese Chinese in May 1978 as an ethnic minority, abolishing the special-category status the Chinese had enjoyed thus far. The change was to indicate the government's firm resolve to integrate the Chinese, along with other ethnic minorities, into the national community. The Chinese community was thus faced with choosing one of two alternatives: the obligations to the state that were implied in the acceptance of a Vietnamese citizenship or the handicaps of an alien status.

The government saw in the mainly urban Chinese community a partial but multifaceted solution to a complex, depressing economic malaise: Because of a shortage of financial resources, the government planned to combat massive urban unemployment by resettling large numbers of city-dwellers—and thus large numbers of ethnic Chinese—in the countryside. Besides, there was the traditional prejudice against the Chinese; a decision to move them to the NEZs close to the Cambodian border where their numbers might dwindle in the cross fire of binational conflict was not likely to arouse resentment among the Vietnamese population. The large-scale hardship and discontent the new policy caused to the Chinese forced many of them to flee the country. A puzzling point of this exodus was that a substantial number of Chinese from North Vietnam also crossed the border into China, indicating that the feeling of insecurity had political roots and had permeated the Chinese community throughout Vietnam, not just in the South.

It is doubtful the Chinese government was genuinely concerned about the plight of the overseas Chinese in Vietnam.[7] To be sure, China had all along maintained its interest in the overseas Chinese but never enough to go to war with any country in Southeast Asia. As for South Vietnam, China had specifically protested against the South Vietnamese government's legislation in 1955 compelling the Chinese community to accept Vietnamese citizenship. In 1965 North Vietnam agreed with China to settle the question in consultation with each other after the "liberation" of South Vietnam. In practice, the Chinese government had done little to protect the overseas Chinese, whether in Indonesia during the second half of the 1960s or in Cambodia before and after the Communist takeover. Vietnam, therefore, may have assumed that its persecution of its Chinese minority would not provoke Beijing. After all, of the 1.5 million Vietnamese Chinese, 90 percent had lived in the South, amassed fortunes by exploiting the prolonged situation created by the Second Indochina War, and had generally supported a capitalist way of life. The indignation of the Chinese government at the "racial" discrimination of Vietnamese Chinese can be explained only in political terms as an attempt to find an additional excuse to attack Vietnam. This is reinforced by the half-hearted manner in which China tried to evacuate the Vietnamese Chinese. Thus in June 1978 China sent two ships, the *Minghua* and the *Changli*, to Saigon and Haiphong to evacuate the Chinese. The two ships remained off the coast during the six weeks of fruitless negotiations with Vietnamese officials over an acceptable evacuation procedure. On July 11, China closed its borders to the thousands of Vietnamese Chinese trying to enter China by land. The Chinese authorities would accept only those refugees who could produce exit visas issued by the Vietnamese government along with repatriation certificates from the Chinese embassy in Hanoi. Insistence on such documentation, particularly repatriation certificates, once again demonstrated that the Chinese government's concern for Vietnamese Chinese was not genuine.

Sino-Vietnamese Conflict

By mid-1978 Sino-Vietnamese relations had sunk to such a precipitously low level that armed conflict appeared imminent. China's actions since the turn of the year had shown that it had decided to take sides in the growing Vietnam-Cambodia dispute not because it was convinced of the rights of either party but because of the impact of the confrontation on the relative influence of the Soviet Union or China in the region. In January 1978 Beijing dispatched Teng Ying Chao, a Central Committee member and widow of former Premier Zhou Enlai, to Phnom Penh to show solidarity with the Pol Pot regime. Soon after, China made large-scale arms shipments, including long-range 130-mm and 150-mm artillery, to Cambodia, even though the former NLF forces had completely pulled out of Cambodia. Hanoi's intelligence sources indicated a Chinese resolve to support Cambodia in what Beijing expected and perhaps hoped would be a protracted war.

At this point in mid-1978, Vietnam openly abandoned its old policy of friendship with both Communist giants. Hanoi contemplated a quick military action to liquidate the Pol Pot regime before it solidified itself further with Chinese military assistance. In order to bolster its own security in the event of a Chinese attack across the Sino-Vietnamese border to coincide with Vietnamese action in Cambodia, Hanoi decided to move closer to Moscow. On June 29, 1978, it joined the Moscow-dominated Council for Mutual Economic Assistance (COMECON, the Communist equivalent of the European Common Market) and on November 3 signed with Moscow a full-fledged, twenty-five-year treaty of friendship and mutual cooperation. A partial price of Soviet assistance was Vietnam's consent to Soviet use and development of Da Nang and Cam Ranh Bay as missile bases.

China retaliated against the first of these actions on July 3, 1978, by formally terminating all its economic, military, and technical assistance to Vietnam and ordering the Chinese personnel there to head home. In the previous month, Vietnam had rejected Chinese requests to open consular offices in Saigon, Da Nang, and Haiphong; in a reciprocal action the Chinese government asked Vietnam to close its consular establishments in Canton, Nanning, and Kunming. Beijing alleged that the USSR and Vietnam had a three-part plan to "encircle" China: first, by removing the Vietnamese Chinese from positions of authority; second, by compelling Laos and Cambodia through military threats to join an Indochinese federation nominally under Vietnamese control but in fact under Soviet domination; and, last, by implementing the Brezhnev Plan for Asian security, thereby bringing all of Southeast Asia into the Soviet sphere of influence. China accused Vietnam of being the "Cuba of Asia," a satellite of the Soviet Union that was assisting the latter in its strategic aims in Asia.

VIETNAM AND THE SOVIET UNION

Toward the end of 1978, the only party that stood to gain from major conflicts in Indochina was the Soviet Union. Moscow's actions to draw Vietnam closer to the Soviet Union politically, economically, and militarily should be seen in the context of its dual policy to weaken the new Sino-U.S. rapprochement and to frustrate Chinese ability to augment its influence in Southeast Asia. The Soviet policy was, in fact, a continuation of its decade-long diplomatic offensive to win all the countries of South and Southeast Asia to its side—or at least wean them away from Beijing. Such efforts were supplemented by an increasingly military (though decidedly low-key) activity, particularly in the Indian Ocean.

The steadily increasing diplomatic and naval activity of the Soviet Union in South and Southeast Asia since 1968 must certainly be seen in the context of the U.S. withdrawal from the region and the growing U.S.-Chinese friendship. Traditionally, Southeast Asia has never figured importantly in Soviet ambitions. But because it is partly an Asian country, the Soviet Union cannot countenance with equanimity the exclusive domination by any other major power, particularly China, over large parts of Asia. Moscow did not want to allow its ideological rival, Beijing, the prestige of becoming the standard-bearer of a Communist revolution not only in Southeast Asia but throughout the world.

But the Soviet Union was far from eager to become the police force of Asia, an ambition any power geographically distant from the region should be able to resist after the glaring failure of the United States. Even during the Vietnam conflict, the Soviet Union begrudged the heavy costs of assisting North Vietnam and the NLF in the form of war materials and sophisticated equipment. The Soviets were also unhappy at the Vietnamese situation in the late 1960s, which impinged upon the progress of Soviet talks with the United States on a wide range of topics aimed at détente. In 1968, a month before the Nixon Doctrine, Soviet leader Leonid Brezhnev proposed a system of collective security for Asia wherein the local military and economic resources would be supplemented by the Soviet Union. No Southeast Asian nation, including North Vietnam, joined the proposed system because none of them wanted to give the impression of ganging up against China, although Moscow denied that the Brezhnev Plan sought to contain the People's Republic of China.

Rationally speaking, the long-term interests of the superpowers, both of them geographically distant from the Southeast Asian region, lay in denying any power an opportunity to dominate the area and to achieve such a goal through promotion of a regional balance of power. In the short run, however, the Sino-U.S. rapprochement, the almost complete withdrawal of U.S. forces from Southeast Asia, and the Sino-Soviet race to win the allegiance of the new Communist regimes in Indochina accelerated immediate Soviet involvement in the region. The Soviet Union had no leverage with the Pol Pot regime, which decried the former's recognition of the Lon Nol regime right up to its downfall in March 1975. China compelled Vietnam to choose between Moscow and Beijing in October 1975, when the general secretary of the Vietnamese Communist Party, Le Duan, visited China. Le Duan refused to comply with his host's wishes to condemn Soviet "hegemonism." Thereafter, China stopped any further aid to Vietnam whereas the Soviet Union came forward to support Vietnam generously, thereby enhancing Vietnamese dependence on the Soviet Union.

During 1978 Moscow apparently persuaded the Hanoi leadership to think that a continuing state of tension between a Chinese-backed Cambodia and Vietnam would constitute a festering economic sore for Vietnam. Moscow urged that the question be resolved expeditiously at least in the interests of economy. In 1978–1979, Vietnam was in dire need of food assistance amounting to 4.3 million tons because of successive crop failures. It was this desperate economic situation that made Vietnam finally succumb to Soviet pressures to join COMECON. Also, because the United States normalized its relations with China, the Soviet Union stepped up its pressure on Vietnam for a formal anti-China military alliance. There is reason to believe that an overt anti-Chinese alliance was the price Moscow extracted for bailing Vietnam out of its economic crisis. The Soviet-Vietnamese treaty of friendship, signed barely six weeks before the Vietnamese march into Cambodia, provided Vietnam a Soviet shield of protection from a Chinese attack. Article 6 of the treaty clearly stated that in the event of an attack or a threat of attack, Vietnam and the Soviet Union would consult with each other and take "appropriate and effective measures" to "eliminate" that threat. The treaty indeed marked a high point of Moscow's diplomatic success in Indochina.

VIETNAM'S OCCUPATION OF CAMBODIA

Armed with its treaty with the Soviet Union, Vietnam was ready for a brisk war aimed at toppling the Pol Pot regime and installing one favorable to itself. First, it brought the Pol Pot regime's genocidal excesses to international attention through a publicity blitz. Second, in order to make its march into Cambodia politically palatable to the world, Vietnam facilitated the creation of the fourteen-member committee called the Kampuchean United Front for National Salvation, under the leadership of dissident pro-Hanoi Communists like Heng Samrin and Chea Sim as well as some exiled Cambodian intellectuals and monks. An important element of the new front would be the support of Khmer Krom, the Cambodian minority of more than .5 million people resident in Cochin China. (It is worth noting that if that minority moved out of Vietnam, it would partly alleviate the food shortages in the country.) Officially, the Vietnamese role would be to help the KUFNS in overthrowing the Pol Pot regime for humanitarian reasons.

Unlike the NLF, the KUFNS did not command large-scale popular support among Cambodians because its patrons were Vietnamese. The organization was clearly a Vietnamese smoke screen created on the eve of Vietnam's invasion of Cambodia to legitimize its action in the eyes of the world. The success of the seventeen-day Vietnamese "blitzkrieg" in Cambodia beginning December 25, 1978, owed little to KUFNS or its few supporters inside that country. If the KUFNS and Vietnamese forces did not encounter much opposition it was because of the public relief over the extinction of the oppressive Pol Pot regime, with its legacy of regimented life, communal kitchens, broken families, and hard, unending labor. Under the leadership of Heng Samrin, the new Cambodian government was successful in controlling most of Cambodia (except the western region) in part because of the presence of an estimated 160,000 Vietnamese occupation troops, who would not brook any measures to crush serious public opposition.

Pol Pot and his cohorts fled to western Cambodia. For a while, China was able to continue supplying military and economic aid to the anti–Heng Samrin guerrillas thanks to the air strip at Siem Reap, passages through Laos and Thailand, and the porous 450-mile Cambodian coastline. The Laotian corridor was soon plugged by the pro-Vietnam government, which also expelled Chinese technical and military personnel from Cambodia. The Pol Pot group had no choice but to league with other foes of the Heng Samrin regime, including Sihanouk moderates and even a right-wing organization called the Khmer Serei, led by the former premier Son Sann. (In 1975 the Pol Pot regime had forced the Khmer Serei to retreat across the Thai border and into the Cardamom Mountains.) The Khmer Serei's hatred of the military occupation of their homeland by the ancient enemy, Vietnam, far surpassed their antipathy toward the Khmer Rouge. Doubts about the ability of the tripartite coalition resistance forces to overthrow the Vietnam-backed Heng Samrin government may have been responsible for the precipitate Chinese invasion of Vietnam in February 1979. China expected Vietnam to withdraw substantial numbers of its troops from Cambodia to move them to the Sino-Vietnamese frontier, thereby relieving pressure on Pol Pot and his allies in western Cambodia.

COMMUNISTS CLASH IN INDOCHINA

The two wars—one at the turn of 1978, the other in early 1979 in Indochina, and both involving Vietnam—made that portion of Asia once more an area of instability and insecurity. For the next decade, China and Vietnam had to keep their forces deployed on two fronts: China on its borders with the Soviet Union and Vietnam, Vietnam on its Chinese borders and against the Chinese-backed Pol Pot forces in Cambodia. All the regional states involved in those conflicts came out losers; only the Soviet Union succeeded in augmenting its influence in the region. Cambodia was the greatest loser of all, its independence and integrity badly compromised, its domestic disorder worsened by a new civil war in which the two sides were supported by China and Vietnam. Vietnam lost on several grounds. Vietnam's military and political domination of Cambodia was achieved at tremendous costs to its own security, stability, economy, and international image. Its Second Five-Year Plan (1976–1980) was practically scrapped as the government had to set new priorities in defense outlay and was forced to postpone several reconstruction projects. The country's military and diplomatic dependence on the Soviet Union and Eastern European countries became as complete as its isolation from most of the Third World. Moreover, its chances of getting developmental assistance from the United States, Western Europe, and Japan disappeared. Additionally, Hanoi's new stance drastically diminished its credibility among ASEAN states as a nation committed to carving a zone of peace in Southeast Asia. Finally, Vietnam's continued control and domination over Laos and Cambodia became contingent on its dependence on Soviet economic and military assistance, thus diluting its own hard-earned independence and making it vulnerable to the charge of being Moscow's agent for acquisition of power and influence in Southeast Asia and for the containment of China.

Vietnam's successful overthrow of the Beijing-backed Pol Pot regime was a serious blow to China. In February 1979, when Chinese forces marched across the border into Vietnam, Beijing's public posture was that it wanted to "teach a lesson" to Vietnam for its behavior toward Cambodia and the ethnic Chinese. On neither count did Hanoi learn any lesson as such. Vietnam did not withdraw its forces from Cambodia. Additionally, it made Laos end China's enormous influence there by asking all Chinese technical personnel to leave the country. Further, Vietnam stepped up its persecution of the ethnic Chinese, causing a mass exodus in the first half of 1979.

The month-long border hostilities did not by any measure establish China's miiltary superiority over its much smaller southern neighbor. Hanoi did not even commit its crack regiments to the border war, most of the fighting being carried out by its militia forces. If anything, the conflict laid bare severe weaknesses in the Chinese military machine, which had not seen action since the border war with India in 1962, had not fully recovered from the severe discipline problems it had experienced during the Cultural Revolution, and perhaps lacked certain categories of equipment previously supplied by the Soviet Union during the days of Sino-Soviet amity and alliance. The Chinese casualties were estimated at 20,000. The little war convinced the Chinese leaders that their defense outlay had to be enhanced even at the expense of their plans to modernize their economy. An additional strain on the economy arising from the conflict with Vietnam was the substantial expenditure on an estimated .25 million Chinese refugees from Vietnam.

THE BOAT PEOPLE

The Problem

Though not arising directly out of the Vietnam-China conflict, the mass exodus between 1978 and 1980 of Vietnamese, principally of Chinese ethnic origin, tarnished Vietnam's international image. A second wave of Vietnamese refugees became an issue of international concern a decade later. Soon after the fall of Saigon in 1975, a relatively small number of people leaving Vietnam's shores in small boats attracted international attention. In the following two years, the total remained below 20,000, mostly absorbed by Malaysia, Thailand, and Hong Kong. In 1978 the number rose sharply to 85,230. The crisis peaked in 1979–1981, with a majority of refugees of Chinese descent, many of them North Vietnamese, who fled either to China or Hong Kong. By the middle of 1979, China alone received 250,000 refugees, Hong Kong 62,000, France 61,000, and the United States 150,000; more than 368,000 were awaiting resettlement in transit camps in Thailand, Malaysia, and Indonesia. At least half that number were presumed to have died of starvation on the high seas or drowned because of leaking boats. From the refugees' accounts, it appeared certain that the Vietnamese government "officially" blessed the exodus—but not before the refugees had each paid in gold the equivalent of $5,000, the government netting nearly $4 billion in the process. Between 1975 and 1990, over 1.5 million Vietnamese, Lao, and Cambodian refugees have been resettled, mostly in Western Europe, North America, and Australia.

Traditionally, refugee resettlement has been a regional concern and has been given a regional solution. Thus most African refugees are resettled in neighboring African countries, refugees from Eastern Europe are settled in Western Europe and by their ethnic relatives in the United States, and so on. The Vietnamese refugee problem, however, was not viewed as a regional problem but as an international problem involving intercontinental resettlement. With the exception of China, the neighboring countries—notably Malaysia, Thailand, and Indonesia (and since 1988 the Philippines)—accepted the refugees on condition that the refugees would be resettled permanently in Western Europe, North America, or Australia. The neighboring countries thus served as first-asylum countries, accommodating the refugees in transit camps but unwilling to provide them a permanent home on grounds that the immigrants would create social and economic problems on a large scale. The non-Communist Southeast Asian countries regarded the refugees not only as a heavy economic burden on their scarce resources but as a potential security risk. This was particularly true of Malaysia, which feared that the influx of Vietnamese-Chinese refugees would upset the already delicate racial balance there.

The Causes of Migration

The causes of the massive emigration from Vietnam were economic, social, and political. During 1975–1977, Vietnam suffered a series of bad harvests. The subsequent two years were marked by natural disasters, and crops in the Mekong Delta suffered from insect pests and fungus diseases. The nonavailability of foodstuffs and their exorbitant price caused great hardship. Both in the North and in the South, the urban population had swelled enormously during the long war. It suffered from inadequate food, large-scale unemployment, and the disruptive government attempts at compulsory resettlement in the NEZs, particularly in the South. The economic situation was worsened by the war in Cambodia and with China. Additionally, the conscription was extended in 1978 to include sixteen- to thirty-five-year-olds, and the period of mandatory service went from three to five years. The war itself produced a large number of refugees willing to try their fortunes on the high seas. Finally, the exodus of Hoa, ethnic Chinese, from South Vietnam was prompted by the government's policy of abolition of private trade in April 1978, and by the growing tension between Vietnam and China in early 1979. Around that time, about 250,000 Hoa, whose ancestors had lived in North Vietnam for generations, fled across the land border into China. Vietnam alleged that many of them had acted as spies in guiding the Chinese invaders along back trails to attack the Vietnamese defenders in the rear. The statement of Deputy Premier Deng Xiaoping of China to UN Secretary General Kurt Waldheim in April 1979 that China might teach Vietnam "another lesson" made the Vietnamese apprehensive of the remaining Hoa, particularly those in the strategic port city of Haiphong and the coastal coal-mining towns of Hongay-Campha further north. They did not want to take chances and therefore expelled ethnic Chinese from those areas and from Hanoi. Of all the refugees and boat people, 80 percent were of Chinese origin.

The Solutions

Several international conferences, in which the Office of the United Nations High Commissioner of Refugees was involved, discussed the crisis in 1979. In May, at the ASEAN-sponsored meeting in Jakarta attended by representatives of twenty-five countries, including Vietnam, Malaysia proposed that a refugee-processing center for 200,000 be established in the United States or a U.S.-controlled territory. In response to calls for organized emigration, Vietnam agreed to send the emigrants directly to the countries of resettlement at the rate of 10,000 a month. It would allow anyone who wished to leave the country, except those who were of age for military conscription, knew state secrets, or were awaiting trial on criminal charges. At the UN-sponsored conference in Geneva in July, attended by representatives of sixty-five countries and international agencies, most Western countries and Japan announced their financial contributions as well as quotas for resettlement of refugees. The United States accepted the bulk of the responsibility. In May 1982, the Geneva-based Inter-Governmental Committee for Migration stated that of the almost 700,000 Indochinese refugees who had been resettled since 1975, over two-thirds (477,000) were accepted by the United States, 82,000 by France, and

60,000 by Canada. The United States instituted an Orderly Departure Program, which did not always work in an orderly fashion because of periodic acrimonious exchanges between Washington and Hanoi over the modalities of emigration. In April 1982, the United States announced new criteria for immigration of Indochinese refugees: Those with close relatives in the United States, former U.S. government employees, and those formerly connected with U.S. activities or with a former non-Communist government in Indochina and who had a specific reason to fear persecution would be allowed to enter the country. By 1982 the emigration by small boats had declined sharply to about 30,000 annually; between 1984 and 1986 there was only a trickle.

Suddenly, from mid-1987, Thailand, Malaysia, and Hong Kong reported alarmingly rapid arrivals of Vietnamese refugees. Thailand related that a large number of these had traveled by land to the Cambodian port of Kompong Som, where they had chartered small boats operated by Thai and Cambodian smugglers for destinations on Thai shores. This time, there were no fountains of sympathy for Vietnamese refugees. Vietnam's ASEAN neighbors, Hong Kong, and the Western countries were allegedly affected by "compassion fatigue," as even after thirteen years of the Communist victory, there seemed to be no end to the refugee exodus out of Vietnam. In the wake of *glasnost*, the Western world had new priorities for settlement of refugees and emigrants from Eastern Europe and the Soviet Union. Malaysia, Thailand, and Hong Kong, who had an excellent record so far of offering a first asylum to refugees from Indochina vociferously complained that most of the new refugees were not political sufferers but economic migrants—peasants, fishermen, as well as professionals— mostly from North Vietnam, who were leaving the country in search of economic betterment in the final resettlement country in the Western world. Although its policy did not change officially, from January 1988 Thailand began to push back into the sea the boats that brought new refugees to its shores. Hong Kong announced that June 1988 would be the cutoff date after which the refugees would be screened to sort out the genuine ones from the economic migrants and that the latter would be forcibly repatriated to Vietnam. In April 1988 Malaysia served one year's notice to the effect that its famous transit camps on the rocky island of Pulau Bidong off the Trengganu coast, which since its opening in 1978 had processed 230,000 refugees, as well as its transit camp at Sungei Besi near Kuala Lumpur would be closed after March 1989.

At the instance of Hong Kong, an international conference was held in June 1989 in Geneva, where sixty nations and international agencies adopted a comprehensive plan of action to work out the special difficulties of the countries of first asylum. The plan included measures to discourage clandestine departures from Vietnam, regional screening in the first-asylum countries to identify genuine political refugees, speedier resettlement of refugees in the West and Australia, and voluntary repatriation, in the first instance, for nonrefugees. Although the Soviet Union, Vietnam, and the United Nations had reservations about compulsory repatriation of nonpolitical refugees, the United States held that as long as conditions in Vietnam "repelled" large segments of the population, the U.S. government would remain "unalterably opposed" to compulsory repatriation. It argued that any Vietnamese refugee who survived the perilous journey on the high seas, involving considerable risk of being robbed or raped by pirates and pursuit by inhospitable governments' patrol boats, was not likely to want to return to Vietnam.

Despite U.S. protests, the British government proceeded to negotiate with Vietnam and sign a "memorandum of understanding" on "involuntary repatriation," under which it sent a group of "economic migrants" to Vietnam. The latter buckled under British pressure to draw a semantic distinction between forced and voluntary repatriation, arguing that there was a "quiet majority" among the refugees who were not for voluntary repatriation but who were not against repatriation as such. In October 1989 Vietnamese Foreign Minister Nguyen Co Thach declared that if such refugees were repatriated with financial help, his government would not regard the action as forcible repatriation. This helped the UN-sponsored voluntary repatriation scheme to return to Vietnam some 867 persons by the end of 1989, giving each person a subsidy of $1,000.

Meanwhile, the United States held bilateral negotiations with Vietnam in July 1989 and announced on January 5, 1990, that it would accept a total of between 400,000 and 450,000 Vietnamese, at the rate of 700 a month, for resettlement. The figure would include a large number of former Vietnamese reeducation-camp inmates, who had served the South Vietnamese and U.S. governments before 1975. The United States agreed not to encourage such emigrants to engage in anti-Vietnamese activities. In all, it has to be recognized that until the basic economic and social adjustment problems are solved in Vietnam, the problem of emigration by desperate people will simply not go away.

CHAPTER 9

The Cambodia Question and U.S.-Vietnamese Relations

If the Sixth National Party Congress of December 1986 marked a watershed in Vietnam's domestic politics, it was also noted for major initiatives in foreign policy. Several factors were responsible for the changes in the international field. First of all was the rise of Mikhail Gorbachev to the helm of affairs in the Soviet Union and his peace offensive, which included improvement of relations with China. One of China's preconditions for normalization of Sino-Soviet relations was withdrawal of Vietnamese forces from Cambodia. Gorbachev put pressure on Vietnam to do so by reducing military and economic aid to Vietnam, thereby making it harder for the latter to continue its military commitment in Cambodia without further deterioration of its economy.

As Hanoi would reveal in September 1989, the eleven-year war in Cambodia had left 23,000 Vietnamese dead and 55,000 wounded. The impact of the war on the Vietnamese economy, despite all the Soviet economic and military assistance, had been disastrous. Nearly 50 percent of Vietnam's military budget was expended in Cambodia. Withdrawal from Cambodia would mean the resumption of trade and investment by West European countries, ASEAN, and Japan, which would greatly improve Vietnam's economy and foreign exchange position. (The United States had, with the help of its allies, successfully blocked loans from the International Monetary Fund to Vietnam.) Above all, Vietnam's withdrawal would pave the way for the normalization of relations with the United States. Thus for domestic as well as diplomatic reasons, it became essential for Vietnam to wind down its political, economic, and military commitments in Cambodia. Such a decision had also become essential to end the military impasse in Cambodia, where the Vietnamese forces would lose during the wet season whatever advances they made on the ground in the dry season.

VIETNAM'S GOALS IN CAMBODIA

Hanoi's invasion and occupation of Cambodia was, in all likelihood, undertaken to enhance Vietnam's security in a variety of ways. It curbed Khmer Rouge attacks on Vietnam's border provinces and removed an unfriendly regime in Phnom Penh. Further, as William Turley puts it, it was strategically important for Vietnam to "deny the use of Cambodia by a country seen as hostile, namely, China. Although China was the immediate threat, Hanoi's transcendent concern, based upon experience in two previous wars, was the threat posed by the susceptibility of regimes on Vietnam's Western flank to non-Vietnamese influence."[1]

Vietnam's security concerns were, however, compounded when China and ASEAN enabled the Khmer Rouge to forge an alliance with two non-Communist Cambodian groups—the Khmer People's National Liberation Front (KPNLF) and the Armée Nationale Sihanoukiste (National Sihanoukist Army)—led respectively by Son Sann and Prince Norodom Sihanouk, to form the Coalition Government of Democratic Kampuchea (CGDK). A new military power equation emerged in the region, with China, the United States, and ASEAN (particularly Thailand) helping the CGDK (which was thus able to secure Cambodia's seat in the UN General Assembly) and the Soviet Union supporting Vietnam and the People's Republic of Kampuchea (PRK).

From the time of its occupation of Cambodia, Vietnam had stressed "security interdependence of the three states of former French Indochina," repeatedly talking of a "special relationship" with Cambodia along the same lines as it had with Laos. With such objectives, Vietnam established trilateral commissions to plan and implement several schemes of economic cooperation that would bring about economic integration among the three states. Vietnam, however, had no intentions of becoming bogged down in Cambodia in the manner that the United States had become mired in Vietnam in the 1960s. Hanoi perceived the wisdom of a policy of reducing, if not eliminating, a permanent presence of its troops and political advisers in Cambodia as soon as practicable and instead promoting political, economic, and military self-reliance on the part of the governments in Cambodia and Laos. Even as the CGDK was formed and Western and ASEAN aid offered to it, Vietnam announced in February, 1982 its plans gradually to withdraw its troops from Cambodia. The withdrawal did not begin, however, until 1985 because of mounting CGDK resistance in western

Cambodia. In that year, Vietnam declared that all of its troops would be pulled out by 1990, a date that would eventually be advanced to September 1989.

Major changes that helped the peace process in Cambodia, however, came in 1989. These were preceded by deliberate conciliatory moves on the part of Vietnam on the MIA question and in improvement of relations with China. The first official Sino-Vietnamese meeting in more than a decade took place in January 1989. In the following month, a joint meeting of foreign ministers of Vietnam, Laos, and Cambodia announced on February 17 that Vietnam would withdraw all the remaining troops from Cambodia before the end of September 1989 "within a framework of a political solution." In May the PRK amended its constitution to change the country's name to the State of Cambodia (SOC), recognize Buddhism as the state religion, and permit private landownership. Such changes were made as a prelude to more serious talks with the two non-Communist elements of the CGDK and to separate them from the murderous Khmer Rouge. On July 20 the PRK, now the SOC, announced a position of "permanent neutrality" in international affairs, thereby virtually ending the Cambodia-Vietnam alliance treaty. Although the Vietnamese withdrawal of troops was not supervised by any international agency, most of the international community, including the United States, ASEAN, and the Western powers, has accepted that, but for the presence of a few hundred military and political "advisers," Vietnam's occupation of Cambodia ended in late 1989.

Vietnam's withdrawal of troops from Cambodia did not mean abandonment of the desire to influence that country's government. In May 1989 the Vietnamese government opened a center in Hanoi to pursue cooperative projects between Vietnam and Cambodia in the fields of economy, science and technology, culture, sports, and tourism. The accomplishments of the Phnom Penh government, particularly since 1986, had encouraged Hanoi to think that it would be able to withstand the political and military opposition of the CGDK, whose solidarity was gravely threatened in 1989 by the possibility that its non-Communist components might break away from it. In case of setbacks, Hanoi would be prepared to rush military and other assistance to Phnom Penh, as it reportedly did in spring 1990 to enable the PRK to defend its position against a major Khmer Rouge offensive in western Cambodia. Apart from its own security concerns, there are no compelling reasons for Hanoi to intervene massively in Cambodia again. Hence Vietnam's genuine efforts since 1989 to establish any kind of government in Phnom Penh that would basically exclude the Khmer Rouge and at least not have unfriendly relations with Hanoi.

PRECONDITIONS TO NORMALIZATION
OF U.S-VIETNAM RELATIONS

Since the "fall" of Saigon in 1975, the official U.S. position has favored normalization of relations with Vietnam. As early as November 1975, U.S. Secretary of State Kissinger declared:

> As for our relations with the new government in that region, these will not be determined by the past; we are prepared to look forward to a more hopeful future. The United States will respond to gestures of goodwill. If these governments show understanding of our concerns and those of their neighbors, they will find us ready to reciprocate. This will be especially the case if they deal constructively with the anguish of thousands of Americans who ask only an accounting for their loved ones missing in action and the return of the bodies of Americans who died in Indochina. We have no interest to continue the Indochina war on the diplomatic front; we envisage the eventual normalization of relations.[2]

Although Kissinger referred to the states of Indochina, his statement was directed mainly to Vietnam. The United States stipulated three conditions for the new Vietnam to meet before the process of normalizing relations could begin: peaceful relations with the ASEAN countries, an accounting of Americans missing in action, and the return of bodies of U.S. troops who had died in Vietnam (the United States lists 1,750 Americans as missing in Vietnam, the total figure in all of Indochina being 2,387).

To these conditions, in the early years of their victory, the Vietnamese added a fourth, namely, reconstruction aid allegedly promised by the United States to Vietnam under Article 21 of the Paris accords of January 1973. In support of its claim, Vietnam publicized a letter of February 1, 1973, from President Nixon to Prime Minister Pham Van Dong confirming the intent of Article 21 and offering reconstruction aid of $3.3 billion over a period of five years.[3]

In mid-1975, within two months of Hanoi's victory in the south, Prime Minister Pham Van Dong called for normalization of relations with the U.S. and the fulfillment of the pledge to provide aid for reconstruction. The United States rejected the Vietnamese demand for aid by arguing that Hanoi had completely violated the understanding at Paris by invading and taking over South Vietnam in April 1975, thereby forfeiting any claim to U.S. assistance. Finding the United States intransigent and badly needing Western assistance for economic development, the Vietnamese government told a visiting U.S. mission under Leonard Woodcock (President Carter's special envoy) in March 1977 that it would not insist on aid as a precondition to normalization of ties.[4]

In an atmosphere of bonhomie at a May 1977 U.S.-Vietnam conference of deputy foreign ministers, the United States declared that it would not exercise its veto on the question of admission of Vietnam to the United Nations. Immediately after that conference, however, the U.S. House of Representatives resolved on May 6 to prohibit the State Department from giving any aid to Vietnam. Such an explicit resolution must have angered Vietnam, which thereupon reverted to its previous position of making the normalization of relations contingent upon U.S. payment of reconstruction aid.

The Vietnamese position, however, changed in the next two years because of its hostile relations with China over the question of Vietnamese occupation of Cambodia and the status of ethnic Chinese in Vietnam. During the period of negotiating its twenty-year friendship treaty with the Soviet Union, Hanoi hoped to counterbalance the increasing Soviet influence in Vietnam by trying to improve its relations with the United States. In July 1978 Vietnam declared its readiness to normalize relations with the United States without any preconditions. Although Cyrus Vance and Richard Holbrooke at the Department of State viewed the new diplomatic development favorably, National Security Adviser Zbigniew Brzezinski opposed any reconciliation with Vietnam; using the same language as had the Chinese, he called Vietnam an "Asian Cuba" that was fighting China and Cambodia as a proxy of the Soviet Union. He argued further that Beijing would view any U.S. understanding with Vietnam as an anti-China move that would help Soviet "hegemonistic" ambitions in Southeast Asia. President Carter opted in favor of the Brzezinski position, thereby reversing on October 11, 1978, the State Department's verbal agreement of September 29 with Vietnam's vice–foreign minister, Nguyen Co Thach, that the U.S. government "in principle" approved normalization of relations with Vietnam from November 1978.[5]

The adoption of a stronger U.S. stand against Vietnam was followed on November 3, 1978, by the signing of the treaty of friendship and cooperation between the Soviet Union and Vietnam. According to Gareth Porter, the conclusion of that treaty had been delayed by Vietnam because of the prospect of normalization of relations with the United States. Washington was at that point involved in normalizing relations with China and feared that a similar move in regard to Vietnam would jeopardize the Sino-American relations. Hanoi interpreted the U.S. adoption of the Brzezinski position to mean that Washington had chosen China over Vietnam, thereby augmenting Vietnam's needs for superior weapons systems from the Soviet Union to combat China.[6] Although the U.S. policy cannot be directly faulted for the Vietnamese-Soviet treaty and the subsequent Vietnamese invasion of Cambodia, it is clear that it both opened the way for closer Vietnamese dependence on the Soviet Union and postponed any prospect for the normalization of U.S.-Vietnamese relations for the next decade.

The Vietnamese invasion of Cambodia brought the United States most vociferously on the side of the ASEAN countries, which not only condemned Vietnam for its aggression but also launched a diplomatic war to ostracize it from international organizations. There were substantial segments of U.S. public opinion, however, that were horrified at the revelations of the genocidal excesses of the Pol Pot regime and therefore opposed its return to power. The Carter administration, adopting Brzezinski's viewpoint, welcomed the Chinese invasion of Vietnam as it could help Vietnam's pullout from Cambodia.

With China's failure to teach Vietnam a "lesson," the Soviet influence in Vietnam increased. It soon extended to the use of Cam Ranh Bay as a naval base. The coalition of anti-Vietnamese forces—the United States, Western Europe, Japan, ASEAN, and China—led to increased Vienamese economic and military dependence on the Soviet Union during the subsequent decade. There was no longer any serious talk of normalization of U.S. relations with Vietnam; indeed, Vietnam's withdrawal from Cambodia became an additional precondition to renewed talks.

THE MIA ISSUE

In the 1980s Hanoi moved specifically to improve relations with the United States by taking action on the MIA issue. In February 1982, for the first time, Vietnam returned MIA remains to a U.S. delegation to Hanoi led by Deputy Secretary of Defense Richard Armitage. In June 1985 Hanoi informed the United States that it was willing to settle the MIA issue within two years. Two months later it released the remains of twenty-six Americans, the largest single transfer since 1982. In November it allowed the first U.S.-Vietnam joint excavation of a B-52 crash site in order to uncover MIA remains.

A major breakthrough on the MIA question came after the Sixth Congress of the Vietnam Communist Party, in December 1986, decided to seek and facilitate a political settlement of the Cambodia problem. In 1987 Vietnam agreed to have the former chairman of the Joint Chiefs of Staff, General John Vessey, visit Hanoi as President Reagan's special representative and discuss the problem of searching for the MIAs. Since that time, General Vessey has been the single most important individual dealing with the MIA question from the U.S. side.

The first Vessey mission, which included several officials and nonofficials, notably representatives of the National League of POW/MIA Families, emphasized the humanitarian issues of mutual interest and resulted in a joint communiqué on August 3, 1987, whereby Vietnam delinked the MIA issue from the question of normalization of relations. Later in the same month, two conferences were held simultaneously in Washington and Hanoi to discuss the MIA question and that of urgent humanitarian assistance for Vietnam.[7] The Reagan administration officially agreed to encourage charitable assistance from the United States to Vietnam, including the establishment of a private foundation to reinforce such activities. These would include an immediate supply of artificial limbs for about 60,000 Vietnamese disabled veterans. It was the first time since 1975 that the United States had offered financial aid of any kind in return for Vietnamese assistance in accounting for MIAs or returning MIA remains. Hanoi also agreed to allow joint U.S.-Vietnam technical teams to work together to find remains of missing persons.

In the two years between September 1988 and the meeting of U.S. Secretary of State James Baker and Vietnamese Foreign Minister Nguyen Co Thach in September 1990 in New York, the United States received from the Vietnamese government the remains of only 100 MIAs. In October 1990 the Vietnamese foreign minister discussed the MIA question with General Vessey in Washington. He agreed to allow the United States to establish an office in Hanoi to gather information about the MIAs. The visiting minister also offered the joint U.S.-Vietnam technical teams free access to war records and archival materials as well as to possible witnesses to the downing of planes or other incidents in which members of the U.S. military disappeared in Vietnam during the war. Nguyen Co Thach, however, pleaded Vietnam's inability to maintain and preserve records, the problem exacerbated by the war and weather conditions, in particular high humidity. In April 1991 General Vessey visited Hanoi and made arrangements to open an office for investigation of the MIAs. Simultaneously, the United States announced the gift of $1 million, to be channeled through humanitarian groups to provide prosthetic devices for Vietnamese war victims. The MIA question, however, continues to sour the U.S.-Vietnamese relations and is an important impediment in the normalization of relations between the two countries.

EFFORTS TOWARD PEACE IN CAMBODIA

By the late 1980s, all the parties directly or indirectly involved in the Cambodian conflict realized that the military impasse did not give anyone any special advantage. The CGDK constituents no longer saw eye to eye. The ASEAN states, notably Thailand, saw no advantage in continuing to be forever a conduit for Chinese arms to the CGDK. On behalf of the ASEAN states, however, Indonesia took the lead to break the political and military impasse by bringing all the Cambodian parties together for informal talks at Jakarta. The first two Jakarta Informal Meetings (JIM-1 in July 1988 and JIM-2 in February 1989) linked the withdrawal of Vietnamese troops to the stoppage of all external aid to the CGDK. The second JIM underlined the need for power-sharing in Phnom Penh as a postwar solution.

Indicative of an all-around desire to find a solution that would include an "honorable" exclusion of the Khmer Rouge from any future government in Cambodia was a UN major initiative. On November 3, 1988, with U.S. and Chinese support, the UN General Assembly passed a significant resolution that Cambodia must not return to "the universally condemned policies and practices of a recent past." The vote was 122 for and 19 against. Apparently, both the United States and China seemed satisfied with the progress in Vietnamese plans for withdrawal from Cambodia. Their support—military, economic, and diplomatic—of the Khmer Rouge markedly dropped thereafter.

If there was no solution found at the first two informal meetings at Jakarta, there was none also at the nineteen-nation international conference at Paris, which opened in July 1989. At that venue, the SOC and Vietnam, backed by the Soviet Union, argued in favor of an international agreement preceding an internal settlement on the sharing of power, while the CGDK, China, and ASEAN insisted on a comprehensive settlement of both the aspects. On the one hand, the CGDK's demand for a quadripartite division of power in the country was not acceptable to the SOC because it would be left with only one-quarter of the authority, which, it argued, was far removed from the "battlefield realities." Moreover, the SOC was totally opposed to any power-sharing that would reward the genocidal Khmer Rouge. On the other hand, the SOC's proposal for a bilateral sharing of power was not acceptable to the CGDK, which claimed total legitimacy of power and sovereignty, in large part based on its holding a seat in the United Nations. One of the few areas of agreement among most of the parties involved was a larger and crucial role for the United Nations not only in the supervision of a cease-fire and disarming of troops but also in the internal administration of the country, on the model of Namibia, pending supervised elections and formation of a coalition government.

The military impasse between the CGDK and the SOC on the battlefields of western Cambodia was now matched by a deadlock at the international negotiations table. Two major international initiatives on the part of the United States and China, the latter's action perhaps as a reaction to the new U.S. stance, most significantly helped the peace process. In a dramatic turnaround marking a change in eleven years of support to the Khmer Rouge, U.S. Secretary of State Baker, at the end of a meeting with the Soviet foreign minister, announced on July 18, 1990, that the United States would no longer support the seating of the CGDK in the UN General

Assembly. Further, the United States declared its readiness to hold direct talks with Vietnam in New York over the Cambodian conflict. Accordingly, on September 29, Foreign Minister Nguyen Co Thach, visiting the UN, met with Baker in New York. He was then "allowed," as an exception to the restriction prohibiting Vietnamese officials from traveling beyond a 25-mile radius of their mission at the UN, to proceed to Washington to discuss the MIA question with General Vessey and to meet with the Senate Foreign Relations Committee for an informal, closed-door session. The Baker-Thach meeting was the first high-level U.S.-Vietnamese meeting since the Paris accords of 1973, indicative of both parties' interest in normalization of relations.

As for China, Mikhail Gorbachev's initiatives in Afghanistan, Vietnam, and indirectly in Cambodia had contributed in the late 1980s to the decline, if not dissipation, of fears of its "encirclement" by the Soviet Union and its ally, Vietnam. In January 1990 the Soviet Union declared that it would no longer use the Cam Ranh Bay base facilities. By April there were reports of the repatriation of about 200,000 Vietnamese workers from the Soviet Union and Eastern Europe, an indication of reduced aid from that quarter to Vietnam. So far, Hanoi had viewed its alliance with the Soviet Union to provide a deterrent to China's use of force against Vietnam. Gorbachev's attempts at forging a Sino-Soviet détente clearly reduced the possibility of the Soviet Union's stepping in if Vietnam and China clashed again. Already, Moscow had manifested a kind of neutrality between Hanoi and Beijing when their rival forces clashed on the offshore Spratly Islands in March 1988.

The visible cracks in the Soviet–Eastern European solidarity and their much-reduced military and economic support to Vietnam eased China's fears. At the same time, it contributed to Vietnam's desire to improve relations with China itself. In May 1990 China and Vietnam arrived at a "basic agreement" to end the Cambodia conflict through international negotiations. In the following week, Moscow announced a normalization of relations with Beijing, implying thereby China's satisfaction that its precondition regarding Vietnam's withdrawal from Cambodia had been met. Reportedly, the two Communist neighbors had agreed to disagree on a number of "minor" points. The much-improved Sino-Soviet relationship prompted Vietnam to open a dialogue with China. Secret talks between the two countries at the highest level, the first since 1976, took place in early September 1990. The Vietnamese delegation, headed by Party General Secretary Nguyen Van Linh, included Prime Minister Du Muoi and the former prime minister, Pham Van Dong; its Chinese counterpart was led by Party Chief Jiang Zemin and Premier Li Peng.

With the change in attitude of the two major supporters of the Khmer Rouge, namely, the United States and China, the international climate became conducive as never before to a settlement of the Cambodian problem. The impasse over the twin questions of power-sharing and the SOC's apprehension of an enhanced UN role in the transitional period was overcome by an Australian proposal presented to a meeting of the five permanent members of the UN interim administration of Cambodia pending general elections. The proposal also suggested that the CGDK be asked to vacate its seat in the UN General Assembly. Although the five permanent members of the Security Council approved the Australian plan in principle, only three of the four Cambodian factions endorsed it, the most vociferous dissenter being the Khmer Rouge. The differences between the Khmer Rouge and its CGDK partners became even sharper at JIM-3 in February 1990. Earlier the same month, Sihanouk announced the renaming of the Coalition Government of Democratic Kampuchea as the National Government of Cambodia, thus distancing the two Communist components of the former CGDK from the Khmer Rouge, whose disreputable government from 1975 to 1978 was known as Democratic Kampuchea.

In spring 1990 there was no appreciable progress toward adoption of the UN plan, despite intense diplomatic pressure on the different Cambodian factions by their former external supporters. Finally, on August 28, 1990, a collective initiative on the part of the five permanent members of the UN Security Council resulted in their unanimous agreement on a "framework" for settlement of the Cambodian conflict. The revised plan entailed a cease-fire, a UN contingent of 10,000 peacekeeping troops, termination of all external military aid, and disarmament of the Cambodian factions—all under UN supervision. A Supreme National Council (SNC) consisting of the four factions was to administer the country until national elections were held. The UN would oversee five of the most important ministries (defense, public security, information, foreign affairs, and finance). About 10,000 UN civilian personnel were expected to be needed for the operation, and it was estimated that implementation of the framework would cost about $10 billion, making it the most elaborate and expensive enterprise in UN history.

On October 15 the General Assembly adopted the framework and welcomed the agreement among the four Cambodian factions to set up the SNC and to send its representative to occupy Cambodia's seat in the United Nations. It was the first unanimous UN resolution on Cambodia since 1978, indicative of global support for the crucial UN role in ending the twelve-year conflict.

The plan was subject to approval by all four Cambodian factions, which met in September 1990 at JIM-4, cochaired by Indonesia and France. The Cambodian parties agreed to form a twelve-member Supreme National Council, which would embody the country's sovereignty and in whose name the UN seat would thereafter be occupied, until the national elections were held and a new government took over. At JIM-4 and subsequent diplomatic parleys, the SOC expressed its apprehension of the UN plan's provisions on demobilization and disarmament of all military forces in Cambodia. It also insisted that the UN plan specifically condemn the genocide that occurred under the Khmer Rouge regime.

Diverse international pressures and the diplomacy of Cambodia's Sihanouk were at last to secure a settlement among all four Cambodian parties meeting at Pattay, outside Bangkok, in June 1991. They consented to a cease-fire and a prohibition on receiving foreign arms. The SOC agreed to allow the SNC to set up its headquarters in Phnom Penh and to allow the three factions of the former CGDK to open their offices in the Cambodian capital. Though the actual implementation of the UN plan had not commenced as of autumn 1991, considerable groundwork had been prepared for the proposed UN Transitional Authority in Cambodia (UNTAC). Peace in Cambodia would open a window of opportunity for Vietnam to improve its relations not only with the United States but also with most of the world interested in promoting prospects of stability in the region.

Chronology

208 B.C.   Zhao Tuo, a Chinese general, conquers Au Lac and styles himself emperor of Nam Viet

111 B.C.–A.D. 939   Nam Viet ruled by China as the province of Giao Chi

A.D. 39–43   Trung sisters' rebellion against China; establish an independent state lasting two years

192   Champa (or Lin-yi) founded after the overthrow of Chinese rule

284   Champa sends its first embassy to China

802   Khmer Empire founded in the Angkor region

939   Vietnamese, under Ngo Quyen's leadership, overthrow the Chinese rule in the Tongking region, send tribute to China

939–968   Ngo dynasty

968   Dinh Bo Linh overthrows Ngo dynasty, calls his state Dai Co Viet

968–980   Dinh dynasty

980–1009   Earlier Le dynasty

1225–1258   The reign of Tran Thai Tong

1282   Mongols attack Champa

1284–1287   Mongols defeated by the Vietnamese

1407–1428   Vietnam under Chinese rule

1428   Le Loi overthrows Chinese rule, establishes a new dynasty

1431   The Thais sack Angkor; the Khmers send tribute to Ayuthaya (Thailand)

1461–1497   The reign of Le Thanh Thong; major legal and administrative reforms

1471   Vietnamese conquest of Champa

1545   Civil war divides Vietnam; China mediates

1603   Establishment of the French East India Company

1615   French Jesuits open a mission at Fai Fo

1627   Alexandre de Rhodes devises *quoc-ngu* to adapt Vietnamese language to Roman script

1720   The Vietnamese absorb the remnant of Champa

1772–1802   The Tayson rebellion

1787   Bishop Pigneau de Béhaine in France to obtain support for Prince Nguyen Anh

1802   Nguyen Anh becomes Emperor Gia Long, unifies the country; reconstruction and reform

1820–1841   The reign of Minh Mang

1825   Minh Mang forbids his subjects' conversion to the Catholic religion, bans Catholic institutions

1836   Minh Mang closes ports to European shipping

1841–1847   The reign of Thieu Tri

1846   French blockade and bombardment of Tourane (Da Nang)

1847–1883   Reign of Tu Duc

1858   Franco-Spanish expedition to Vietnam to save missionaries

1862   Vietnam cedes three provinces of Cochin China to France

1863, AUGUST 11   French protectorate over Cambodia

1866, JUNE   De Lagrée-Garnier Mekong expedition begins

1867   Franco-Thai treaty recognizes French protectorate over Cambodia

1884   Vietnam signs the protectorate treaty with France

1885, JUNE 9   Franco-Chinese treaty establishing a French protectorate over Annam and Tongking

1887   France creates the Indochinese Union consisting of Cochin China, Annam, Tongking, and Cambodia

1890   Ho Chi Minh born

1893   France extends protectorate over Laos

1900   Boxer Uprising

1913   Ho Chi Minh leaves for Europe, remains out of Vietnam for three decades

1913   Phan Boi Chau establishes the Association for the Restoration of Vietnam

1919   Ho Chi Minh at Versailles peace conference, tries to present a petition demanding self-determination for Vietnam

1920   Ho Chi Minh joins the French Communist Party

1923   Ho Chi Minh goes to Moscow to attend an international conference and remains there

1924   Ho Chi Minh accompanies Borodin to China and stays on to organize a movement against French rule in Vietnam

1925   Ho Chi Minh forms the Association of Vietnamese Revolutionary Youth; Phan Boi Chau sentenced to life imprisonment

1927   Vietnam Nationalist Party founded

1930, JANUARY   Ho Chi Minh unites Vietnamese Communist groups into one Communist Party later to be named the Indochina Communist Party (ICP)

1930, FEBRUARY 10   Yen Bay uprising; VNQDD suppressed; leaders flee to China

1930, MAY 1   ICP organizes strikes in plantations and factories; ICP-led rebellions severely repressed by the French; leaders flee to China

1932, SEPTEMBER   Prince Bao Dai returns from France

1940, AUGUST   Japan occupies Indochina but leaves the pro-Vichy French officials in charge

1941, MAY   Viet Minh established

1944, DECEMBER   Vo Nguyen Giap founds the Viet Minh army

1945, MARCH   Japan assumes direct control of French Indochina, interns French officials

1945, AUGUST 7   Japan surrenders; the Viet Minh elects a national liberation committee to serve as a provisional government

1945, AUGUST 25   Bao Dai abdicates in favor of the provisional government

1945, AUGUST 29   Ho Chi Minh proclaims provisional government with Bao Dai as supreme counselor

1945, SEPTEMBER   China occupies Vietnam north of the 16th parallel; British troops occupy Vietnam south of the 16th parallel

1945, SEPTEMBER 2   Democratic Republic of Vietnam proclaimed

1945, NOVEMBER 11   ICP dissolved and replaced by Association of Marxist Studies

1946, MARCH 6   Franco–Viet Minh agreement; France recognizes Vietnam as a "free state" within the French union; French allowed to return to North Vietnam as China agrees to withdraw its troops

1946, NOVEMBER 23   French bombing of Haiphong

1946, DECEMBER 19   Viet Minh attack French troops in Hanoi; the DRV government moves out of Hanoi

1946–1954   First Indochina War

1949, MARCH 8   Elysée agreement signed by France and Bao Dai creates the "state" of Vietnam as an associated state within the French union

1949, OCTOBER   People's Republic of China established

1950   Franco-U.S. treaty; United States aids France directly in Indochina

1950, JANUARY 14   China and the Soviet Union recognize the DRV

1950, FEBRUARY 7   Britain and the United States recognize Bao Dai's government

1951, FEBRUARY   Ho Chi Minh founds the Lao Dong (Workers') Party

1953, MARCH 5   Stalin dies

1953, OCTOBER   France grants Laos "full independence" as a member of the French union

1953, NOVEMBER 9   Prince Sihanouk declares Cambodia independent

1954, MAY 7   Viet Minh defeat the French at Dien Bien Phu

1954, MAY 8   Geneva conference on Indochina opens

1954, JUNE 16   Ngo Dinh Diem appointed premier of the "state" of Vietnam

1954, JUNE 17   Pierre Mendès-France becomes premier of France, vows to resign if a settlement on Indochina is not reached by July 20

1954, JULY 21   Geneva agreements on Indochina signed

1954, SEPTEMBER 8   Southeast Asia Treaty Organization founded

1955, FEBRUARY 19   Eisenhower writes to Diem offering unconditional support

1955, OCTOBER 23   Diem becomes president of the Republic of Vietnam

1957   Diem launches a mopping up campaign, uses emergency powers

1960   Birth of the National Liberation Front

1963, MAY 8   South Vietnamese troops shoot at Buddhist demonstrators at Hué; Buddhist agitation builds up

1963, NOVEMBER 1   Diem and Nhu assassinated

1964–1975   Second Indochina War

1964, AUGUST 2   United States charges that the U.S.S. *Maddox* and *Turner Joy* were attacked by North Vietnam

1964, AUGUST 5   U.S. Congress passes the Gulf of Tongking Resolution, giving the president extraordinary powers to act in Southeast Asia

1965, FEBRUARY 7   Viet Cong attack U.S. base at Pleiku

1965, FEBRUARY 24   United States launches Operation Rolling Thunder; sustained bombing of North Vietnam

1967, SEPTEMBER 3   Nguyen Van Thieu elected president of South Vietnam, with Nguyen Cao Ky as vice-president

1968, JANUARY 31   The Tet offensive begins

1968, MARCH 28   President Johnson announces decision not to seek re-election

1968, JUNE 8   First withdrawal of U.S. troops announced

1969, JULY 25   Nixon Doctrine enunciated in Guam

1969, SEPTEMBER 3   Ho Chi Minh dies

1970, FEBRUARY 20   Kissinger begins secret talks in Paris with Le Duc Tho

1970, MARCH 18   Sihanouk overthrown; Lon Nol establishes a pro-U.S. government

1970, APRIL 30   U.S. and South Vietnamese forces invade Cambodia in search of Communist sanctuaries

1971   Withdrawal of U.S. forces from Vietnam begins

1971, JULY   Sino-U.S. rapprochement begins; Kissinger visits Beijing

1971, OCTOBER 3   Thieu reelected president of South Vietnam

1972, FEBRUARY   Nixon visits China

1973, JANUARY 27   Paris peace accords signed; cease-fire in Vietnam, Laos, and Cambodia

1973, MARCH 29   Withdrawal of U.S. troops from Vietnam completed

1973, SEPTEMBER   South Vietnam incorporates the Spratly Islands

1974, JANUARY   China occupies the Paracel Islands

1975, APRIL 17   Khmer Rouge overthrows the Lon Nol regime; Cambodia renamed Kampuchea

1975, APRIL 21   Thieu resigns and leaves South Vietnam; neutralist government established under General Duong Van Minh

1975, APRIL 30   Communists take over Saigon and assume reins of power in South Vietnam

1976, JANUARY 2   Vietnam formally reunited

1976, APRIL   Elections held for the National Assembly of all Vietnam

1976, JULY   Establishment of the Socialist Republic of Vietnam (SRV)

1977, JANUARY   Kampuchea attacks Vietnam's border provinces

1978, MAY   The special minority status of the Vietnamese-Chinese abolished

1978, MAY   The integration of currencies of North and South Vietnam

1978, JUNE 29   Vietnam joins the Moscow-dominated COMECON

1978, JULY   China terminates all aid to Vietnam, closes its borders with Vietnam

1978, NOVEMBER 3   Soviet-Vietnamese treaty of friendship and cooperation signed

1978, DECEMBER 25   Vietnam invades Kampuchea

1979, FEBRUARY–MARCH   China invades Vietnam

1982   Fifth Congress of the Vietnamese Communist Party

1986, MAY   Truong Chinh, Pham Van Dong, and Le Duc Tho take over the duties of Le Duan

1986, JULY 10   Le Duan dies; Truong Chinh becomes the general secretary of the VCP

1988, MARCH 10   Pham Hung, premier since June 1987, dies

1988, JUNE 22   Du Muoi becomes premier

1988, JULY 25–30   Jakarta Informal Meeting (JIM-1) held

1988, SEPTEMBER 30   Truong Chinh, president of Vietnam since 1981, dies

1989, FEBRUARY   JIM-2 held

1989, JUNE 13–14   Geneva conference on Indochinese refugees

1989, JULY–AUGUST   Nineteen-nation International Conference on Cambodia in Paris

1989, SEPTEMBER   Vietnam announces completion of withdrawal of forces from Cambodia

1990, FEBRUARY 26–MARCH 1   JIM-3 held

1990, JULY 18   United States withdraws support of CGDK seat in the UN

1990, AUGUST 28   Permanent members of the UN Security Council approve a "framework" for peace in Cambodia

1990, SEPTEMBER 9–10   JIM-4 held

1990, OCTOBER 15   UN General Assembly unanimously approves the plan for Cambodian peace

1991, APRIL   United States opens an office in Hanoi for investigation of MIAs, offers Vietnam $1 million for prosthetic devices

1991, JUNE 24   Cambodian factions agree to a cease-fire

Notes

CHAPTER 1

1. Georges Coedès, *The Making of South East Asia* (Berkeley: University of California Press, 1966), p. 79.

2. David Marr, *Vietnamese Anti-Colonialism, 1885–1925* (Berkeley: University of California Press, 1971), p. 9.

3. Lê Thanh Khoi, *Le Viet-Nam, histoire et civilisation* (Paris: Editions de Minuit, 1955), p. 86, refutes the theory that the Viets are the only ancestors of the Vietnamese.

4. Quoted in Thomas Hodgkin, *Vietnam: The Revolutionary Path* (London: Macmillan, 1981), p. 21.

5. King C. Chen, *Vietnam and China, 1938–1954* (Princeton: Princeton University Press, 1969), p. 12.

6. Hodgkin, *Vietnam*, p. 29.

7. Jean Chesneaux, *Contribution à l'histoire de la nation vietnamienne* (Paris: Editions Sociales, 1962), pp. 26–27.

8. Joseph Buttinger, *Vietnam: A Political History* (New York: Praeger, 1968), p. 29.

CHAPTER 2

1. Quoted in Ralph Smith, *Viet-Nam and the West* (London: Heinemann, 1968), p. 9.

CHAPTER 3

1. Charles Maybon, *Histoire moderne du pays d'Annam, 1592–1820* (Paris: Plon-Nourrit, 1919).

2. Translations of this edict vary. One version reads, "The wicked religion of the Western people casts its malicious spell on the minds of the people; the Catholic

missionaries wrong the people's mind, violate the country's good customs and result in a great harm for the nation." See Marvin E. Gettleman, ed., *Vietnam: History, Documents and Opinions on a Major World Crisis* (Greenwich, Conn.: Fawcett Publications, 1965), p. 28; and Georges Taboulet, *La geste française en Indochine*, vol. 1 (Paris: Adrien-Maisonneuve, 1956), pp. 328–329.

3. John F. Cady, *The Roots of French Imperialism in Eastern Asia* (Ithaca: Cornell University Press, 1954), p. 29.

4. Joseph Buttinger, *The Smaller Dragon: A Political History of Vietnam* (New York: Praeger, 1958), p. 133.

5. *Catholic Digest*, February 1962, p. 17.

6. Henri Blet, *France d'Outre-mer*, vol. 2 (Paris: Arthaud, 1950), p. 281.

7. Bernard Fall, *The Two Viet-Nams: A Political and Military Analysis*, 3d ed. (New York: Praeger, 1967), p. 16.

8. Lê Thanh Khoi, *Le Viet-Nam, histoire et civilisation* (Paris: Editions de Minuit, 1955), p. 365.

9. Francis Garnier, *Voyage d'exploration en Indochine* (Paris: Librairie Hachette, 1885), 2 vols.

10. H. I. Priestly, *France Overseas: A Study of Modern Imperialism* (New York: Appleton-Century, 1938), p. 217.

11. Ella S. Laffey, "French Adventurers and Chinese Bandits in Tonkin: The Garnier Affair in Its Local Context," *Journal of Southeast Asian Studies* 6 (March 1975), p. 41.

12. Ibid., p. 39.

13. Taboulet, *La geste française*, vol. 2, p. 709.

14. M. Dutreb, *L'Amiral Dupré et la conquête du Tonkin* (Paris: E. Leroux, 1924), pp. 94–96.

15. Lois E. Bailey, *Jules Ferry and French Indo-China* (Madison: University of Wisconsin Press, 1946), p. 24.

16. Thomas F. Power, Jr., *Jules Ferry and the Renaissance of French Imperialism* (New York: Octagon Books, 1966), p. 191.

CHAPTER 4

1. David Marr, *Vietnamese Anti-Colonialism, 1885–1925* (Berkeley: University of California Press, 1971), p. 4.

2. Truong Buu Lam, *Patterns of Vietnamese Response to Foreign Intervention, 1858–1900* (New Haven: Yale University Press, Southeast Asia Studies, 1967), p. 3.

3. For a detailed analysis along these lines, see Marr, *Vietnamese Anti-Colonialism*, pp. 95–97.

4. Hoang Van Chi, *From Colonialism to Communism* (New York: Praeger, 1964), p. 18; P. J. Honey, ed., *North Vietnam Today: Profile of a Communist Satellite* (New York: Praeger, 1962), p. 4.

5. King Chen has compiled a list of Ho's nineteen aliases, some repeated at different times in his life. King C. Chen, *Vietnam and China, 1938–1954* (Princeton: Princeton University Press, 1969), pp. 37 and 40, footnotes.

6. Pham Van Dong and the Committee for the Study of the History of the Vietnamese Workers' Party, *President Ho Chi Minh* (Hanoi: Foreign Languages Publishing House, 1960), pp. 41–42.

7. M. E. Gettleman, ed., *Vietnam* (New York: Penguin, 1965), p. 37.

8. Ibid., p. 39.

9. Quoted from a Viet Minh pamphlet by Jean Lacouture, *Ho Chi Minh: A Political Biography* (New York: Vintage Books, 1968), p. 88.

10. Quoted in Ellen Hammer, *The Struggle for Indochina* (Stanford: Stanford University Press, 1954), p. 102.

11. At this point, the Indochina Communist Party is believed to have had 5,000 members. The number jumped to 210,000 in 1946 and to 365,000 in the following year. According to Joseph Buttinger, these 365,000 became the "founding members" of the Lao Dong (Workers Party), the name under which the Vietnamese Communist Party was officially re-formed on March 3, 1951. *Vietnam: A Political History* (New York: Praeger, 1968), p. 336.

12. Quoted in David Halberstam, *Ho* (New York: Vintage Books, 1971), pp. 84–85.

13. Milton E. Osborne, *Region of Revolt: Focus on Southeast Asia* (Rushcutters Bay, Australia: Pergamon Press, 1970), p. 100.

14. *Le monde*, August 24, 1949.

15. New China News Agency, Daily News Release, November 23, 1949.

16. U.S. Department of State, *Department of State Bulletin* 22 (February 13, 1950), p. 244.

17. The Geneva agreements were signed in the early hours of July 21. The French premier's plane engines were buzzing at that time, ready to take him from Geneva to Paris to submit his resignation in case the talks failed.

CHAPTER 5

1. For a detailed study of the commission's work, see D. R. SarDesai, *Indian Foreign Policy in Cambodia, Laos and Vietnam, 1947–1964* (Berkeley: University of California Press, 1968).

2. Statement of the U.S. representative at Geneva, Bedell Smith, as given in *Further Documents Relating to the Discussion of Indochina at the Geneva Conference*, Cmd. 9239, 1954, pp. 6–7.

3. The five principles were mutual respect for each other's territorial integrity and sovereignty, nonaggression, noninterference in each other's internal affairs, equality and mutual benefit, and peaceful coexistence. The Sino-Indian agreement of 1954 began a friendship between the two Asian countries that lasted until 1962. The principles outlined in the accords were later included in numerous agreements between Communist and nonaligned countries.

4. Victor Bator, *Vietnam: A Diplomatic Tragedy* (New York: Oceana Publications, 1965), p. 172.

5. U.S. Senate Committee on Foreign Relations, *Report on Indochina by Senator Mike Mansfield, October 15, 1954*, 82d Congress, 2d session (Washington, D.C.: Government Printing Office, 1954), p. 14.

6. *New York Times*, November 18, 1954. See also Robert Sheer, *How the United States Got Involved in Vietnam* (Santa Barbara: Center for the Study of Democratic Institutions, 1965), quoted in Marvin E. Gettleman, ed., *Vietnam: History, Documents and Opinions on a Major World Crisis* (Greenwich, Conn.: Fawcett Publications, 1965), p. 241.

7. President Eisenhower to Bao Dai, February 19, 1955, in *Department of State Bulletin* 32 (March 14, 1955), p. 423.

8. Graham Greene, "Last Act in Indo-China," *New Republic* 132, May 9, 1955, p. 10.

9. Dwight D. Eisenhower, *Mandate for Change, 1953–56* (New York: Signet Books, 1965).

10. Douglas Pike, *Viet Cong* (Cambridge: MIT Press, 1966), p. 76.

11. George M. Kahin and John W. Lewis, *The United States in Vietnam* (New York: Dial Press, 1967), p. 119.

12. Frances Fitzgerald, *Fire in the Lake* (New York: Vintage Books, 1972), p. 18.

13. Ibid.

14. U.S. Department of State, *A Threat to the Peace* (Washington, D.C.: Government Printing Office, 1961), p. iii.

15. *Pentagon Papers*, vol. 2 (New York: Bantam Books, 1971), p. 75.

16. David Halberstam, *The Making of a Quagmire* (New York: Random House, 1965), p. 68.

CHAPTER 6

1. John Galloway, *The Gulf of Tongking Resolution* (Cranbury, N.J.: Associated University Press, 1970), pp. 36–37.

2. The United States was helped by token forces from its allies: New Zealand (500), Australia (7,000), the Philippines (no combat troops, only a hospital corps and an engineer battalion), South Korea (10,000), and Thailand (2,500).

3. *Pentagon Papers* (New York: Bantam Books, 1971).

4. Clark Clifford, "A Vietnam Reappraisal," *Foreign Affairs* 47 (July 1969), p. 612.

5. John G. Stoessinger, *Henry Kissinger: The Anguish of Power* (New York: Norton, 1976), pp. 51–52.

6. For an analysis of the U.S. policy of the time, see Stephen P. Gilbert, "Implications of the Nixon Doctrine for Military Aid Policy," *Orbis* 16, 3 (Fall 1972), pp. 660–681. See also Richard Nixon, *U.S. Foreign Policy for the 1970's: A New Strategy for Peace—A Report to the Congress by Richard Nixon, February 18, 1970* (Washington, D.C.: Government Printing Office, 1970), pp. 55–56.

7. Norodom Sihanouk, "Cambodia Neutral: The Dictate of Necessity," *Foreign Affairs* 36 (July 1958), pp. 582–586.

8. For short biographies of the eight most prominent members of the Khmer Rouge High Command, see John Barron and Anthony Paul, *Murder of a Gentle Land: The Untold Story of Communist Genocide in Cambodia* (New York: Reader's Digest Press, 1977), pp. 43–45.

9. Pol Pot's speech, September 28, 1977, *BBC Summary of World Broadcasts* October 3, 1977.

10. Norodom Sihanouk, *My War with the CIA* (Harmondsworth, UK: Penguin Press, 1973).

11. Nguyen Cao Ky, *How We Lost the Vietnam War* (New York: Stein and Day, 1984), p. 108.

CHAPTER 7

1. For detailed statistical information on postwar South Vietnam, see Huynh Kim Khanh, "Restructuring the Economy of South Vietnam," *Southeast Asian Affairs, 1976* (Singapore: Institute of Southeast Asian Studies, 1976), pp. 467–484.

2. Huynh Kim Khanh, "Year One of Post-Colonial Vietnam," *Southeast Asian Affairs, 1977* (Singapore: Institute of Southeast Asian Studies, 1977), p. 290.

3. Ibid., p. 291.

4. The conversion rate was 1.2 dongs to the dollar in 1980.

5. *Documents of the Sixth Congress of the Communist Party of Vietnam, 15–18 December 1986* (Hanoi: Foreign Languages Publishing House, 1987), p. 51.

6. International Institute for Strategic Studies, *The Military Balance, 1990–91* (London: IISS, 1991), pp. 180–181.

CHAPTER 8

1. William Shawcross, "The Third Indochina War," *New York Review of Books,* April 6, 1978, p. 16. Shawcross was a correspondent in Vietnam and the author of the well-known book *Sideshow.*

2. Nayan Chanda, *Brother Enemy: The War After the War—A History of Indochina Since the Fall of Saigon* (San Diego: Harcourt Brace Jovanovich, 1986), pp. 72–73.

3. For details, see Ben Kiernan, *How Pol Pot Came to Power: A History of Communism in Kampuchea, 1930–1975* (London: Verso, 1985).

4. Deng's speech, as reported by the New China News Agency, June 30, 1975.

5. *Straits Times* (Singapore), July 31, 1975.

6. For a detailed review of rival Chinese and Vietnamese claims, see Chang Pao-min, *The Sino-Vietnamese Territorial Dispute* (New York: Praeger, 1986), pp. 13–23.

7. Charles McGregor, *The Sino-Vietnamese Relationship and the Soviet Union,* Adelphi Papers 232 (London: International Institute for Strategic Studies, 1988), pp. 23–24.

CHAPTER 9

1. William S. Turley, "The Khmer War: Cambodia After Paris," *Survival* 32, 5 (September-October 1990), p. 445.

2. *Department of State Bulletin,* December 15, 1975, p. 847.

3. Ibid., June 27, 1977, pp. 674–675.

4. *New York Times,* March 24, 1977.

5. Zbigniew Brzezinski, *Power and Principle: Memoirs of the National Security Advisor, 1977–1981* (New York: Farrar, Straus and Giroux, 1983), pp. 227–229.

6. Gareth Porter, "Vietnamese Policy and the Indochina Crisis," in David W. P. Elliot, ed., *The Third Indochina Conflict* (Boulder, Colo.: Westview Press, 1981), p. 108.

7. Christopher Goscha, "Letter from Reagan: U.S. Encourages Private Aid to Vietnam and Presses MIA Issue," *Far Eastern Economic Review,* January 21, 1988, pp. 29–30.

Bibliography

SOUTHEAST ASIA—GENERAL

Bayard, D. T., ed. *Southeast Asian Archaeology at the XV Pacific Science Congress.* Otago University Studies in Prehistoric Anthropology. Dunedin, New Zealand: Otago University, 1984.

Brimmell, J. H. *Communism in Southeast Asia.* London: Oxford University Press, 1959.

Cady, John F. *Southeast Asia: Its Historical Development.* New York: McGraw-Hill, 1964.

Chen, King. "North Vietnam in the Sino-Soviet Dispute." *Asian Survey* (September 1964).

Coedès, Georges. *The Making of South East Asia.* Berkeley: University of California Press, 1966.

Cotter, M. G. "Towards a Social History of the Vietnamese Southward Movement." *Journal of Southeast Asian History* 9, 1 (1968).

Coughlin, M. "Vietnam in China's Shadow." *Journal of Southeast Asian History* 6, 2 (1967).

Elsbree, Willard H. *Japan's Role in Southeast Asian Nationalist Movements, 1940–1945.* Cambridge: Harvard University Press, 1953.

Emerson, Rupert, ed. *Government and Nationalism in Southeast Asia.* New York: Institute of Pacific Relations, 1942.

Hall, D.G.E. *A History of South-East Asia.* 3d ed. London: Macmillan, 1968.

_____ . *Atlas of South-East Asia.* New York: St. Martin's Press, 1964.

_____ , ed. *Historians of South-East Asia.* London: Oxford University Press, 1961.

Hanks, L. M. *Rice and Man: Agricultural Ecology in Southeast Asia.* Chicago: Aldine, 1972.

Hanna, Willard A. *Eight Nation Makers: Southeast Asia's Charismatic Statesmen.* New York: St. Martin's Press, 1964.

Higham, Charles. *The Archaeology of Mainland Southeast Asia from 10,000 B.C. to the Fall of Angkor.* Cambridge: Cambridge University Press, 1989.

Holland, William L., ed. *Asian Nationalism and the West.* New York: Macmillan, 1953.

Institute of Southeast Asian Studies. *Southeast Asian Affairs, 1977.* Singapore: Institute of Southeast Asian Studies, 1977.

————. *Southeast Asian Affairs, 1976.* Singapore: Institute of Southeast Asian Studies, 1976.

Lebar, F., G. Hickey, and J. Musgrave. *Ethnic Groups of Mainland Southeast Asia.* New Haven: Human Relations Area Files, 1964.

McVey, Ruth T. *The Calcutta Conference and the South East Asian Uprisings.* Ithaca: Cornell University. Mimeograph. 1958.

Morrison, Charles, and Astri Suhrke. *Struggles of Survival: The Foreign Policy Dilemmas of Smaller Asian States.* New York: St. Martin's, 1978.

Osborne, Milton E. *Region of Revolt: Focus on Southeast Asia.* Rushcutters Bay, Australia: Pergamon Press, 1970.

Panikkar, K. M. *Asia and Western Dominance.* London: Allen and Unwin, 1953.

Purcell, Victor. *The Chinese in Southeast Asia.* London: Oxford University Press, 1965.

Pye, Lucian W. *Southeast Asia's Political Systems.* Englewood Cliffs, N.J.: Prentice-Hall, 1967.

SarDesai, D. R. *Southeast Asia, Past and Present.* 2d ed. Boulder, Colo.: Westview Press, 1989.

Silverstein, J., ed. *Southeast Asia in World War II.* New Haven: Yale University Press, 1966.

Smith, R. B., and W. Watson, eds. *Early South East Asia.* London: Oxford University Press, 1979.

Steinberg, David J. *In Search of Southeast Asia.* 2d ed. Honolulu: East-West Center, 1985.

Tilman, Robert O. *Man, State and Society in Contemporary Southeast Asia.* New York: Praeger, 1969.

Trager, Frank N., ed. *Marxism in Southeast Asia.* Palo Alto: Stanford University Press, 1960.

Von der Mehden, Fred R. *Religion and Nationalism in Southeast Asia: Burma, Indonesia, the Philippines.* Madison: University of Wisconsin Press, 1963.

Williams, Lea. *The Future of the Overseas Chinese in Southeast Asia.* New York: McGraw-Hill, 1966.

VIETNAM—GENERAL

Beresford, Melanie. *Vietnam: Politics, Economics, and Society.* London: Pinter, 1988.

Buttinger, Joseph. *The Smaller Dragon: A Political History of Vietnam.* New York: Praeger, 1958.

Gheddo, Piero. *The Cross and the Bo Tree.* New York: Sheed and Ward, 1970.

Hickey, Gerald C. *Village in Vietnam.* New Haven: Yale University Press, 1964.

Hodgkin, Thomas. *Vietnam: The Revolutionary Path.* London: Macmillan, 1981.

Karnow, Stanley. *Vietnam: A History.* New York: Viking, 1983.

Lê Thanh Khôi. *Le Viet-Nam, histoire et civilisation.* Paris: Editions de Minuit, 1955.

Masson, André. *Histoire de l'Indochine*. Paris: Presses Universitaires de France, 1950.

Smith, Ralph. *Viet-Nam and the West*. London: Heinemann, 1968.

United Nations. *Atlas of Physical, Economic and Social Resources of the Lower Mekong Basin*. Washington, D.C.: UN Agency for International Development, 1968.

PREHISTORIC AND TRADITIONAL VIETNAM

Adams, J., and N. Hancock. "Land and Economy in Traditional Vietnam." *Journal of Southeast Asian History* 1, 2 (1970).

Aurousseau, Leonard. "La première conquête chinoise des pays annamites." *Bulletin de l'école française d'Extrême-Orient* 23 (1923).

Buttinger, Joseph. *Vietnam: A Political History*. New York: Praeger, 1968.

Cadière, L. "Le mur de Dong-Hoi, étude sur l'établissement des Nguyen Cochinchine." *Bulletin de l'école française d'Extrême-Orient* 6 (1906).

Coedès, Georges. *The Indianized States of Southeast Asia*. Honolulu: East-West Center Press, 1968.

_____ . *The Making of South East Asia*. Berkeley: University of California Press, 1966.

Ha Van Tan. "The Hoabinhian in the Context of Viet Nam." *Vietnamese Studies* 46 (1976), pp. 127–197.

Jamieson, N. "A Perspective on Vietnamese Pre-history Based upon the Relationship Between Geological and Archaeological Data." *Asian Perspectives* 24 (1981), pp. 187–192.

Janse, J. M. "On the Origins of Traditional Vietnamese Music." *Asian Perspectives* 6 (1962), pp. 145–162.

_____ . *Archaeological Research in Indo-china: The Ancient Dwelling Site of Dong-S'on*. Cambridge: Harvard University Press, 1958.

_____ . *Archaeological Research in Indo-china: The District of Chiu-Chen During the Han Dynasty*. 2 vols. Cambridge: Harvard University Press, 1947, 1951.

Kalgren, B. "The Date of the Early Dongson Culture." *Bulletin of the Museum of Far Eastern Antiquities* 45 (1942), pp. 1–29.

Le May, Reginald. *The Culture of South-East Asia*. London: Allen and Unwin, 1954.

Maspero, M. G. *Le royaume de Champa*. Paris: Librairie Nationale, 1928.

Maybon, Charles. *Histoire moderne du pays d'Annam, 1592–1820*. Paris: Plon-Nourrit, 1919.

Mus, Paul. "Cultes indiens et indigènes au Champa." *Bulletin de l'école française d'Extrême-Orient* 33 (1933), pp. 367–410.

Nguyen Ngoc Huy. *The Le Code: Law in Traditional Vietnam*. Athens: Ohio University Press, 1987.

O'Harrow, S. "From Co-loa to the Trung Sisters' Revolt: Viet-Nam as the Chinese Found It." *Asian Perspectives* 22, 2 (1979), pp. 140–164.

Pelliot, Paul. "Les grands voyages maritimes chinois au debut du XVème siècle." *T'oung Pao* 30 (1933).

Pham Minh Huyen. "Various Phases of the Development of Primitive Metallurgy in Viet Nam." In D. T. Bayard, ed., *Southeast Asian Archaeology at the XV Pacific*

Science Congress. Otago University Studies in Prehistoric Anthropology. Dunedin, New Zealand: Otago University, 1984.

Quaritch-Wales, H. G. *The Making of Greater India*. 2d ed. London: Bernard Quaritch, 1961.

Smith, Ralph. *Viet-Nam and the West*. London: Heinemann, 1968.

Taylor, Kenneth W. *The Birth of Viet Nam*. Berkeley: University of California Press, 1983.

Tran Van Giap. "Le bouddhisme en Annam." *Bulletin de l'école française d'Extrême-Orient* 32 (1932).

Truyen Mai Tho. *Le bouddhisme au Viet-Nam*. Saigon: National Publishers, 1952.

Woodside, Alexander B. *Vietnam and the Chinese Model*. Cambridge: Harvard University Press, 1970.

THE FRENCH PERIOD

Bailey, Lois E. *Jules Ferry and French Indo-China*. Madison: University of Wisconsin Press, 1946.

Betts, R. F. *Assimilation and Association in French Colonial Theory, 1890–1914*. New York: Columbia University Press, 1961.

Blet, Henri. *France d'Outre-mer*. Paris: Arthaud, 1950.

Briggs, L. P. "Aubaret and the Treaty of July 15, 1867, Between France and Siam." *Far Eastern Quarterly* 4 (1947), pp. 122–138.

Buttinger, Joseph. *A Dragon Embattled: A History of Colonial and Post-Colonial Vietnam*. 2 vols. New York: Praeger, 1967.

Cady, John F. *The Roots of French Imperialism in Eastern Asia*. Ithaca: Cornell University Press, 1954.

Dutreb, M. *L'Amiral Dupré et la conquête du Tonkin*. Paris: E. Leroux, 1924.

Ennis, Thomas E. *French Policy and Development in Indochina*. Chicago: University of Chicago Press, 1936.

Fall, Bernard B. *Hell in a Very Small Place: The Siege of Dien Bien Phu*. New York: Lippincott, 1967.

Garnier, Francis. *Voyage d'exploration en Indochine*. 2 vols. Paris: Librairie Hachette, 1885.

Grauwin, Paul. *Doctor at Dien Bien Phu*. London: Hutchinson, 1955.

Honey, P. J. "French Historiography and the Evolution of Colonial Vietnam." In D.G.E. Hall, ed., *Historians of Southeast Asia*. London: Oxford University Press, 1961.

Laffey, Ella S. "French Adventurers and Chinese Bandits in Tonkin: The Garnier Affair in Its Local Context." *Journal of Southeast Asian Studies* 6 (March 1975), pp. 38–51.

Ngo Vinh Long. *Before the Revolution: The Vietnamese Peasants Under the French*. Cambridge: Harvard University Press, 1973.

Norman, C. B. *Tonkin or France in the Far East*. London: Chapman and Hall, 1884.

Osborne, Milton E. *The French Presence in Cochin-China and Cambodia: Rule and Response, 1859–1905*. Ithaca: Cornell University Press, 1969.

Pham Cao Duong. *Vietnamese Peasants Under French Domination, 1861–1945.* Berkeley: University of California Press, 1989.

Power, Thomas F., Jr. *Jules Ferry and the Renaissance of French Imperialism.* New York: Octagon Books, 1966.

Priestley, H. I. *France Overseas: A Study of Modern Imperialism.* New York: Appleton-Century, 1938.

Robequain, Charles. *The Economic Development of French Indo-China.* London: Oxford University Press, 1954.

Roberts, Stephen H. *The History of French Colonial Policy, 1870–1925.* 2 vols. London: P. S. King, 1929.

Smith, Ralph. *Viet-Nam and the West.* London: Heinemann, 1968.

Taboulet, Georges. *La geste française en Indochine.* 2 vols. Paris: Adrien-Maisonneuve, 1955–1956.

Thompson, Virginia. *French Indochina.* New York: Macmillan, 1937.

Truong Buu Lam. *Patterns of Vietnamese Response to Foreign Intervention, 1858–1900.* New Haven: Yale University Press, Southeast Asia Studies, 1967.

Tuck, Patrick J. N., ed. *French Catholic Missionaries and the Politics of Imperialism in Vietnam, 1857–1914.* Liverpool: Liverpool University Press, 1987.

NATIONALIST AND COMMUNIST MOVEMENTS
TO DIEN BIEN PHU AND GENEVA

Artaud, Denise, and Lawrence Kaplan, eds. *Dienbienphu: The Atlantic Alliance and the Defense of Southeast Asia.* Wilmington, Del.: Scholarly Resources, 1989.

Billings-Yun, Melanie. *Decision Against War: Eisenhower and Dien Bien Phu, 1954.* New York: Columbia University Press, 1988.

Blum, Robert M. *Drawing the Line: The Origins of American Containment Policy in East Asia.* New York: Norton, 1982.

Cable, James. *The Geneva Conference of 1954 on Indochina.* New York: St. Martin's, 1986.

Chen, King C. *Vietnam and China, 1938–1954.* Princeton: Princeton University Press, 1969.

Chesneaux, Jean. *Contribution à l'histoire de la nation vietnamienne.* Paris: Editions Sociales, 1962.

Davidson, Phillip B. *Vietnam at War: The History, 1946–1975.* Novato, Calif.: Presidio Press, 1988.

Devillers, Philippe, and Jean Lacouture. *End of a War: Indochina, 1954.* New York: Praeger, 1969.

Devillers, Philippe, and Jean Lacouture. "The Struggle for the Unification of Vietnam." *China Quarterly* (January-March 1962), pp. 2–23.

Duiker, William J. *The Rise of Nationalism in Vietnam, 1900–1941.* Ithaca: Cornell University Press, 1976.

Fall, Bernard B., ed. *Ho Chi Minh on Revolution: Selected Writings, 1920–1966.* New York: Praeger, 1967.

Fischer, Ruth. "Ho Chi Minh: Disciplined Communist." *Foreign Affairs* 33 (October 1954), pp. 86–97.

Gardner, Lloyd C. *Approaching Vietnam: From World War II Through Dienbienphu, 1941–1954*. New York: Norton, 1988.

Halberstam, David. *Ho*. New York: Vintage Books, 1971.

Hammer, Ellen J. *The Struggle for Indochina*. Stanford: Stanford University Press, 1956.

Hess, Gary R. *The United States' Emergence as a Southeast-Asian Power, 1940–1950*. New York: Columbia University Press, 1987.

Hinton, Harold C. *China's Relations with Burma and Vietnam*. New York: Institute of Pacific Relations, 1958.

Ho Chi Minh. *Prison Diary*. Trans. Aileen Palmer. Hanoi: Foreign Languages Publishing House, 1961.

Hoang Van Chi. *From Colonialism to Communism*. New York: Praeger, 1964.

Huyen N. Khac. *Vision Accomplished? The Enigma of Ho Chi Minh*. New York: Macmillan, 1971.

Huynh Kim Khanh. *Vietnamese Communism, 1925–1945*. Ithaca: Cornell University Press, 1986.

Irving, Ronald E. *The First Indochina War: French and American Policy, 1945–1954*. London: Croom Helm, 1975.

Lacouture, Jean. *Ho Chi Minh: A Political Biography*. New York: Vintage Books, 1968.

Lancaster, Donald. *The Emancipation of French Indochina*. London: Oxford University Press, 1961.

Le Duan. *On the Socialist Revolution in Vietnam*. 2 vols. Hanoi: Foreign Languages Publishing House, 1965.

McAlister, John T., Jr., and Paul Mus. *The Vietnamese and Their Revolution*. New York: Harper and Row, 1970.

Marr, David G. *Vietnamese Anti-Colonialism, 1885–1925*. Berkeley: University of California Press, 1971.

Mus, Paul. *Viet-Nam, sociologie d'une guerre*. Paris: Editions du Seuil, 1952.

———. "The Role of the Village in Vietnamese Politics." *Pacific Affairs* 23 (September 1949), pp. 265–272.

Navarre, Henri. *Agonie de l'Indochine, 1953–54*. Paris: Plon, 1956.

Neumann-Hoditz, Reinhold. *Portrait of Ho Chi Minh*. Trans. John Hargreaves. New York: Herder and Herder, 1972.

Nguyen Duy Thanh. *My Four Years with the Viet Minh*. Bombay: Democratic Research Service, 1950.

Pham Van Dong, and the Committee for the Study of the History of the Vietnamese Workers' Party. *President Ho Chi Minh*. Hanoi: Foreign Languages Publishing House, 1960.

Pike, Douglas. *History of the Vietnamese Communism, 1925–1976*. Palo Alto: Hoover Institution Press, 1978.

Rotter, Andrew J. *The Path to Vietnam: Origins of American Commitment to Southeast Asia*. Ithaca: Cornell University Press, 1987.

Roy, Jules. *The Battle of Dien Bien Phu*. Trans. Robert Baldick. New York: Harper and Row, 1965.

Sainteny, Jean. *Ho Chi Minh and His Vietnam: A Personal Memoir*. Chicago: Cowles Book Company, 1970.

_____ . *Histoire d'une paix manquée indochine.* Paris: Aniot Dumont, 1953.

Shaplen, Robert. *The Lost Revolution, 1946–1966.* New York: Harper and Row, 1965.

Tanham, George K. *Communist Revolutionary Warfare: The Vietminh in Indo-China.* New York: Praeger, 1961.

Tran Dan Tien. *Glimpses of the Life of Ho Chi Minh.* Hanoi: Foreign Languages Publishing House, 1958.

Truong Buu Lam. *Patterns of Vietnamese Response to Foreign Intervention, 1858–1900.* New Haven: Yale University Southeast Asia Studies, 1967.

Truong Chinh. *The August Revolution.* Hanoi: Foreign Languages Publishing House, 1958.

Vo Nguyen Giap. *People's War, People's Army.* New York: Praeger, 1962.

Warbay, William. *Ho Chi Minh and the Struggle for a Free Vietnam.* London: Merlin Press, 1972.

VIETNAM FROM THE GENEVA CONFERENCE TO 1975

Ashmore, Harry S., and William C. Baggs. *Mission to Hanoi.* New York: G. P. Putnam, 1968.

Bator, Victor. *Vietnam: A Diplomatic Tragedy.* New York: Oceana Publications, 1965.

Berman, Larry. *Lyndon Johnson's War.* New York: Norton, 1989.

_____ . *Planning a Tragedy: The Americanization of the War in Vietnam.* New York: Norton, 1982.

Bodard, Lucien. *The Quicksand War: Prelude to Vietnam.* Boston: Little, Brown, 1967.

Boettcher, Thomas D. *Vietnam: The Valor and the Sorrow, from the Home to the Front Lines in Words and Pictures.* Boston: Little, Brown, 1985.

Brown, Sam, and Len Akland, eds. *Why Are We Still in Vietnam?* New York: Random House, 1970.

Bui Diem. *In the Jaws of History.* Boston: Houghton Mifflin, 1987.

Butler, David. *The Fall of Saigon: Scenes from the Sudden End of a Long War.* New York: Simon and Schuster, 1985.

Chawla, S., M. Gurtov, and A. Marsot, eds. *Southeast Asia Under the New Balance of Power.* New York: Praeger, 1974.

Clarke, Jeffrey J. *Advice and Support: The Final Years, 1965–1973.* Washington, D.C.: Center for Military History, 1988.

Clifford, Clark. "A Vietnam Reappraisal." *Foreign Affairs* 47 (July 1969), pp. 601–622.

Clodfelter, Mark. *The Limits of Air Power: The American Bombing of North Vietnam.* New York: Free Press, 1989.

Coleman, J. D. *Pleiku: The Dawn of Helicopter Warfare in Vietnam.* New York: St. Martin's Press, 1988.

Cooper, Chester L. *The Lost Crusade: America in Vietnam.* New York: Dodd Mead, 1970.

Dacy, Douglas C. *Foreign Aid, War, and Economic Development: South Vietnam, 1955–1975.* Cambridge: Cambridge University Press, 1986.

Davidson, Phillip B. *Vietnam at War: The History, 1946–1975.* Novato, Calif.: Presidio Press, 1988.

Duiker, William. *The Communist Road to Power in Vietnam*. Boulder, Colo.: West-view Press, 1981.

Eisenhower, Dwight D. *Mandate for Change, 1953–56*. New York: Signet Books, 1965.

Falk, Richard A., ed. *The Vietnam War and International Law*. Princeton: Princeton University Press, 1968.

Fall, Bernard B. *The Two Viet-Nams: A Political and Military Analysis*. 3d ed. New York: Praeger, 1967.

_____ . *Last Reflections on a War*. New York: Doubleday, 1963.

_____ . "Power and Pressure Groups in North Vietnam." *China Quarterly* (January-March 1962), pp. 37–46.

_____ . "The Political-Religious Sects of Vietnam." *Pacific Affairs* 28 (September 1955), pp. 235–253.

_____ , ed. *Ho Chi Minh on Revolution: Selected Writings, 1920–1966*. New York: Praeger, 1967.

Fifield, Russell H. *Americans in Southeast Asia: The Roots of Commitment*. New York: Thomas Crowell, 1973.

_____ . *Southeast Asia in United States Policy*. New York: Praeger, 1963.

Fitzgerald, Frances. *Fire in the Lake*. New York: Vintage Books, 1972.

Fulbright, J. William. *The Arrogance of Power*. New York: Random House, 1967.

Galloway, John. *The Gulf of Tonkin Resolution*. Cranbury, N.J.: Associated University Press, 1970.

Gettleman, Marvin E. *Vietnam and America: Documented History*. New York: Grove Press, 1985.

_____ , ed. *Vietnam*. New York: Penguin, 1965.

_____ , ed.*Vietnam: History, Documents and Opinions on a Major World Crisis*. Greenwich, Conn.: Fawcett Publications, 1965.

Gilbert, James W. *The Perfect War: The War We Couldn't Lose and How We Did*. Boston: Atlantic Monthly Press, 1986.

Gilbert, Stephen P. "Implications of the Nixon Doctrine for Military Aid Policy." *Orbis* 16, 3 (Fall 1972), pp. 660–681.

Gittinger, J. Price. "Communist Land Policy in North Vietnam." *Far Eastern Survey* 27 (August 1959), pp. 113–126.

Goodwin, Richard N. *Triumph or Tragedy: Reflections on Vietnam*. New York: Random House, 1966.

Greene, Graham. "Last Act in Indo-China." *New Republic* 132, May 9, 1955, pp. 9–11.

Gruening, Ernest, and Herbert W. Beaser. *Vietnam Folly*. Washington, D.C.: National Press, 1968.

Gurtov, Melvin. *The First Vietnam Crisis*. New York: Columbia University Press, 1967.

Halberstam, David. *The Making of a Quagmire: America and Vietnam During the Kennedy Era*. New York: Random House, 1965.

_____ . *The Best and the Brightest*. Greenwich, Conn.: Fawcett Publications, 1969.

Hammer, Ellen J. *A Death in November: America in Vietnam, 1963*. New York: E. P. Dutton, 1987.

Henderson, William. "South Vietnam Finds Itself." *Foreign Affairs* 35 (January 1957), pp. 283–294.

Herring, George C. *America's Longest War: The United States and Vietnam, 1950–1975.* Philadelphia: Temple University Press, 1986.

Hess, Gary R. *Vietnam and the United States: Origins and Legacy of War.* Boston: Twayne Publishers, 1990.

Hinton, Harold C. *China's Relations with Burma and Vietnam.* New York: Institute of Pacific Relations, 1958.

Honey, P. J. *Communism in North Vietnam: Its Role in the Sino-Soviet Dispute.* Cambridge: MIT Press, 1963.

Isaacs, Arnold R. *Without Honor: Defeat in Vietnam and Cambodia.* Baltimore: Johns Hopkins University Press, 1983.

Joes, Anthony James. *The War for South Vietnam, 1945–1975.* New York: Praeger, 1989.

Kahin, George M. *Intervention: How America Became Involved in Vietnam.* New York: Knopf, 1986.

Kahin, George M., and John W. Lewis. *The United States in Vietnam.* New York: Dial Press, 1967.

Kiernan, Ben. *How Pol Pot Came to Power: A History of Communism in Kampuchea, 1930–1975.* London: Verso, 1985.

Kolko, Gabriel. *Anatomy of a War: Vietnam, the United States, and the Modern Historical Experience.* New York: Pantheon, 1985.

Kurland, Gerald, ed. *Misjudgment or Defense of Freedom? The United States in Vietnam.* New York: Simon and Schuster, 1975.

Lacouture, Jean. *Vietnam Between Two Truces.* New York: Vintage Books, 1966.

Laniel, Joseph. *Le drame indochinois: De Dien Bien Phu au Pari de Genève.* Paris: Plon, 1957.

Le Duan. *Letters to the South.* Hanoi: Foreign Languages Publishing House, 1986.

———. *On the Socialist Revolution in Vietnam.* 2 vols. Hanoi: Foreign Languages Publishing House, 1965.

Maclear, Michael. *The Ten Thousand Day War.* New York: St. Martin's, 1981.

Mangold, Tom. *The Tunnels of Cu Chi.* London: Hodder and Stoughton, 1985.

Nghiem Dang. *Viet-Nam, Politics and Public Administration.* Honolulu: East-West Center Press, 1966.

Nguyen Cao Ky. *How We Lost the Vietnam War.* New York: Stein and Day, 1984.

Nixon, Richard. *U.S. Foreign Policy for the 1970's: A New Strategy for Peace—A Report to the Congress by Richard Nixon, February 18, 1970.* Washington, D.C.: Government Printing Office, 1970.

Nolting, Frederick. *From Trust to Tragedy.* New York: Praeger, 1988.

Palmer, Bruce, Jr. *The Twenty-Five-Year War: America's Military Role in Vietnam.* Lexington: University Press of Kentucky, 1984.

Papp, Daniel S. *Vietnam: The View from Moscow, Peking, Washington.*Salisbury, N.C.: McFarland, 1981.

Pentagon Papers. New York: Bantam Books, 1971.

Pike, Douglas. *Viet Cong.* Cambridge: MIT Press, 1966.

Porter, Gareth. *A Peace Denied: The United States and the Paris Agreements*. Bloomington: Indiana University Press, 1975.

————. *The Myth of the Bloodbath: North Vietnam's Land Reform Considered*. Ithaca: Cornell University International Relations of East Asia Project. Mimeograph. 1972.

Race, Jeffrey. *War Comes to Long An: Revolutionary Conflict in a Vietnamese Province*. Berkeley: University of California Press, 1972.

Rust, William J. *Kennedy in Vietnam*. New York: Scribner, 1985.

SarDesai, D. R. *Indian Foreign Policy in Cambodia, Laos and Vietnam, 1947–1964*. Berkeley: University of California Press, 1968.

Schlesinger, Arthur M., Jr. *The Bitter Heritage: Vietnam and American Democracy, 1941–1966*. Boston: Houghton Mifflin, 1967.

Scigliano, Robert. *South Vietnam: Nation Under Stress*. Boston: Houghton Mifflin, 1963.

Shabad, Theodore. "Economic Development in North Vietnam." *Pacific Affairs* (March 1958), pp. 36–54.

Shaplen, Robert. *The Lost Revolution, 1946–1966*. New York: Harper and Row, 1965.

Shawcross, William. *The Quality of Mercy: Cambodia, Holocaust, and Modern Conscience*. New York: Simon and Schuster, 1984.

————. *Sideshow: Kissinger, Nixon and the Destruction of Cambodia*. New York: Pocket Books, 1979.

Short, Anthony. *The Origins of the Vietnam War*. London: Longman, 1989.

Sihanouk, Norodom. *My War with the CIA*. Harmondsworth, UK: Penguin Books, 1973.

————. "Cambodia Neutral: The Dictate of Necessity." *Foreign Affairs* 36 (July 1958), pp. 582–586.

Smith, Ralph B. *An International History of the Vietnam War*. Vol. 1, *Revolution Versus Containment, 1955–1961*. New York: St. Martin's, 1983.

Smyser, W. R. *The Independent Vietnamese: Vietnamese Communism Between Russia and China, 1955–1969*. Athens: Ohio University Press, 1980.

Spector, Ronald H. *Advice and Support: The Early Years of the United States Army in Vietnam, 1941–1960*. New York: Free Press, 1985.

Stoessinger, John G. *Henry Kissinger: The Anguish of Power*. New York: Norton, 1976.

Thayer, Thomas C. *War Without Fronts: The American Experience in Vietnam*. Boulder, Colo.: Westview Press, 1985.

Thompson, James Clay. *Rolling Thunder: Understanding Policy and Program Failure*. Chapel Hill: University of North Carolina Press, 1980.

Truong Chinh. *Resolutely Taking the North Vietnam Countryside to Socialism Through Agricultural Cooperation*. Hanoi: Foreign Languages Publishing House, 1959.

Truong Nhu Tang. *Journal of a Vietcong*. London: Cape, 1986.

————. *A Vietcong Memoir*. San Diego: Harcourt Brace Jovanovich, 1985.

Turley, William S. *The Second Indochina War: A Short Political and Military History, 1954–1975*. Boulder, Colo.: Westview Press, 1986.

United Kingdom. Foreign Office. *Further Documents Relating to the Discussion of Indochina at the Geneva Conference, June 16–July 21, 1954*. Cmd. 9239. London: HMSO, 1954.

U.S. Department of State. *A Threat to the Peace.* Washington, D.C.: Government Printing Office, 1961.

U.S. Senate Committee on Foreign Relations. *Report on Indochina by Senator Mike Mansfield, October 15, 1954* 82d Congress, 2d session. Washington, D.C.: Government Printing Office, 1954.

Vickerman, Andrew. *The Fate of the Peasantry: Premature "Transition to Socialism" in the Democratic Republic of Vietnam.* New Haven: Yale University Press, Southeast Asia Studies, 1986.

Vietnam, Socialist Republic of. *History of the Communist Party of Vietnam.* Hanoi: Foreign Languages Publishing House, 1986.

Warbay, William. *Ho Chi Minh and the Struggle for a Free Vietnam.* London: Merlin Press, 1972.

Warner, Denis. *The Last Confucian.* New York: Macmillan, 1963.

Westmoreland, William C. *A Soldier Reports.* New York: Doubleday, 1976.

Woodside, Alexander B. *Community and Revolution in Modern Vietnam.* Boston: Houghton Mifflin, 1976.

Yang Sam. *Khmer Buddhism and Politics from 1954 to 1984.* Newington, Conn.: Khmer Studies Institute, 1987.

Zagoria, Donald. *Vietnam Triangle: Moscow, Peking, Hanoi.* New York: Pegasus, 1967.

VIETNAM AND CAMBODIA SINCE 1975

Albin, David A., and Marlowe Hood, eds. *The Cambodian Agony.* Armonk, N.Y.: M. E. Sharpe, 1987.

Barron, John, and Anthony Paul. *Murder of a Gentle Land: The Untold Story of Communist Genocide in Cambodia.* New York: Reader's Digest Press, 1977.

Basu, Sanghamitra. *Kampuchea as a Factor in the Sino-Soviet Conflict, 1975–1984.* Calcutta: Firma KLM, 1987.

Becker, Elizabeth. *When the War Was Over: The Voices of Cambodia's Revolution and Its People.* New York: Simon and Schuster, 1986.

Brzezinski, Zbigniew. *Power and Principle: Memoirs of the National Security Advisor, 1977–1981.* New York: Farrar, Straus and Giroux, 1983.

Carney, Timothy M., ed. *Communist Party in Kampuchea, Documents and Discussion.* Cornell University Southeast Asia Program Data Paper, 1977.

Chanda, Nayan. *Brother Enemy: The War After the War—A History of Indochina Since the Fall of Saigon.* San Diego: Harcourt Brace Jovanovich, 1986.

Chandler, David P., Ben Kiernan, and Chanthou Boua, eds. *Pol Pot Plans the Future: Confidential Leadership Documents from Democratic Kampuchea, 1976–1977.* New Haven: Yale University Press, Southeast Asia Studies, 1988.

Chang Pao-min. *Kampuchea Between China and Vietnam.* Singapore: Singapore University Press, 1985.

———. *The Sino-Vietnamese Territorial Dispute.* New York: Praeger, 1986.

Dellinger, David T. *Vietnam Revisited: From Covert Action to Invasion to Reconstruction.* Boston: South End Press, 1986.

Duiker, William J. *China and Vietnam: The Roots of Conflict*. Berkeley: University of California Press, 1986.

———. *Vietnam Since the Fall of Saigon*. Athens: Ohio University Center for International Studies, 1985.

Etcheson, Craig. *The Rise and Demise of Democratic Kampuchea*. Boulder, Colo.: Westview Press, 1984.

Fforde, Adam. *The Agrarian Question in North Vietnam, 1974–1979*. Armonk, N.Y.: M. E. Sharpe, 1989.

Goscha, Christopher. "Letter from Reagan: U.S. Encourages Private Aid to Vietnam and Presses MIA Issue." *Far Eastern Economic Review*, January 21, 1988, pp. 29–30.

Hayslip, Le Ly. *When Heaven and Earth Change Places: A Vietnamese Woman's Journey from War to Peace*. New York: Doubleday, 1989.

Hildebrand, George C. *Cambodia: Starvation and Revolution*. New York: Monthly Review Press, 1976.

International Institute for Strategic Studies. *The Military Balance, 1990–91*. London: IISS, 1991.

Jackson, Karl D., ed. *Cambodia, 1975–1978: Rendezvous with Death*. Princeton: Princeton University Press, 1989.

Kelley, Gail Paradise. *From Vietnam to America: A Chronicle of the Vietnamese Immigration to the United States*. Boulder, Colo.: Westview Press, 1977.

Kiljunen, Kimmo, ed. *Kampuchea: Decade of the Genocide*. London: Zed, 1984.

Klintworth, Gary. *Vietnam's Withdrawal from Cambodia*. Canberra: Australian National University, 1987.

Leifer, Michael. *Cambodian Conflicts: The Final Phase?*. London: Center for Security and Conflict Studies, 1989.

Long, Robert Emmet, ed. *Vietnam Ten Years After*. New York: Wilson, 1986.

McGregor, Charles. *The Sino-Vietnamese Relationship and the Soviet Union*. Adelphi Papers 232. London: International Institute for Strategic Studies, 1988.

Ngor Haing S. *Surviving the Killing Fields: The Cambodian Odyssey*. London: Chatto and Windus, 1988.

Nguyen Khac Vien. *Southern Vietnam, 1975–1985*. Hanoi: Foreign Languages Publishing House, 1985.

Picq, Laurence. *Beyond the Horizon: Five Years with the Khmer Rouge*. New York: St. Martin's Press, 1989.

Pike, Douglas. *Vietnam and the Soviet Union: Anatomy of an Alliance*. Boulder, Colo.: Westview Press, 1987.

Ponchaud, François. *Cambodia, Year Zero*. New York: Holt and Rinehart, 1977.

Porter, Gareth. "Vietnamese Policy and the Indochina Crisis." In David W. P. Elliot, ed., *The Third Indochina Conflict*. Boulder, Colo.: Westview Press, 1981.

Pradhan, P. C. *Foreign Policy of Kampuchea*. New Delhi: Radiant, 1985.

Ross, Robert S. *The Indochina Tangle: China's Vietnam Policy, 1975–1979*. New York: Columbia University Press, 1988.

Schanberg, Sydney Hillel. *The Death and Life of Dith Pran*. New York: Penguin, 1985.

Silber, Irwin. *Kampuchea: The Revolution Rescued*. Oakland: Line of March Publications, 1986.

Stuart-Fox, Martin. *The Murderous Revolution: Life and Death in Pol Pot's Kampuchea.* Denver: Alternate Publishing Company, 1986.

Tan Teng Lang. *Economic Debates in Vietnam: Issues and Problems in Reconstruction and Development (1975–84).* Singapore: Institute of Southeast Asian Studies, 1985.

Thrift, Nigel, and Dean Forbes. *The Price of War: Urbanization in Vietnam, 1954–1985.* London: Allen and Unwin, 1985.

Tran Van Don. *Our Endless War: Inside South Vietnam.* Novato, Calif.: Presidio Press, 1978.

Turley, William S. "The Khmer War: Cambodia After Paris." *Survival* 32, 5 (September-October 1990), pp. 437–453.

_____ , ed. *Confrontation or Coexistence: The Future of ASEAN-Vietnam Relations.* Bangkok: Chulalongkorn University, 1985.

Vickery, Michael. *Kampuchea: Politics, Economics, and Society.* London: Pinter, 1986.

_____ . *Cambodia, 1975–1982.* Boston: South End Press, 1984.

Vietnam, Socialist Republic of. *Documents of the Sixth Congress of the Communist Party of Vietnam, 15–18 December 1986.* Hanoi: Foreign Languages Publishing House, 1987.

_____ .*Vietnam Ten Years After.* Hanoi: Foreign Languages Publishing House, 1985.

Yang Sam. *Khmer Buddhism and Politics from 1954 to 1984.* Newington, Conn.: Khmer Studies Institute, 1987.

About the Book & Author

Vietnam, with its recent history of continual conflict, has stirred intense interest among scholars and statesmen, journalists and general readers alike. Millions of Vietnamese children have grown to adulthood carrying memories of bloodshed, terror, bombing, and dislocation. The U.S. intervention there divided public opinion throughout the world, affecting human values, national economies, presidential prospects, and military strategies. The spectacle of Third World people with outmoded weaponry immobilizing the most militarily advanced nation in the world cast doubt on the very basis of modern strategic defense.

What motivated the Vietnamese people to wage such a protracted battle at such great economic and emotional cost? Was it communism, nationalism, or a combination of both? And how does one explain the conflicts among the Communist regimes in the region? What are the prospects of Hanoi emerging as a major political and ideological center in Southeast Asia?

This concise introduction attempts to answer these questions by bringing a historical perspective to the Vietnam War that is often lacking in other works. The author situates the country in the context of the traditional Sino-Vietnamese cultural and colonial relationship and the more recent experience under the French. Arguing that the quest for national identity has been a recurring theme throughout Vietnamese history, the author asserts that nationalism, even more than communism, fueled the recent struggles against France, the United States, and China. A major portion of the study deals with the postwar era of Vietnam's reconstruction, administrative reorganization, its decade-long occupation of Cambodia and the subsequent UN settlement, and its relations with major powers. This thoughtful and accessible text will be valuable for students of both Vietnamese history and contemporary politics.

D. R. SarDesai is professor of history at the University of California–Los Angeles.

Index